To Pastor Toby,

From your fellow Pastor

Rick Stanley

Matt 6:33

AMERICA IN THE BALANCE
AMERICAN DREAM vs. WOKE NIGHTMARE

Rick Scarborough

Steve Feazel

AMERICA IN THE BALANCE

AMERICAN DREAM VS. WOKE NIGHTMARE

21stCENTURY
P   R   E   S   S
READING YOU LOUD AND CLEAR

Dedication

To Fred Dailey, former Director of
Agriculture in Ohio and one of my
political mentors
— Steve Feazel

To Art Ally and his wife and best friend
for 62 years, Bonnie Jean Ally, who was
promoted to Heaven on March 12, 2023
and is now with their son, Stephen, who
was received into Heaven on September
26, 2019. Their impact on me and
Tommye, my beloved wife, of 52 years is
immeasurable.
— Rick Scarborough

What Leaders Are Saying About This Book

"Rick Scarborough is truly a modern-day watchman on the wall. In his latest book, America in the Balance, he issues well-researched warnings that the survival of the American Dream is possible only if it rests on Biblical principles. This book will provoke thought and conversation. As Christians, we are called to be change agents. The Gospel is the tip of our Sword. How can we pierce hearts for Christ if we have no point of truth?

"Thankfully, we have dedicated servants like Rick Scarborough and Steve Feazel, who have written a clarion call to all who serve God and love this country. The thesis is evident in the subtitle: American Dream vs. Woke Nightmare. These authors wisely expose the differences in ideology, but don't leave us there, instead, they offer practical recommendations to implement change!"
—— Dr. Ed Young, Senior Pastor, Second Baptist Church, Houston, Texas

"The authors expose how positions on vital issues by liberals are in direct opposition to biblical truths. They provide practical advice and actions which Christians and liberty-minded Americans can take to become more engaged in civic affairs and help our nation regain its original values and aspirations. A must read before you vote."
—Mike Huckabee, Former Governor of Arkansas and Host of *Huckabee TV Show*

"Rick Scarborough and Steve Feazel have produced a book that everyone who is concerned about America's future should read before voting in 2024. They expose the wicked agenda of the Left and what we must do to counter their efforts."
—Tony Perkins. President of Family Research Council

"Rick Scarborough and his co-author, Steve Feazel, have given us a timely and important tool for pushing back on the assault of the god haters in America who are seeking to destroy the church and our country. Every chapter builds on the preceding chapter as they present their case that our country is at tipping point, and the next election may very well decide whether America remains the land of freedom or falls to the Communists in our midst who are indoctrinating and sexualizing our children.

"Both are pastors and they lay the blame for the receding decline in our nation's morals where it belongs…at the feet of her pastors who have forsaken their calling to preach Christ and His word without compromise. They define the issues of our day, and they offer solutions.

"I have known Rick Scarborough for many years and I know him to be a frontline warrior for Christ. We will be encouraging our vast network of pastors and supporters to read this book. I believe it is that important."
—Tim Wildmon, President of American Family Association

"This book could not be more timely. *America in the Balance* not only diagnoses the ideological disease infecting America, it also explains the protocol to heal our land. This book is a must read. Everyone realizes that something is terribly wrong with the direction of our nation. America in the Balance provides the roadmap to restore the broken system. There is an urgency to read this book and follow its roadmap to restore the principles of freedom. Rick Scarborough and Steve Feazel have written a masterful book that helps the reader understand the current issues facing America but also providing a solution to the problems. This is an invaluable resource."
—Mat Staver, Chairperson of the Liberty Counsel

"Rick Scarborough has been leading the charge of pastors combating the godless attack on Christianity in America for three decades. *America in the Balance* is a straightforward, easy to follow refutation of the 'woke' cultural assault on our Judeo-Christian foundation. It is a must read and reference for every Christian!"
—Paul K. Blair, Senior Pastor, Liberty Church, Edmond OK

"America in the Balance: American Dream vs Woke Nightmare by Rick Scarborough and Steve Feazel is a timely resource and call to action. I encourage fellow Christians to be encouraged and equipped by this book. As the battle for not only life, but souls, and our culture, rages on, we need to stand firm in our beliefs and be prepared to defend biblical truths. Let this book be your foundation for supporting normalcy in a world that has lost its moral compass."
—Melissa Ohden, Executive Director of Abortion Survivors Network

"Proverbs 29:2 has significance for us that it doesn't have in many other nations around the world. It says, 'When the righteous are in authority, the people rejoice: but when the wicked beareth rule, the people mourn.' (KJV) Interwoven throughout the fabric of our founding are timeless Biblical principles that if followed assisting us in keeping this nation as Abraham Lincoln said, 'the last best hope of earth.'

"America in the Balance is a timely reminder of the part we are called to play. Though we did not ask to be born in America or to be given a government of which we are the stewards; nevertheless, God has given it to us, and He will call us to account for our stewardship of this important trust. Steve Feazel and Rick Scarborough have reminded us of the incredible deference that each of us must make!"
—Rev. Tim Throckmorton, National Director of Community Impact at the Family Research Council.

Contents

Important Note by the Authors

Demystifying the Leftist and the Liberal

The terms "**Leftist**" and "**Liberal**" are often used interchangeably in contemporary political discussions, but this usage is incorrect and can be misleading.

In our examination of the current political landscape, particularly with regard to informing pastors and Christians about the gravity of our existing political divisions, we aim to use these terms accurately. Through collaboration with a knowledgeable educator and theologian, we have established the following definitions:

Both Liberals and Leftists belong to the Left-wing of politics, but they differ in certain aspects. Liberals generally accept that tax breaks for the wealthy, while not ideal, are permissible. They advocate for limited government intervention overall and prioritize individual freedom to make personal choices.

On the other hand, Leftists desire a strong and expansive government that plays a dominant role in the economy. They believe that increased centralization of power signifies progress and often identify themselves as "Progressives." They advocate for greater government involvement in the economy, viewing it as beneficial. Leftists argue that the wealthy should contribute their "fair share" in taxes to enable redistribution of wealth, ensuring that those who earn less receive their fair portion from public funds.

If taken to its extreme conclusion, the economic philosophy of Leftism leads to Communism. In practice, present-day Leftists frequently resort to insults and verbal abuse when confronted with opposing viewpoints. Liberals, on the other hand, are more open to debates and disagreements, maintaining a friendly demeanor throughout. Leftists tend to be guided by emotions rather than logical reasoning. They often label those who disagree with them as hatemongers, using terms like "homophobic" or similar labels. Critical Race Theory is seen as an undeniable truth by Leftists, and they believe that the current generation has a moral obligation to provide reparations. They often broadly criticize white individuals, asserting that they have benefited solely due to their race.

Leftists can be characterized as the aggressors in today's political debates, and it is crucial for Christians to understand these distinctions if they aspire to reclaim their country and restore their nation. This book aims to illuminate these differences and their implications.

Foreword

Mike Huckabee
Former Governor of Arkansas
Host of the TV Show, Huckabee

The prophet Isaiah said, "Woe to those who call evil good and good evil" (Isa 5.20 NIV). The words of this biblical sage are relevant to our nation today as we see discord throughout our society. Things that were once regarded as unlawful and indecent are being embraced by people in ever-increasing numbers. Sadly, Leftist politicians have supported and even promoted this major cultural change. Abortion, same-sex marriage, gender transition, and making prayer unlawful in schools are all examples of what the Old Testament prophet was addressing. We are not a better nation because of it.

In their book, *America in the Balance,* Rick Scarborough and Steve Feazel tackle this problem head-on. They remind us of our godly heritage and how it shaped the original intent of our Founding Fathers to bring forth a nation conceived in liberty and rooted in the morality of the Christian faith. They expose how positions on vital issues by Leftists directly oppose biblical truths. They provide practical advice and actions that Christians and liberty-minded Americans can take to become more engaged in civic affairs and help our nation regain its original values and aspirations.

The subtitle of the book, *The American Dream vs. The Woke Nightmare,* indicates that the book will engage in a discussion centered around contrasting perspectives, specifically those aligned with the extreme right and the

Left. Just a casual stroll through America's early history reveals that the three foundation stones of faith, family, and freedom related to our republic were indeed treasured by our Founding Fathers. If we examine the efforts of those on the Left today, we quickly realize these three gems of liberty are under assault and are no longer valued. It is a sad thought when one realizes the foundation of the greatest nation the world has ever seen is being weakened by members of both major political parties as they attack these once cherished icons of our founding, some aggressively driving the assault on our Christian values and others by refusing to stop it.

The United States is not an accurate description of our nation today. "The Divided States of America" seems more fitting, and our Lord, on three occasions, stated that a house divided against itself cannot stand. There are calls for unity during every election season. It must be pointed out that there is no benefit when people are united around the wrong things. The Bible is filled with stories of kings who forsook the God who gave the Ten Commandments as they introduced false gods and idols to the people. The unity in this false faith resulted in God's judgment. We as a nation would benefit from unity if that unity were around the Founding Fathers' original intent. What is going on in our schools and streets puts people in danger. Radical policies are atrocious and could not have been imagined ten years ago. That is why it makes sense to choose normal over crazy. Our future well-being depends on it.

Several books have boldly exposed the sinister actions of those who have used public office to serve themselves instead of the people. Rick and Steve do not shy away from this. Still, refreshingly, they also present a call to action for Christian and conservative voters to become active in the political arena during election season. They stress the need for those who value our Christian heritage to be active at the local level. County and city offices and school board positions all matter, especially the school boards. If we are to turn back the menacing efforts of the Left, we must realize that education is ground zero in the cultural war. If we are to protect our children, we must go to the frontline of the fight. Securing positions on school boards is a key factor in ending the indoctrination and sexualization of our children. Most parents have no idea what wicked pro-homosexual activists are pumping into classrooms. Rick and Steve pull no punches.

When he gave his Gettysburg Address, Abraham Lincoln called for America to "have a new birth of freedom." Do we ever need this today! American history shows us that recovering from a national crisis begins in its pulpits. The First Great Awakening fanned the flames of freedom before the American Revolution through the preaching of the great evangelist George Whitefield. The Second Great Awakening led to the abolition of slavery and was ignited by the preaching of Charles Finney. We have such voices in our pulpits today to call us to repentance and renewal, and some will be cited in this book, but they are too few. Wokeism has seeped deeply into many churches as many preachers prefer to be popular rather than prophetic. We pray that *America in the Balance* will be a spark to kindle the flames of the third great awakening, bringing America back to its Christian moorings. I pray for that to happen.

AMERICA IN THE BALANCE

Introduction

The Declaration of Independence laid the cornerstone of human government upon the first precepts of Christianity.[1]
– John Adams

As the sun rises over Washington, DC, it illuminates the east side of the Washington Monument, where the Latin phrase "Laus Deo" is engraved. This powerful expression translates to "Praise be to God" and serves as a poignant reminder of our country's Christian heritage. The monument was erected in 1884, during a time when the "Separation of Church and State" movement was not as vehement as it is today. If such a movement existed during the monument's construction, it is doubtful that the capstone would have been inscribed with those sacred words. Our nation has strayed far from its Christian roots, and it is imperative that we return to our spiritual foundations.

The late Rush Limbaugh was renowned for his politically insightful mind, making him one of the most prominent voices ever on the airwaves. He frequently emphasized that the two major political parties in the US no longer shared anything in common. As someone who remembers past presidential campaigns, such as the Nixon-Kennedy election in 1960 and the Johnson-Goldwater contest during my college years, I recall a time when both parties were pro-life and did not discuss issues like abortion and homosexuality. The sanctity of marriage, defined as a union between one man and one woman, was the norm, and transgender topics were not even on the political agenda. There were also similarities in economic issues, such as Kennedy's decision to lower taxes to boost national prosperity.

However, as Limbaugh observed, the current political reality is vastly different. The absence of any shared principles between the two major parties is not only disappointing but also alarming. The principles upon which our nation was founded are incredibly valuable to the success of our republic, and it is essential that each party upholds them. Sadly, this is not the case today. The Democratic Party has changed its core values and moved away from the wisdom of the Founding Fathers. It has become a home for progressives and Liberals, two terms now synonymous with Democrats. Regardless of the nomenclature, these positions consistently find a place on the left side of the political spectrum and continue to shift further left each year.

The term "progressive" is intriguing, as it derives from "progress." However, upon close analysis, it becomes apparent that it does not accurately describe Democrats. Progress implies something positive, yet the policies and goals of Democrats lead to regression.

When the colonies were established in the 1600s and 1700s, individuals bade farewell to their loved ones, taking a perilous six-week ocean voyage to own their land. They left behind their mother country, England, where 10% of the population owned 90% of the land under the Feudal System.

If so-called progressives succeed in their aims, they will establish a small ruling elite class and a vast underclass, much of whom would be dependent on a big government. The once-thriving capitalist economy would be eradicated, and a modern-day Feudal System would take its place. This is not progress. Instead, it represents a return to authoritarian rule, where individuals are less free and less prosperous. This is a regressive, not a progressive, path.

The use of language by Liberal politicians is a masterful way to control the narrative, despite the baseless foundation upon which their arguments rest. The term "homophobe" has been coined by these individuals to label anyone who holds traditional views on marriage and sexuality, regardless of their religious beliefs. Similarly, they have created the term "Islamophobia" to shame anyone who dares to harbor negative thoughts about Muslims in the aftermath of terrorist attacks.[2] While it is important to condemn any violence or ill will towards peaceful Muslims, the Democrats have taken it further, demanding that even derogatory terms for Islamic terrorists be avoided. One wonders why they are so protective of the Islamic community, even to the point of sympathizing with terrorists who have committed evil acts.

The answer is simple: the Democrats know that by 2040, more Muslims will be voting in America than Jews.[3] They are courting this future voting bloc, which may also explain their recent disregard for the nation of Israel. But their tactics have evolved beyond traditional identity politics. They have now embraced the term "Woke" to promote their ideology, defined as "the behavior and attitudes of people who are sensitive to social and political injustice."[4] This may sound noble. Still, it camouflages corruption, undermines Christian principles, and distorts the truth.

Christians and lovers of decency must awaken to the deception of these Liberal politicians and become engaged in the political process. This book exposes the falsehoods of wokeism and provides a rallying cry for those who wish to preserve traditional values and stand up for truth and justice.

Steve Feazel once attended a meeting at a church in central Ohio before the 2022 midterm election. The event featured prominent conservative radio talk show hosts from the Salem Radio Network as well as Representative Jim Jordan. One of the hosts, Eric Metaxas delivered a powerful message, asserting that the election was not just about Republicans versus Democrats but rather a battle between good and evil. He argued that calling out evil actions or policies, such as allowing Fentanyl into the country, supporting human trafficking, releasing dangerous criminals, promoting immoral sexual behavior to young children, and endorsing transgender activities in schools without parental notification, was necessary.

Rick Scarborough, a Southern Baptist minister, was ordained shortly before Jimmy Carter became president in 1976. Scarborough launched an evangelistic ministry called United Church Evangelistic Ministries after completing seminary, and preached over 500 Crusades worldwide, leading many to faith in Christ. He initially admired Carter for his outspoken devotion to Jesus Christ. Still, he soon realized that his personal faith did not translate into effective leadership when Carter pursued Left-leaning policies resulting in high inflation, long gas lines, and a failure to resolve the Iran hostage crisis. Scarborough and others worked hard to replace Carter with Ronald Reagan, whose policies were more Christian-friendly and beneficial for the average American, despite not being regarded as strong an evangelical as Carter.

Liberal Democrats' radical positions on key issues often conflict with the standards laid out in the Bible, and Christians must oppose such positions, including at the ballot box. In the opening quote at the top of this Introduction famed theologian Francis Schaeffer introduced the concept of the "Great Shift." Franklin Graham agrees, as evidenced in his quote in *Decision Magazine*:

If progressives continue to hold both houses of Congress for several more years, I can only imagine the damage they will do. Already the White House, with its Liberal policies on abortion, gay and transgender rights, and attacks on the sanctity of marriage, has sought to drive an immoral and godless agenda.

...The lines are well drawn on critical moral issues, so I encourage you to pray and to cast your ballot for those men or women who are not afraid to take a stand on the truth of Biblical principles.[5]

The quote presents thought-provoking ideas. First, it argues that neutrality is not an option for Christians in politics at present. Franklin Graham's list of Liberal policies is presented as contradicting biblical truths and opposing God's standards. This view aligns with Eric Metaxas' belief that the 2022 midterm election was a battle between good and evil. Second, the quote recommends that Christians should vote for candidates who uphold biblical principles, which it suggests would not include those affiliated with the Liberal progressive political party.

The quote then explores why American politics has become so polarized that an election could be framed as a contest between good and evil. It cites theologian Francis Schaeffer's concept of the "Great Shift," which he believed had a negative cultural and political impact on the United States. Schaeffer argued that America was originally founded on a Christian consensus that established national morality and societal norms, which even non-religious citizens followed. These standards were integrated into the country's laws and were reinforced by two religious great awakenings before the Revolutionary and Civil Wars.

However, the quote suggests that the 1900s marked a shift towards humanism, a purely secular worldview that places man at the center of everything and as the measure of all things. This ideology does not recognize a God-Creator as the ultimate authority over the universe. Schaeffer contrasted this with the Christian consensus and argued that the two worldviews conflicted. Schaeffer emphasizes the importance of holding to God's standards as absolutes to be obeyed when he writes:

The Christian consensus held that neither the majority nor the elite is absolute. God gives the standards of value, and His absolutes are binding on both the ordinary person and those in all places of authority.

… because the Christian consensus has been put aside, we face a flood of personal cruelty today. As we have noted, the Christian consensus gave great freedoms without leading to chaos – because society in general, functioned within the values given in the Bible, especially the unique value of human life. Now that humanism has taken over, the former freedoms run riot, and individuals, acting on what they are taught, increasingly practice their cruelties without restraint. And why shouldn't they? If the modern humanistic view of man is correct and man is only a product of chance in a universe that has no ultimate values, why should an individual refrain from being cruel to another person, if that person seems to be standing in his or her way?[6]

Schaeffer's words explain the stark differences between today's two major political parties. The Democratic Party has fully embraced humanism, allowing it to dictate their core values and openly support actions such as abortion, gay rights, and transgender advancement. On the other hand, while the Republican Party is not without fault, it still gives Christian values a place at the policy table.

The danger of wokeness lies in its close connection to humanism. It masquerades as noble causes while surreptitiously pushing humanistic and Leftist agendas. It has infiltrated corporations, public schools, and Christianity, including the evangelical church and its colleges. Both wokeism and humanism reject biblical principles and instead believe in relative morality, leading to chaos and ultimately, authoritarianism.

Three pastors, Dr. D. James Kennedy, Dr. Jerry Falwell, and Dr. Tim LaHaye, have significantly influenced the authors' ministries by preaching the Word and getting involved in politics. Despite opposition to pastors engaging in politics, these three pastors set an example by advancing the gospel and fighting for Christian values in the national culture. Their legacies debunk the myth of the separation of church and state, inspiring us to take action today.

Proverbs 14.34 reminds us that "Righteousness exalts a nation, but sin is a disgrace to any people." Christians must apply this verse as they vote and live in today's culture. With God's Holy Spirit, we can awaken our nation to the evils that seek to strip it of its Christian heritage established by the Founders. We must reject crazy wokeism and choose normalcy to preserve the original intent of our nation's Founding Fathers.

It is time to choose normal over crazy.

Part One

America is a Divided Nation

CHAPTER 1

America Stands on a Christian Foundation

Religion is the only solid base of morals, and Morals are the only possible Support for free governments.[1]
– Gouverneur Morris

Psalm 33.12;16-22: 12 **Blessed is the nation whose God is the** L<small>ORD</small>, the people he chose for his inheritance…16 No king is saved by the size of his army; no warrior escapes by his great strength. 17 A horse is a vain hope for deliverance; despite all its great strength, it cannot save. 18 But the eyes of the L<small>ORD</small> are on those who fear him, on those whose hope is in his unfailing love 19 to deliver them from death and keep them alive in famine. 20 We wait in hope for the L<small>ORD</small>; he is our help and our shield. 21 In him our hearts rejoice, for we trust in his holy name. 22 May your unfailing love be with us, L<small>ORD</small>, even as we put our hope in you.

Our Founding Fathers understood that if they were to succeed in forging a free and independent nation, they must have God's aid, for the Psalmist taught them that:

> 16…No king is saved by the size of his army; no warrior escapes by his great strength. 17 A horse is a

vain hope for deliverance: despite all its great strength, it cannot save. 18 But the eyes of the LORD are on those who fear him, on those whose hope is in his unfailing love, 19 to deliver them from death.

They believed their only hope of defeating the mighty British war machine was to invoke God's help and that God would provide for them if they honored Him. Those who claim that America was not founded on the principles of Christianity are either naively misled or purposefully determined to undermine the nation's origins and alter the meaning of being an American. The *Declaration of Independence* acknowledges that our rights come from God, not the government. The Signers believed in self-evident truths, including the central foundational truths that *"all men are created equal, that they are endowed by their Creator with certain unalienable Rights, that among these are life, liberty, and the pursuit of happiness."*[2] If these truths are self-evident, then only a fool would fail to see and embrace them. Our Founding Fathers believed in them enough to fight and die for them. America needs people of truth to rise again today and protect her from those maliciously determined to separate the people of America from these truths.

God deniers must disregard these truths to advance their nefarious humanist agenda. If God endowed every person with fundamental human rights, then the humanist agenda crumbles like a house of cards. Facts are a troublesome thing for those who refuse to accept the truth. If one looks honestly at our nation's history, America was founded on Christian principles. That's not to say those who founded America were perfect men because they were not. Some enslaved people and all were flawed with a sinful nature, as is all of humankind. Romans 3:23 reminds us that "all have sinned," God revealed to the Apostle Paul that man's sinful nature required a Savior.

2

America was not founded by perfect white men but by sinners who acknowledged their flaws and relied on God to guide their paths. Today's generation ignores this critical fact at their peril. To avoid this mistake, one must examine the clues that history has preserved for us.

Christ Bearer

Christopher Columbus discovered the Americas in 1492 while sailing under the Spanish flag in search of a shorter and more direct route to India, China, Japan, and the Spice Islands. Labeled a dreamer by his critics, Columbus was inspired by his Christian faith. His name, Christopher, means "Christ Bearer." While it is not appropriate to defend all of Columbus's actions during his voyages to the "New World," it is evident that he desired to spread the gospel to the ends of the earth. In his journal, he wrote:

> Thursday, October 11 (1492)
> …Presently, many inhabitants of the island assembled…*that we might form a great friendship, for I knew that they were a people who could be more easily freed and converted to our holy faith by love than by force,* gave to some of them red caps, and glass beads to put round their necks, and many other things of little value, which gave them great pleasure, and made them so much our friends that it was a marvel to see. They afterward came to the ship's boats where we were, swimming and bringing us parrots, cotton threads in skeins, darts, and many other things, and we exchanged them for other things that we gave them, such as glass beads and small bells. In fine, they took all and gave what they had with goodwill.[3] (Italics added by authors)

Unfortunately, Columbus also found gold, spices, and other valuable commodities that his Spanish benefactors, King

Ferdinand, and Queen Isabella, would want to offset their investment and enrich themselves. Gold clouds many clear minds; some have discredited Columbus for exploiting the new world's inhabitants. Other European explorers followed his courageous example across previously unchartered waters to the Americas and ravaged the new world's inhabitants in search of treasure and fortune. Unlike the men who followed, Columbus was driven by his desire to present the gospel of the Lord Jesus Christ to the new world's inhabitants. Others came to the New World seeking gold, using their superior weaponry on the indigenous people causing terror and submission. Their actions are well documented and indefensible, but there were thousands more who came to America seeking God, and the United States of America, the greatest and freest nation the world has ever known, was the product of their willingness to brave the waters and dangers of the New World to advance the gospel and live in freedom.

The Scripture makes it clear that one generation is never responsible for the sins of the previous. We hear much today about reparations. In fact, the Democratic Party has become a coalition of the exploited classes led by an elite ruling class that promises them money, safety, and security in exchange for their loyalty, especially at election time. The Left has no hesitation in giving away other people's money to buy favor and support from their coalition of victimized groups.

In Vivek Ramaswamy's excellent book, *Nation of Victims*, he asserts: "So the main way victimhood causes national decline is by making the economic pie smaller as everyone focuses on grabbing as much of it as they can instead of by growing it.[4]" The Left encourages such victimhood and promises to repay them for their losses instead of encouraging self-reliance and refusing to be a victim. By making such promises, they keep their coalition

4

together. Fortunately for America, many are waking up to such empty promises and decades of failure to keep them.

The children of Israel dealt with this same issue. They were told that they were responsible for their father's sins. It became such a stumbling block to their lives that Ezekiel, the Prophet, addressed the matter. Ezekiel 18:1-4 states the following:

> 1The word of the Lord came to me: 2 "What do you people mean by quoting this proverb about the land of Israel: "'The parents eat sour grapes, and the children's teeth are set on edge'? 3 "As surely as I live, declares the Sovereign Lord, you will no longer quote this proverb in Israel. 4 For everyone belongs to me, the parent as well as the child—both alike belong to me. The one who sins is the one who will die.

We often hear talk from the Left about reparations and the responsibility that White America must bear in compensating the descendants of slaves for the mistreatment that African Americans endured at the hands of slaveholders in America over 150 years ago. There is a similar argument regarding the treatment of America's Indigenous inhabitants, who were conquered as the nation expanded westward until it reached the Pacific coastline.

In 1823, President James Monroe invoked the term "Manifest Destiny" when he spoke before Congress, warning European nations not to interfere with America's westward expansion. He threatened that any attempt by Europeans to colonize the "American continents" would be considered an act of war. This policy of an American sphere of influence and non-intervention in European affairs became known as the "Monroe Doctrine."

Clearly, many atrocities were committed against the Indigenous people by Americans who embraced the idea of

"Manifest Destiny." They believed that God had destined the United States to expand its dominion and spread democracy and capitalism across the entire North American continent. However, today's inhabitants are not responsible for the crimes and sins of their forebears. We are responsible for our behavior, particularly in our interactions with people of different ethnicities and lifestyles. Christians should be known for their love, kindness, and forthright stance on truth.

Our responsibility is to ensure we address racial issues fairly and justly in our generation. America is a nation of many ethnicities, all united by the common belief that "all men are created equal and endowed by their Creator with certain unalienable rights." The ultimate solution to all victimhood is not reparations but forgiveness, as taught in God's Word. Until that happens, America will continue to slide toward national suicide. Those who argue otherwise are mistaken; some do so intentionally because they reject the notion of God altogether. They despise the idea of America as it was originally designed.

We, the authors, believe the only hope we have for securing a future of blessings and freedom is to see millions of Americans return to the original intent of our Founding Fathers. Our national motto, printed on our National Seal and many coins, is *E Pluribus Unum*, a Latin phrase that means "Out of many, One."

Let's move forward and discuss those who sought God, not gold. England was a Roman Catholic nation until 1534 when King Henry VIII, one of England's most tyrannical kings, who reigned from 1509-1547, decided to break away from the Roman Catholic Church and form the Church of England. King Henry VIII is best remembered for his six wives, two of whom were executed at the Tower of London. His numerous indiscretions and fondness for beautiful women meant that he struggled to commit to one woman

6

for life, and the Catholic Church refused his many annulment requests. His solution was to replace the Roman Catholic Church with the Church of England, naming himself as the head of his new church.

Aided by his daughter, Queen Elizabeth I, who reigned from 1558-1603, he introduced changes that differentiated the Church of England from the Church of Rome while retaining many of the rituals and teachings of the Roman Catholic Church. Some thoughtful English worshipers felt that many of these rituals and teachings were unbiblical and sought relief from them. They were known as dissidents. Many of these devoted dissidents were called Puritans because they wanted to purify the Church of England.

Another more radical group was known as the Separatists. They wanted nothing to do with the Church of Rome or the Church of England, seeking instead the freedom to pursue personal faith and a simpler approach to Scripture and worship. The advent of the printing press and the Reformation that swept across Europe, ending the Dark Ages, opened many people's eyes by making the Bible available to the common man, allowing them to see God's truth and the differences between divine and human approaches to worship. Their growing resistance to Church authority resulted in fines, beatings, imprisonment, and for some, death.

Eventually, a group of Separatists moved to the Netherlands, where they found religious freedom. This group included William Bradford and the small band that would eventually land at Plymouth Rock in the New World. They lived in the Netherlands for over a decade, a period characterized by poverty and hard work when opportunities arose. Life in the Netherlands was difficult, with a language that was challenging for older members to learn, though easier for the young. The redeeming factor was religious freedom.

Contrary to popular belief, they did not go to America to find religious freedom but left the Netherlands because their children were being naturalized by their surroundings and losing their English identity. To live and worship as English people, they had to establish their own colony in the New World, which they decided to do. Some could not face the journey across the Atlantic and chose to remain. The following is a portion of the sermon Rev. John Robison gave to those of his church who would stay in Holland:

> I charge you before God and his blessed angels that you follow me no further than you have seen me follow Christ. If God reveals anything to you by any other instrument of His, be as ready to receive it as you were to receive any truth from my ministry, for I am verily persuaded the Lord hath more truth and light yet to break forth from His holy word. The Lutherans cannot be drawn to go beyond what Luther saw. Whatever part of His will our God has revealed to Calvin, they (Lutherans) will rather die than embrace it; and the Calvinists, you see, stick fast where they were left by that great man of God, who yet saw not all things. This is a misery much to be lamented.[5]

He wanted his people to understand that truth is not confined to one person or moment in history. The truth that swept across Europe, ending the Dark Ages, was still being revealed as people read the Bible for themselves, and he wanted his followers to have open hearts to the truth God was making known to all people. Rev. Robinson possessed a genuine pastor's heart.

While the church of the founding era advanced freedom, much of the church today is aiding and abetting the demise of liberty in America. It is doing so on two very different fronts. First, there are the preachers and churchgoers who avoid involvement in anything that may be construed as "political." Then, there are the preachers and active church members who have embraced "wokeism." The first group wants nothing to do with anything political for fear of offending some. To be loved and accepted, even if it means downplaying biblical truth, is desired by many.

The Church Growth Movement in the seventies gave birth to this notion when well-intentioned theologians and church leaders sought to better understand the mechanics of how to grow a church, forgetting that the pastor's sole responsibility is to faithfully proclaim that Jesus is the Christ, the Son of the Living God, and leave the growth of the Church to Him (see Matthew 16:13-18). Who among people can measure the true growth of a church? Nickels and noses do not always measure it. Some of the greatest churches in America are small but led by courageous Patriot Pastors who, like the sons of Issachar, understand the times and know what they should do, and they are doing it (see 1 Chronicles 12:32).

Woke pastors are activists who embrace Black Lives Matter and Liberal anti-law enforcement policies because "blacks and minorities have been unfairly targeted" by traditional law and order. They advocate for open borders and assert that homosexuality is not a choice. They embrace gender fluidity and socialism while allowing big government and bureaucrats to run their lives and direct their churches.

The COVID lockdowns revealed how easily many pastors would comply to gain favor with big government and avoid conflict. During the lockdown, we were told by our government that liquor stores and big box stores were essential and, therefore, could remain open, while churches were not and must be closed. God's Word says, "Do not forsake the assembling of ourselves together, as the manner of some is; but exhorting one another: and so much the more, as you see the day approaching" (Hebrews 10:25). We could understand a church closing for a few Sundays for a virus we knew little about to slow the spread, but after the first month, it became clear that the spread of COVID-19 was no greater among the churches that remained open than among the general public, and in many cases, it was less. Courageous pastors reopened their churches despite the mandate that they must remain closed.

The authorities began levying fines on some. Rev. Steve Smothermon, the Senior pastor of Legacy Church in Albuquerque, New Mexico, with multiple campuses across Albuquerque and New Mexico, publicly defied the Governor of New Mexico and refused to close his church and abide by her draconian measures, which ultimately destroyed many small businesses across the state.[6] After numerous threats of arrest and levying fines on his church, the Governor finally conceded she had no authority to shut down his church, and the fines were dismissed.

There were other wonderful examples of courage exhibited by men of God, like Pastors John McArthur and Jack Hibbs in Liberal California and Pastors Steve Riggle and Edwin Young, both in Houston. Many other pastors of large and small churches stood tall, risking it all, and are known to God for their courage. But many other pastors hid in the shadows and obeyed man rather than God. May they see the error of their ways and join the ranks of the courageous before it is too late.

The members of Rev. Robinson's church, who embarked on their journey to the New World, were about to face a strenuous trial beyond anything they could have imagined. They planned to meet with some other fellow Separatists in Southampton and depart together on the Speedwell and the Mayflower. Twice, the Speedwell returned to port because it leaked water. The Speedwell was declared unseaworthy, meaning all the Pilgrims would have to squeeze into the compact quarters of the Mayflower for the 3,000-mile transatlantic journey in a ship that was only 106 feet long.

They embarked on the 66-day perilous journey on June 26, 1620. When the Pilgrims left England, they obtained permission from the King of England to settle on land near the mouth of the Hudson River (in present-day New York). Due to currents and wind, the sailing vessel landed at Cape Cod on November 11, 1620. A few weeks later, they sailed up the coast to Plymouth and started to build their town where a group of the Wampanoag tribe had lived before a sickness had killed most of them. On November 11, 1620, needing to maintain order and establish a civil society, the adult male passengers signed the Mayflower Compact, the first official document signed by colonists in the new world, which became known as their "New" England. The text read:

In the name of God, Amen. We whose names are underwritten, the loyal subjects of our Sovereign Lord King James, by the Grace of God of Great Britain, France, and Ireland King, Defender of the Faith, etc.

Having undertaken for the Glory of God and advancement of the Christian Faith and Honour of our King and Country, *a Voyage to plant the First Colony in the Northern Parts of Virginia, do by these presents solemnly and mutually in the presence of God and one of another, Covenant and Combine ourselves together in a Civil Body Politic, for our better ordering and preservation and* furtherance of the ends aforesaid; and by virtue hereof to enact, constitute and frame such just and equal Laws, Ordinances, Acts, Constitutions and Offices from time to time, as shall be thought most meet and convenient for the general good of the Colony, unto which we promise all due submission and obedience. In witness whereof, we have hereunder subscribed our names at Cape Cod, the 11th of November, in the year of the reign of our Sovereign Lord King James, of England, France, and Ireland the eighteenth, and of Scotland the fifty-fourth. Anno Domini 1620.[7]

Early America was characterized by deeply religious men who sought guidance from God and aimed to introduce the new world's inhabitants to Christianity. A closer examination of the founding documents of each colony and subsequent state constitutions offers strong evidence that Christians founded America. Many state constitutions demanded more testimony of faith from office seekers than many seminaries require of their students today. Let's take a look at the founding documents of some of the original states and those of their leaders.

Starting with Pennsylvania, William Penn received a charter from King Charles II of England, which marked the first English charter to colonize land in the New World. Today, that colony is known as Pennsylvania. William Penn was a prominent member of the American upper class and supported the Society of Friends, also known as the Quakers. His father had loaned money to the King before his death, and many saw this charter as a way for the King to repay the debt. Quakers rejected rituals and oaths and opposed war. As a member of the Society of Friends or the Quakers, Penn wanted to create a safe haven for his persecuted friends in the New World and asked the King to grant him land in the territory between the Province of Maryland and the Province of New York.[8]

The Pennsylvania Constitution of 1776 stated that:
Each member, before he takes his seat, shall make and subscribe to the following Declaration: "I do believe in one God, the creator and governor of the

universe, the rewarder of the good and the punisher of the wicked. And I acknowledge the Scriptures of the Old and New Testament to be given by Divine inspiration."[9]

The Delaware Constitution, 1776 stated that:
Every person who shall be chosen a member of either house, or appointed to any office or place of trust, before taking his seat, or entering upon the execution of his office, shall take the following oath, or affirmation, if conscientiously scrupulous of taking an oath, to wit: "I, do profess faith in God the Father, and in Jesus Christ His only Son, and in the Holy Ghost, one God, blessed for evermore; and I do acknowledge the holy scriptures of the Old and New Testament to be given by divine inspiration.[10]

The North Carolina Constitution, 1776 stated:
That no person, who shall deny the being of God or the truth of the Protestant religion, or the divine authority either of the Old or New Testaments or who shall hold religious principles incompatible with the freedom and safety of the State, shall be capable of holding any office or place of trust or profit in the civil department within this State.[11]

The Vermont Constitution, 1777 stated:
And each member, before he takes his seat, shall make and subscribe to the following Declaration, "I ____ do believe in one God, the Creator and Governor of the Diverse, the rewarder of the good and punisher of the wicked. And I do acknowledge the Old and New Testament scriptures to be given by divine inspiration and own and profess the protestant religion.[12]

The Massachusetts Constitution, 1780 stated:

Any person chosen governor, lieutenant-governor, councilor, senator, or representative, and accepting the trust, shall before he proceeds to execute the duties of his place or office, make and subscribe the following Declaration: "I . . . do declare that I believe the Christian religion, and have a firm persuasion of its truth; and that I am seized and possessed, in my own right, of the property required by the Constitution, as one qualification for the office or place to which I am elected.[13]

Undoubtedly, the founding figures of America desired their states to be led by individuals who respected and feared God. They believed that fearing God was far more effective in curbing corruption than any man-made law they could conceive. They understood that without the fear of God's judgment, the hearts of all people could potentially transgress. This spiritual accountability, expressed in their creeds, was reaffirmed in the constitutions of the colonies.

Today's society clearly demonstrates the accuracy of their beliefs; as we have distanced ourselves from God and His moral laws revealed in Scripture, corruption and deceit have become increasingly commonplace. Let's examine the character and beliefs of some of the prominent individuals who made America the most blessed nation the world has ever known.

Introducing American Patriot George Washington:

Revered as the Father of our Country, George Washington had a profound and unwavering faith in Jesus Christ as his Savior and Lord. While addressing a Delaware Chief who brought three young people to be educated in American schools, he stated, "You do well to learn our arts and ways

14

of life, and above all, the religion of Jesus Christ. These will make you a greater and happier person than you are." During the War for Independence, his troops recognized him as a devout man of prayer, and his enemies believed he was divinely protected from harm. *The Bulletproof George Washington* is a book that recounts the experiences of a relative of Washington, who confirmed the legendary general's remarkable fortune on the battlefield.[14] The book tells a story from the French and Indian War before America gained independence from Great Britain. This tale was once taught in our schools but is now removed due to efforts to eliminate any reference to the supernatural aspects of our history.

It was the most lopsided battle in American history. 714 British soldiers were killed and 37 wounded. 26 officers out of 86 were killed, and 37 were wounded. Only 30 men and three officers were killed among the French and Indians.

Upon Washington's return to Fort Cumberland (120 miles from the battle scene), he wrote a letter to his mother to allay her fears, as news of the rout had preceded them. On the same day (July 18, 1755), he also wrote to his brother, John A. Washington: "As I have heard since I arrived at this place [Fort Cumberland], a circumstantial account of my death and dying speech, I take this early opportunity of contradicting the first, and of assuring you that I have not yet composed the latter. But, by the all-powerful dispensations of Providence, I have been protected beyond all human probability or expectation; for I had four bullets through my coat, and two horses shot under me, yet escaped unhurt, although death was leveling my companions on every side of me!"

Fifteen years later, an old respected Indian Chief sought counsel with Washington when he heard he was in the area. Through an interpreter, he explained that he had set out on a long journey to meet Washington personally and to speak to him about the battle 15 years earlier. He said: "I am a chief and ruler over my tribes. My influence extends to the waters of the great lakes and to the far Blue Mountains. I have traveled a long and weary path that I might see the young warrior of the great battle. It was on the day when the white man's blood mixed with the streams of our forest that I first beheld this chief [Washington]. I called to my young men and said; mark yon tall and daring warrior? He is not of the red-coat tribe–he hath an Indian's wisdom, and his warriors fight as we do–himself is alone exposed. Quick, let your aim be certain, and he dies. Our rifles were leveled, rifles which, but for you, knew not how to miss–'twas all in vain, a power mightier far than we shielded you. Seeing you were under the special guardianship of the Great Spirit, we immediately ceased to fire at you. I am old and soon shall be gathered to the great council fire of my fathers in the land of shades, but ere I go, there is something that bids me speak in the voice of prophecy. Listen! The Great Spirit protects that man [pointing at Washington] and guides his destinies–he will become the chief of nations, and a people yet unborn will hail him as the founder of a mighty empire. I have come to pay homage to the man who is the favorite of Heaven and who can never die in battle."[15]

In his lengthy farewell address at the end of Washington's long and distinguished career as a soldier/politician, he stated:

Of all the dispositions and habits which lead to political prosperity, religion, and morality are indispensable supports. In vain would that man claim the tribute of patriotism who should labor to subvert these great pillars of human happiness-- these firmest props of the duties of men and citizens. The mere politician, equally with the pious man, ought to respect and cherish them. A volume could not trace all their connections with private and public felicity. Let it simply be asked, where is the security for property, for reputation, for life, if the sense of religious obligation *desert* the oaths which are the instruments of investigation in courts of justice? And let us, with caution, indulge the supposition that morality can be maintained without religion. Whatever may be conceded to the influence of refined education on minds of peculiar structure and reason and experience both forbid us to expect that national morality can prevail in exclusion of religious principle.[16]

Meet American Patriot, Ben Franklin

Franklin was a member of the Second Continental Congress and served on the *Committee of Five,* which was charged with drafting the *Declaration of Independence.* He served as the First Postmaster General and was an Ambassador to France. He was also a member of the Constitutional Convention and a signer of the *Declaration of Independence.* No other Founder has been labeled as more irreligious and secular than Ben Franklin. In his autobiography, he wrote that the concept of God becoming embodied in human form through Jesus Christ and coming to Earth was a stumbling block to Christianity that he could not overcome.

His thoughts and interactions with Christianity were far

17

from those of an unbeliever. In Christ Church in Philadelphia, he reserved Pew 70 and regularly attended church there, along with many of our most prominent Founders. One of Franklin's most famous examples of faith occurred as the Founding Fathers grappled with the words of the Constitution for the new nation. Having defeated the British on the battlefield, they now struggled with building the government of their new nation. Ben Franklin stood before the Assembly and made the following recommendation that completely changed everything and laid the foundation for the longest-lasting Constitution the world has ever known:

Mr. President:
At the beginning of the contest with G. Britain, when we were sensible of danger, we prayed daily in this room for Divine Protection. -- Our prayers, Sir, were heard, and they were graciously answered. All of us who were engaged in the struggle must have observed frequent instances of a Superintending providence in our favor. To that kind providence, we owe this happy opportunity of consulting in peace on the means of establishing our future national felicity. And have we now forgotten that powerful friend? Or do we imagine that we no longer need His assistance? I have lived, Sir, a long time, and the longer I live, the more convincing proofs I see of this truth -- that *God governs in the affairs of men.* And if a sparrow cannot fall to the ground without [H]is notice, is it probable that an empire can rise without [H]is aid? We have been assured, Sir, in the sacred writings that "except the Lord build they labor in vain that build it." I firmly believe this, and I also believe that without [H]is concurring aid, we shall succeed in this political building no better than the

18

Builders of Babel: We shall be divided by our little partial local interests; our projects will be confounded, and we ourselves shall become a reproach and a bye word down to future age. And what is worse, mankind may, hereafter from this unfortunate instance, despair of establishing Governments by Human Wisdom and leave it to chance, war, and conquest. I, therefore, beg leave to move -- that henceforth prayers imploring the assistance of Heaven, and its blessings on our deliberations, be held in this Assembly every morning before we proceed to business, and that one or more of the Clergy of this City be requested to officiate in that service.[17]

Those do not sound like the words of someone who denies that God lives and involves Himself in the affairs of men. Speaking of the power and impact of Franklin's speech, Jonathan Dayton stated:

The Doctor sat down, and never did I behold a countenance at once so dignified and delighted at that of Washington at the close of the address, nor were the convention members generally less affected. The word of the venerable Franklin fell upon our ears with a weight and authority even greater than we suppose an oracle to have had in a Roman Senate.[18]

The friendship between Ben Franklin and the Rev. George Whitefield, who is credited with the Great Awakening that swept the colonies just before the war with England broke out, is legendary. Whitefield was preaching across America at the time. His crowds grew to sizes that no building in the Colonies could hold, so he went to open fields and preached.

Perhaps Franklin just found Whitefield to be a compelling speaker and was drawn to him, but it is hard to imagine such a rich friendship between two of the most famous men of their era could have flourished without some agreement on the truth Whitefield preached. After impacting all of England, he arrived on the shores of the Colonies, where he drew large crowds and many converts. It's hard to imagine a friendship developing between Franklin and Whitefield without the truth of what Whitefield preached penetrating the heart of Franklin. We won't put Franklin in Heaven—that's not our business here. However, we do have an opinion and believe that, despite the words of Franklin in his autobiography, he struggled intellectually with the incarnation; perhaps sometime late in life, he found the Gospel that Whitefield preached relevant to his own life as well. Regardless, he certainly lived by the Bible's teachings, respected its power in men's affairs, and advanced Christianity's principles.

Meet American Patriot Noah Webster:

American Patriot Noah Webster was the author of America's first dictionary, *An American Dictionary of the English Language*. He strongly advocated for America to separate from Great Britain and served as a soldier in the War for Independence. He was known as the "Schoolmaster of the Republic" and stressed that the Bible be used as a textbook. He became very influential in politics following the war. In a book he wrote in 1832, he attributed almost all liberty in the world to the Christian religion. He wrote: "The religion which has introduced civil liberty is the religion of Christ."[19]

Meet American Patriot Samuel Adams:

Samuel Adams was known as the voice of American Independence. In November 1772, Samuel Adams and other leading patriots formed the Boston Committee of Correspondence in response to the news that governors, judges, and other high officials in Massachusetts Bay Province would be paid their salaries by the Crown rather than by colonial legislatures. He was one of the early agitators in the colonies, calling for separation from British rule. Samuel Adams was also a devout orthodox Christian who was very active in the Congregationalist church. He believed in the stern patriarchal God worshiped by the Puritans who fled the Church of England. Unfortunately, today Samuel Adams is better known for beer than his deep personal devotion to Christ, which drove him to action for freedom and liberty. He famously stated: "[Divine] Revelation assures that righteousness exalteth a nation. Communities are dealt with in this world by the wise and just Ruler of the Universe. He rewards or punishes them according to their general character."[20] In 1772, he wrote in his *The Right of the Colonists as Christians* pamphlet:

> The right to freedom being the gift of God Almighty, the rights of the Colonists as Christians may best be understood by reading and carefully studying the institutions of The Great Law Giver and the Head of the Christian Church, which are to be found clearly written and promulgated in the New Testament.[21]

As a delegate to the Continental Congress, Adams signed the *Declaration of Independence*, and in a fiery 1776 speech in Philadelphia, he castigated Americans who sided with the Crown.

Meet American Patriot John Adams:

John Adams was also a member of the Committee of five appointed to draft the *Declaration of Independence*. Few did more to promote liberty and advance the American Revolution than did this devout Puritan Christian. He and his wife, Abigail, were known for their great love of God and Country. He was America's first Vice President and second President. He wrote in his diary, "The Christian religion is, above all the religions that ever prevailed or existed in ancient or modern times, the religion of wisdom, virtue, equity, and humanity."[22]

Adams, in a speech delivered to the Militia of Massachusetts on October 11, 1798, stated:

We have no government armed with power capable of contending with human passions unbridled by morality and religion. Avarice, ambition, revenge, or gallantry would break the strongest cords of our Constitution as a whale goes through a net. Our Constitution was made only for moral and religious people. It is wholly inadequate to the government of any other.[23]

In a letter to Thomas Jefferson, Adams shared what he believed united the army of the United States in their battle for freedom:

The general principles of Christianity, in which all those sects (denominations) were united, and in the general principles of English and American liberty, in which all those young men united, and which had united all parties in America, in majorities sufficient to assert and maintain their independence. Now I will avow that I then believed and now believe that those general principles of Christianity are as eternal and immutable as the existence and attributes of God; and that those principles of liberty are as unalterable as human nature and our terrestrial, mundane system.[24]

22

In another letter to Thomas Jefferson, Adams wrote, "I have examined all religions, and the result is that the Bible is the best book in the world."[25]

The Reconciliation of Adams and Jefferson: A Lesson for Today

One of the greatest stories of friendship born then lost and finally reconciled America has ever known is the story of the friendship between John Adams and Thomas Jefferson. These two men, more than any others, wrestled over the text of the *Declaration of Independence.* When the Republic was born, John Adams was elected the second president. His second term was lost to Thomas Jefferson in a bitter campaign over policy disputes, which severed their friendship in 1801.

One of history's unsung heroes and one of America's most devout Christians deserve thanks for reconciling the two Founding Fathers. His name is Benjamin Rush, a medical doctor known as the father of the Sunday School Movement in America called *The First Day Society*. Like Adams and Jefferson, Rush was a signer of the *Declaration of Independence*. He stayed close to both men in the years following the American Revolution. According to Founding Brothers author Joseph Ellis, he started encouraging former friends to reach out to each other in 1809.

The correspondence began with a New Year's Day letter from Adams, himself a dedicated follower of Christ, to Jefferson in 1812. For the next 14 years, the two men exchanged 158 remarkable letters to each other. In God's sovereignty, the two great men both passed away on the same day, July 4, 1826. The 83-year-old Jefferson died first, just after noon, at his mansion, Monticello. The 90-year-old Adams passed away several hours later. Political division separated these two great men for many years until a

23

Christian Founding Father, understanding Paul's words recorded in 2 Corinthians 5:14-21, put them into practice:

> 14 For Christ's love compels us because we are convinced that one died for all, and therefore all died. 15 And he died for all, that those who live should no longer live for themselves but for him who died for them and was raised again. 16 So from now on we regard no one from a worldly point of view. Though we once regarded Christ in this way, we do so no longer. 17 Therefore, if anyone is in Christ, the new creation has come: The old has gone, the new is here! 18 All this is from God, who reconciled us to himself through Christ and gave us the ministry of reconciliation: 19 that God was reconciling the world to himself in Christ, not counting people's sins against them. And he has committed to us the message of reconciliation. 20 We are therefore Christ's ambassadors, as though God were making his appeal through us. We implore you on Christ's behalf: Be reconciled to God. 21 God made him who had no sin to be sin for us, so that in him we might become the righteousness of God.

If America is going to be saved, it is up to Christians, led by their pastors, to take up the ministry of reconciliation once again and demonstrate to the world what it means to truly forgive. After all, [21]"God made him who had no sin to be sin for us, so that in him we might become the righteousness of God."

Meet American Patriot Patrick Henry

Patrick Henry served as the Governor of Virginia and led the fight for liberty as a Colonel in the Virginia Regiment.

24

He served as a member of the Continental Congress. And as a member of the Virginia House of the Burgesses, he gave his famous speech, which included the phrase, "Give liberty or give me death!" [26]

Henry once said, "Being a Christian…is a character which I prize above all this world has or can boast."[27] In a letter to his daughter dated August 20, 1796, he wrote:

> Amongst other strange things said of me, I hear it is said by the deists that I am one of their numbers; and, indeed, that some good people think I am no Christian. This thought gives me much more pain than the appellation of Tory; because I think religion is of infinitely higher importance than politics, and I find much cause to reproach myself that I have lived so long and have given no decided and public proofs of my being a Christian. But, indeed, my dear child, this is a character I prize far above all this world has or can boast.[28]

On his deathbed, Patrick Henry was reported to have said:

> Doctor, I wish you to observe how real and beneficial the religion of Christ is to a man about to die…. I am … much consoled by reflecting that the religion of Christ has been attacked in vain from its first appearance in the world by all the wits, philosophers, and wise ones, aided by every power of man, and its triumphs have been complete.[29]

Some of the Founders were deists, who believed in God, but not one who involved himself in the affairs of men. But Patrick Henry wanted the world to know he was a follower of Jesus.

AMERICA IN THE BALANCE

Meet American Patriot Rev. John Witherspoon

John Witherspoon was the first College of New Jersey President, now Princeton University. He was educated in Edinburgh, graduating in 1745. Upon graduation, he came to America, where he was a great advocate for the new nation. He presided over the Somerset County Committee of Correspondence (1775–76), was a member of two provincial congresses, and was a delegate to the Continental Congress (1776–79, 1780–82), wherein 1776 he was a persuasive advocate of adopting a resolution of independence. He was the only clergyman among the signers of the *Declaration of Independence*. As a result of his signing the *Declaration*, the British ransacked the College and almost destroyed it. After the war, he devoted his life to rebuilding the College and serving in the state legislature.

Witherspoon wrote extensively on religious and political topics. His works include *Ecclesiastical Characteristics* (1753) , *Considerations on the Nature and Extent of the Legislative Authority of the British Parliament* (1774), as well as numerous essays, sermons, and pamphlets.[30]

Meet American Patriot Rev. John Peter Muhlenberg

He is a favorite colonial character of the authors. In 1774, Muhlenberg was a member of the Virginia House of Burgesses and a pastor who regularly preached on Christian responsibility. His father, Henry Muhlenberg, was one of the founders of the Lutheran Church in America. In 1775, he preached out of Ecclesiastes 3. In verse one, it says: *"For everything there is a season and a time for every matter under Heaven."* He closed his message by saying: "In the language of the Holy Writ. There is a time for all things. There is a time to preach, and there is a time to fight."

He then took off his clerical robe, revealed he was wearing a Revolutionary Army uniform, and announced he was prepared to join General George Washington, who made him a Colonel of the Eight Virginia Regiment. He served throughout the war and achieved the rank of Major General, serving General Washington's staff. He is pictured sitting on his horse in the famous painting by John Trumbull of the surrender of Lord Cornwallis at Yorktown to General Washington. After the war, he held numerous political offices, including US Senator from Virginia. His portrait hangs in the National Statuary Hall in the Rotunda of the US Capitol.

There can be no argument from the historical record that Christians and men who feared God established America on Christian principles. Those Christian principles gave birth to a Constitution that disallowed the State to establish a national church and protected those who did not believe in God to speak without restraint. Constitutional Convention delegate James McHenry (1753-1816) wrote in his diary, "A lady asked Dr. Franklin, "Well Doctor, what have we got? A republic or a monarchy?' – 'A republic, if you can keep it, replied the Doctor'"[31]

How strong Christianity was in early America can be seen in the observation of Alexis de Tocqueville, who came from France in 1831 to observe how this new nation was faring under its republican form of democracy. He published his findings in his two-volume work entitled, *Democracy in America.* This French historian and social philosopher was impacted by the influence religion had on American citizens:

> Upon my arrival in the United States, the religious aspect of the country was the first thing that struck my attention; and the longer I stayed there, the more I perceived the great political consequences resulting from this new state of things. In France, I had almost always seen the spirit of religion and the spirit of freedom marching in opposite directions. But in

America, I found they were intimately united and
that they reigned in common over the same country.[32]

For this French historian, Christianity defined the nation's
character and identity. He believed it to be the most
important element in the nation's success and would
determine its future status:

> I sought for the key to the greatness and genius of
> America in her harbors...; in her fertile fields and
> boundless forests; in her rich mines and vast world
> commerce; in her public school system and
> institutions of learning. I sought for it in her
> democratic Congress and in her matchless
> Constitution. Not until I went into the churches of
> America and heard her pulpits flame with
> righteousness did I understand the secret of her
> genius and power. America is great because America
> is good, and if America ever ceases to be good,
> America will cease to be great.[33]

This Frenchman gives valuable insight into what America
was like in its first fifty years of existence. It is a shame that
most Americans are ignorant of this account of the early
years of our country.

Chapter 2

The Assault – Separation of Church and State

Of all the dispositions and habits which lead to political
prosperity, Religion, and morality are indispensable
supports. In vain would that man claim the tribute of
Patriotism who should labor to subvert these great
Pillars of human happiness ...[1]
- George Washington

Leftists often employ the tactic of targeting children as a means of shaping attitudes and instilling humanistic values and situational ethics. They aim to persuade young people to adopt relative morality, hoping that it will influence their beliefs as they mature. To achieve their goals, the Left sees the public school system as a valuable tool for exerting its influence. They have distorted the interpretation of the Constitution and propagated the myth of the "Separation of Church and State" to attack schools and other cultural institutions.

Target Christianity

The concept of Separation of Church and State is a fundamental principle for the Liberal Left, as important to them as the virgin birth of Christ is to Christianity.

Historically, schools have had a positive and cooperative relationship with Christianity and its values since the time of the Founding Fathers up until the mid-1900s. For Liberals to exert their influence in schools, they needed to neutralize or, ideally, eradicate the impact of Christianity in public education. They employed the Separation of Church and State as a weapon, shaking the cultural landscape and transforming the Liberal Left into a formidable force. A significant turning point occurred on June 25, 1962, when the Supreme Court ruled that prayer in public schools was unconstitutional.[2]

Liberals attempt to present their interpretation of the Separation of Church and State as indisputable and aligned with the Founding Fathers' original intentions. They argue that anyone who disagrees lacks reasonable intelligence. While they haven't convinced most Americans, they are inching closer. They maintain the advantage as long as they can sway enough judges to support their position.

The notion of Separation of Church and State is essentially a reinterpretation of history combined with a strategic marketing plan. It is unfounded. The United States was built upon strong moral and religious principles that would impact the nation's laws and way of life. Liberals seek to remove any religious influence on the country's laws and culture. To gain the upper hand in this debate, a side must win the historical argument, which is essential for understanding the full scope of the controversy.

Liberal politicians aim to prove that the Founding Fathers intended to create a secular government and a constitution that limited the role of religion in public affairs. They argue that religion should not be taught or mentioned in public schools, linked to national mottos, pledges of allegiance, national holidays, government practices, or displayed in any government building. According to proponents of the Separation of Church and State, the

Founding Fathers sought a purely secular government devoid of religious influence, particularly Christianity. They believe the First Amendment established a barrier to prevent religion from encroaching on government matters.

The Heart of the Debate

A sincere examination of history leads to a different conclusion. The "establishment clause" in the First Amendment states, "Congress shall make no law respecting an establishment of religion …" This was intended to prevent the government from declaring a specific sect or denomination as the official national church, similar to Britain's Church of England. The subsequent phrase, "…or prohibiting the free exercise thereof…" was seen as a restriction on Congress, preventing it from interfering with religious practices. If a wall existed, it was not to prevent religion from influencing the government and its policies but to keep the government from meddling with religious activities.

The "establishment of religion" interpretation lies at the heart of this controversy. The Left considers any reference or tribute to any religion or religious activity as an establishment of religion. For them, even a moment of silence at the beginning of a school day is unacceptable because it could be perceived as a suggestion for prayer. In contrast, those supporting Christian values believe the "establishment of religion" refers to Congress not officially endorsing a specific denomination as the national church or granting it preferential status. This perspective does not preclude religion from playing a valued and welcome role in the nation's life, culture, and law.

The outcome of this Separation of Church and State debate is crucial, as the winning side will have the upper hand in shaping the nation's culture and values.

Unfortunately, the Christian faith is losing ground. The original intent of the First Amendment's authors should determine the outcome, but their words reveal that the modern-day concept of Separation of Church and State is unfounded.

Although a careful study of history should resolve the issue, the situation is more complex. Liberals have become adept at "spinning" news to garner favorable opinions for their viewpoints, and they do the same with history. They have repeated the phrase "Separation of Church and State" so often that some surveys indicate two-thirds of Americans believe it is in the Constitution. However, this is false, as the words "Separation of Church and State" does not appear in the Constitution or any official documents related to the nation's founding.

The radical Left's approach to history mirrors the Liberal media's approach to the present. They research the subject, select supporting evidence, present it as the final word, and ignore the rest. If they uncover information that does not benefit their cause and cannot be hidden, they spin it. For the Left, repeating falsehoods as truth over time can eventually lead people to accept them as true.

Getting It Wrong

Liberals delved into history to find a champion for their "Separation of Church and State" doctrine, and they believed they discovered one in the third president of the United States, Thomas Jefferson, the author of the *Declaration of Independence*. They saw him as the Founding Father who provided historical evidence supporting their claim that the Founders intended a completely secular government.

When Jefferson was elected president, he received a letter from the Baptist Association of Danbury, Connecticut, expressing approval of his election and voicing a concern.

The Danbury Baptists worried that the religious rights granted to them by the State might not be the unalienable rights (from God) mentioned in the *Declaration of Independence*. They asked Jefferson for clarification regarding the government's potential interference in their religious activities and whether it could choose a national church, disadvantaging smaller denominations. He stated this:

> But, sir, our constitution of government is not specific . . . Therefore, what religious privileges we enjoy (as a minor part of the State), we enjoy as favors granted and not as inalienable rights.[3]

The Constitution in the First Amendment proclaims "free exercise of religion." The Danbury Baptists were calling for a point of clarification because they feared it might be interpreted that the State could change this "free exercise of religion" if it indeed were conceived that it was a right based on governmental policy. The Baptists asked, "Can the government intrude in our religious activity in the future?" They were also concerned that, as a small denomination, they could be disadvantaged if the government chose another denomination as a national church. It is quite clear that they were asking, "What reach does the government have into religion?" and not, "What restrictions are on religion regarding its involvement in public life and government activity?"

This distinction is significant because today's advocates of the Separation of Church and State use Jefferson's response to the Danbury Baptist letter as the all-important document proving their belief, even though they misinterpret the letter's meaning. The Baptists feared the intrusiveness of a strong government. At the same time, the secularists of the Liberal Left wanted to turn the emphasis to religion not being allowed any influence on government policy or activity.

Jefferson's response to the Baptists contained a phrase that stated his understanding of why the Constitution declared that Congress could not make a law that would establish a national religion or any law that would prohibit the free exercise of religion. That phrase was "thus building a wall of separation between Church and State."[4] This phrase from a response to an inquiry letter is hardly a document worthy of being compared to the *Declaration of Independence* or the Constitution. Still, it is what the Left must rely on for their Separation of Church and State doctrine. They point to the "wall," which Jefferson wrote as what needs to stand to prevent religion from touching any part of government and public policy. However, they got it all wrong! The "wall" in Jefferson's mind was not to prevent religion from touching the government but to prevent the government from interfering in religious activity or how a person expresses their faith.

One might wonder why Liberals are gaining traction and effortlessly achieving their goals. Why are religious practices increasingly limited in public affairs? Why are traditional references to God, essential to our national heritage, being challenged? These are puzzling questions in a representative republic where the people's voice is heard through the legislature, and public opinion is continually measured.

The Left has made significant progress with their unfounded Separation of Church and State idea because they recognize that they don't need to persuade lawmakers or the general public to succeed. All they need is for one of their lawyers to convince five judges on the Supreme Court to agree with their perspective. This is why Liberals view a conservative-leaning Court as a threat.

If this is the case, then why do Liberals have so much momentum and seem to be advancing their cause at will? Why does religion appear to face increasing restrictions concerning public affairs? Why are traditional references to God, which have been part of our national heritage, now under attack?

One Phrase Out of Context

The Liberal Left took one small phrase from Jefferson's response and used it as a springboard for a national policy. They disregarded the context in which the phrase appears, a common practice for those on the Left. They ignore anything that goes against their cause or even disproves it.

We will not ignore the context here. Below is a larger portion of Jefferson's response, which provides the context and understanding that undermines the Left's cause:

> Gentlemen,—The affectionate sentiments of esteem and approbation which you are so good as to express towards me on behalf of the Danbury Baptist Association give me the highest satisfaction … Believing with you that religion is a matter which lies solely between a man and his God; that he owes account to none other for his faith or his worship; that legislative powers of government reach action only and not opinions, I contemplate with sovereign reverence that act of the whole American people which declared that their legislature should "**make no law respecting an establishment of religion or prohibiting the free exercise thereof,**" thus building a wall of separation between Church and State. Adhering to this expression of the supreme will of the nation on behalf of the rights of conscience, I shall see with sincere satisfaction the progress of those sentiments which tend to restore to man all his natural rights, convinced he has no natural right in opposition to his social duties. I reciprocate your

kind prayers for the protection and blessings of the common Father and Creator of man and tender you for yourselves and your religious association assurances of my high respect and esteem.[5]

Jefferson used the phrase "natural rights," which the Founding Fathers often employed to describe unalienable rights originating from God rather than the State. This suggests that Jefferson understood the Baptists' concerns about the government potentially passing a law infringing on their religious freedom. Jefferson reassured them that the Constitution prevented the government from doing so, and the wall safeguarded religion from the State, not vice versa. Importantly, Jefferson acknowledged "the common Father and Creator of man" in his response, affirming his belief in God as the creator of humanity and the universe and rejecting the notion that life emerged by chance. However, Liberals often neglect to mention this aspect as they misuse his "wall" phrase.

Overwhelming evidence indicates that the Founding Fathers aimed to protect religion from the government while embracing it as a valuable participant in public affairs and culture. Jefferson's actions as founder of the University of Virginia challenged the Separation of Church and State advocates. He allocated space in the University of Virginia's Rotunda for chapel services.[6] and welcomed religious schools to be located near and on the university's property, enabling students to participate in religious activities.[7] He endorsed the use of the Charlottesville courthouse for church services. These actions by Jefferson would be condemned by Liberal activists today and banned by their allies in the judiciary.

Jefferson's actions demonstrate that he welcomed religion as a valuable participant in public affairs and did not perceive it as conflicting with government operations.

As he once wrote in a letter to Captain John Thomas in 1807, his words provide further evidence that religion was "deemed in other countries incompatible with good government and yet proved by our experience to be its best support."[8] Why hasn't this document been brought to light in this debate?

True Intent

Some of the same men in Congress that approved the First Amendment also passed the act creating the Northwest Ordinance in 1789 when George Washington was president.[9] The Northwest Territory would give the nation the states of Ohio, Indiana, Illinois, Wisconsin, and Michigan. Article III of the Ordinance contains the following words:

"Religion, morality, and knowledge being necessary to good government and the happiness of mankind; schools and the means of education shall forever be encouraged."[10]

The Congress of the United States approved an act where religion and morality are considered necessary for good government. Yet, this was the same Congress that the Liberal Left claims fully endorses their total Separation of Church and State concept. The latter part of the quote further complicates things for separation advocates, as the writers and approvers of the Act link religion and morality as subjects to be taught in schools.

The Founding Fathers did not want a national church, i.e., a national denomination; they sought to dispel this in the "establishment clause" of the First Amendment while still allowing religion to influence the government. They had witnessed the legacy of national churches in the countries they and their ancestors came from. The religious wars, special taxation, and sectarian rivalry were all undesirable to them. Founding Father Joseph Story wrote:

37

"The real object of the First Amendment was not to countenance, much less to advance, Mahometanism (Islam), or Judaism, or infidelity by prostrating Christianity but to exclude all rivalry among Christian sects."[11]

Could it be any clearer what the intention of those who wrote the First Amendment was? The issue of establishing an official religion was related to a particular denomination, not all religions in general. By the way, in case you are wondering who Joseph Story was. Check out some of his resume highlights:

• Son of one of the "Indians" of the Boston Tea Party

• Harvard graduate

• Delivered eulogy at George Washington's Funeral

• Member of the Massachusetts Legislature

• U.S. House of Representatives 1808-09

• Appointed to the U.S. Supreme Court by President Madison 1811-45

• Founder of the Harvard Law School

• Has been called the "Father of American Jurisprudence"[12]

Joseph Story, a prominent figure in American legal history, clearly articulates the framers' original intent. It raises questions about the judgments of activist judges that the Liberals use to advance their Separation of Church and State ideas.

Jefferson echoed Story's view on the First Amendment, emphasizing that the issue was related to specific denominations and not a religion in general. He wrote on this subject to a fellow signer of the *Declaration of Independence,*

Dr. Benjamin Rush:

> The clause of the Constitution which, while it
> secured the freedom of the press, also covered the
> freedom of religion, had given the clergy a very
> favorite hope of a particular form of Christianity
> through the United States, and as every sect believes
> its own form the true one, everyone perhaps hoped
> for his own, but especially the Episcopalians and
> Congregationalists. The returning good sense of our
> country threatens abortion to their hopes, and they
> believe that any portion of power confided to me
> will be exerted in opposition to their schemes. And
> they believe rightly.[13]

Once again, the crux of the issue is evident. The concern
was to prevent the establishment of a particular
denomination as a national church and not to eliminate
religion in general from public and political spheres. It is
helpful to study the issue as those at the Constitutional
Convention debated it to understand whether the focus was
on competing denominations rather than religion. George
Mason, known as "The Father of the Bill of Rights,"
suggested wording for the First Amendment:

> "All men have an equal, natural, and unalienable
> right to the free exercise of religion, according to
> the dictates of conscience, and that no particular
> sect or society of Christians ought to be favored or
> established by law in preference to others."[14]

Mason's words reveal that the "establishment clause"
debate was related to various sects and not excluding
Christianity as a whole. The historical evidence
overwhelmingly counters the position of Liberal leaders
and their secularist cohorts, but it hasn't slowed them down
from pressing their views.

Massachusetts, You Once Shined

An important aspect to consider in the Separation of Church and State is the actions of individual states after the U.S. Constitution was in operation. Today, those calling for strict observance of total Separation of Church and State demand that the laws passed federally related to this issue are immediately adhered to by all states. If the Supreme Court rules on a case involving one state, its ruling is considered the law of the land for the rest of the states. However, this concept was not held nor practiced in the early years of our nation.

Jefferson believed states had jurisdiction regarding religious exercise. He stated that the "power to prescribe any religious exercise . . . must rest with the States."[15] Many states had words in their state constitutions encouraging religious involvement and influence on civil affairs. There was a strong belief that religion improved the quality of government for the people and was welcomed. An example comes from the Massachusetts State Constitution during the founding era:

"As the happiness of a people and the good order and preservation of civil government essentially depend upon piety, religion, and morality, and as these cannot be generally diffused through a community but by the institution of the public worship of God and of public instructions in piety, religion, and morality: Therefore to promote happiness and to secure the good order and preservation of their government, the People of this Commonwealth have a right to invest their Legislature with power to authorize and require . . . the several towns, parishes, precincts, and other bodies politic or religious societies, to make suitable provision at their own expense for the institution of the public worship of God and for the support and maintenance of public Protestant teachers of piety, religion, and morality."[16]

This passage makes several points:

- The preservation of government depends upon piety, religion, and morality. The lawmakers in Massachusetts didn't think the Federal Government should prevent them from having religion play a vital part in the operation of their state government.

- The people have a right to demand that their Legislature require towns, parishes, etc., to provide for the public worship of God. The state government considered itself responsible for encouraging and promoting the worship of God. Such an action today would be declared unconstitutional. It wasn't deemed unconstitutional back then because it was clearly understood that the "establishment clause" pertained to a specific denomination receiving favored status and not removing religion entirely from the civic scene.

- The government encouraged and promoted the support and maintenance of piety, religion, and morality teachers. One thing the Left is firmly against is teaching religion to young people. However, an original state in the years following the ratification of the U.S. Constitution felt it was well within its parameters to do so.

For years, there was no challenge to their position. Religion was allowed to influence life and law with the blessings of the government.

All this time, they had no idea that they were being unconstitutional. It took the Liberal Left of our day and a handful of high Court judges who chose to ignore the obvious to make that call. History records that the state of Massachusetts willingly promoted the worship of God and the support of religious teachers. Isn't this the state that gave us Ted Kennedy, Michael Dukakis, John Kerry, and Elizabeth Warren? Maybe the citizens of this state should revisit their history for a reality check.

Clobbered by the Courts

It is unfortunate that some individuals on the Liberal Left have used the First Amendment as a means to further their own socialistic and morally questionable agenda. Prior to the appointment of three conservative justices by President Trump, the Supreme Court leaned in favor of the Liberal Left, leading to the erosion of long-standing practices and freedoms cherished by the American people for over 180 years. In his book, *Original Intent,* author David Barton provides a comprehensive list of the consequences resulting from judgments made by courts that have embraced a misguided interpretation of the separation of Church and State. Here are just a few examples:

- If a student prays over his lunch, it is unconstitutional for him to pray aloud. (REED v. VAN HOVEN, 1965)

- It is unconstitutional for a war memorial to be erected in the shape of a cross. (LOWE v. CITY OF EUGENE, 1969) (This ruling was reversed in 2023.}

- It is unconstitutional for a public cemetery to have a planter in the shape of a cross, for if someone were to view that cross, it could cause "emotional distress" and thus constitute an "injury-in-fact." (WARSAW v. TEHACHAPI, 1990)

- Even though the wording may be constitutionally acceptable, a bill becomes unconstitutional if the legislator who introduced it had a religious activity in his mind when it was authored. (WALLACE v. JAFFREE, 1985)

- It is unconstitutional for a classroom library to contain books dealing with Christianity or for a teacher to be seen with a copy of the Bible at school. (ROBERTS v. MADIGAN, 1976)

- Artwork may not be displayed in schools if it depicts something religious - even if that artwork is considered a historical classic. (WASHEGESIC v. BLOOMINGDALE PUBLIC SCHOOLS, 1993)

- It is unconstitutional for a kindergarten class to ask whose birthday is celebrated by Christmas. (FLOREY v. SIOUX FALLS SCHOOL DISTRICT, 1979)[17]

If the Founding Fathers were to read these items, would they say, "Yes, that's exactly what we had in mind when we put the Constitution together"? These court decisions are evidence that the radical Left has gained much ground in the culture war, and they did it all without swaying public opinion or passing a law in a legislature. It is also the reason why they are so concerned about the Supreme Court taking a conservative bend during the Trump years.

It needs to be pointed out that not all judges on the high Court have remained silent on this issue, even though they were on the minority side. The late former Chief Justice William Rehnquist has described the Separation of Church and State as a misleading metaphor.

> But the greatest inquiry of the "wall" notion is its mischievous diversion of judges from the actual intentions of the drafters of the Bill of Rights. . . . The "wall of separation between church and State is a metaphor based on bad history, a metaphor which has proved useless as a guide to judging. It should be frankly and explicitly abandoned.[18]

The words "mischievous diversion of judges,," tell us that the former United States Chief Justice gets it. He understood what the Founding Fathers had in mind and that wiping out 180 years or more of practices that were a vital part of our culture and rooted in our heritage was ridiculous. Liberals have found the Achilles Heel of our Republican representative form of government to be the judiciary system and have exploited it effectively. Now you know why some have called for stacking the Supreme Court by expanding the number of justices on it.

Jefferson is the great hero to the separation secularist crowd as they extract chosen words from his response to the Danbury Baptists to try and legitimize their position. Still, they must quote him when he speaks out about the judiciary system. Jefferson realized the dangers that the judicial branch held when it was not accountable to an electorate, a point he strongly made in a letter to William Jarvis.

> You seem . . . to consider the judges as the ultimate arbiters of all constitutional questions; a very dangerous doctrine indeed, and one which would place us under the despotism of an oligarchy. Our judges are as honest as other men and not more so. They have, with others, the same passions for party, for power, and the privilege of their corps. . . . And their power is more dangerous as they are in office for life and not responsible, as the other functionaries are, to the elective control. The Constitution has erected no such single tribunal.[19]

During the revolutionary war and to, the present-day motto of Jefferson's home state of Virginia was and is, "Thus always to tyrants," meaning their demise. According to Jefferson's words, some judges would not fare well today. Jefferson saw that the Supreme Court had the potential to

44

be misused. I don't think he would approve of the present radical tactics of the Democrat Party, of which he is considered the founder. They take his words out of context and then misuse the courts to advance their cause without the electorate's check. If Jefferson were alive today, these people would not be on his Christmas card list (holiday greeting card list for the politically correct Liberals).

The Founding Fathers wanted a government of the people, for the people, and by the people. Today, we get government by the judges, for the Liberal Left, despite the people. As it is now being executed, the Separation of Church and State policy has separated our country from its true heritage and the foundation of its greatness.

Chapter 3

The Radical Attack of the Left

I can no longer remain in today's Democratic Party that's under the complete control of an elitist cabal of warmongers who are driven by cowardly wokeness, who divide us by racializing every issue and stroking anti-white racism, who actively work to undermine our God given freedoms that are enshrined in our Constitution...[1]
- Tulsi Gabbard

The word "radical" is defined as "relating to or affecting the fundamental nature of something; far-reaching or thorough: 'a radical overhaul of the existing regulatory framework.'"[2] The current Democrat Party's actions are undeniably transformative and intended to overhaul the nation's laws, life, and culture. The Liberal Progressives are committed to completely restructuring America despite the precariousness of drastically altering a country hailed as the greatest in history. Nevertheless, the radicals who have taken over the traditional Democratic Party are undeterred and evil, willing to harm anyone to gain and retain power.

A Revisit to 1960

When you look back to 1960, it is apparent that the Democrat Party of today is far removed from its roots. The party's radical leftward shift has turned it into an anti-American movement rather than a political party. A simple comparison of the party then and now is sufficient to substantiate this claim. The 1960 party convention in Los Angeles nominated John F. Kennedy as President, and the party platform presented positions that would now be considered anathema to the Liberal mindset that controls the party. Today's Conservatives would be proud to run on the 1960 Democrat Party platform, which upheld values the current party has since abandoned. Three critical issues from the 1960 platform illustrate the drastic shift that has taken place within the party.

1. Military

The new Democratic Administration will recast our military capacity in order to provide forces and weapons of diversity, balance, and mobility sufficient in quantity and quality to deter both limited and general aggressions.[3]

The Democrat Party of 1960 prioritized maintaining a strong and fully equipped military, armed with state-of-the-art weaponry and fully mobile, to be prepared for any situation. Today's Democrat Party, however, seems more concerned with soldiers using the correct pronouns than weapon advancements. The COVID vaccine mandates have resulted in thousands of military personnel being discharged. At the same time, the Afghanistan fiasco left behind $80 billion worth of state-of-the-art military equipment for the Taliban and 13 dead military personnel. Consequently, recruitment in all branches of the military is now down. Andrew Abbott of the Association of Mature American Citizens articulated the Democrats' departure from their 1960 military stance, indicating a cause for concern:

48

Even as the military struggles to fill its ranks, Pentagon bureaucrats and Biden administration officials have also plowed ahead with their plans to "wokeify" the military, alienating vast swaths of Americans. The Army and Navy have pushed Critical Race Theory texts like Ibram X. Kendi's *How to Be An Anti-Racist* on their "recommended reading list." CRT has also entered the curriculum at West Point and other military academies. Recently, the Navy was slammed for forcing recruits to watch training videos on "proper pronoun usage." Several Republicans in Congress have also raised concerns about woke policies in this year's military funding bill.[4]

The President serves as the military's Commander-in-Chief, and his perceived weakness can have far-reaching consequences for our nation's security, particularly on the world stage. Hostile countries such as Russia, Iran, North Korea, and China become emboldened when they sense weakness. Unlike during the Kennedy years, the military no longer commands global respect. Russia has invaded Ukraine, and China is strengthening ties with Russia, Iran, and North Korea, leading many to anticipate their invasion of Taiwan by the end of 2023. These actions were unthinkable during the Trump presidency. An axis of evil similar to pre-World War II is forming, and only a strong America can prevent another catastrophic global conflict.

2. Economy

The new Democratic Administration will confidently proceed to unshackle American enterprise and to free American labor, industrial leadership, and capital to create an abundance that will outstrip any other system.

Free competitive enterprise is the most creative and productive form of economic order that the world has seen. The recent slow pace of American growth is due not to our free economy's failure but to our national leadership's failure.

We, Democrats, believe that our economy can and must grow at an average rate of 5% annually, almost twice as fast as our average annual rate since 1953. We pledge ourselves to policies that will achieve this goal without inflation.

Economic growth is how we improve the American standard of living and produce added tax resources for national security and essential public services.

...We believe that except in periods of recession or national emergency, these needs can be met with a balanced budget, with no increase in present tax rates, and with some surplus for the gradual reduction of our national debt.

... we shall bring in added Federal tax revenues by expanding the economy. Each dollar of additional production puts an additional 18 cents in tax revenue in the national treasury.[5]

The opening statement advocates for generating prosperity that surpasses any other system. This resembles the notion of "American Exceptionalism," criticized by Liberals. The passage commends the virtues of "free competitive enterprise" (capitalism) as the finest system in existence. It's doubtful that the progressive faction led by AOC would endorse this 1960 economic tenet, as they prefer a socialist model with elements of communism.

The 1960 Democrats pursued economic expansion without inflation or tax hikes. Such ideas are unfamiliar to today's Democratic Party, who often support new taxes and utilize inflation as a political tool by increasing the money supply to garner votes through government assistance.

The 1960 Democratic Platform included a call for a balanced budget, marking a historic moment for the party. It's hard to imagine that this concept was once part of the Democratic Party's legacy. Along with the balanced budget, reducing national debt was a key objective. No wonder numerous Americans voted Democrat in the 1960 election, and they would likely do so again if contemporary Democrats presented similar solutions. Modern Democrats aspiring to eliminate the national debt would be embarking on a fantastical journey. The notion of boosting tax revenue by expanding the economy without raising taxes is a conservative talking point, yet it is present in the 1960 Democratic Platform. It is unlikely that Nancy Pelosi and Chuck Schumer would adhere to the economic principles of this platform.

The current energy policy comes to mind whenever we refuel our vehicles or pay our electricity bills. It's hard to fathom that in 1960, gasoline cost 31 cents per gallon and stayed at that price until 1965. The energy ideas of the 1960 Democrats would probably result in their expulsion from today's party. There was no "Green New Deal;" instead, they put forth a strategy of energy self-reliance using domestic resources, as demonstrated by the following excerpt from their 1960 Platform:

> The Democratic Administration instead will foster the development of efficient regional giant power systems from all sources, including water, tidal, and nuclear power, to supply low-cost electricity to all retail electric systems, public, private, and cooperative.
>
> ...We will resume research and development work on using low-grade mineral reserves, especially

oil shale, lignite, iron ore taconite, and radioactive minerals.[6]

The 1960 Democratic Platform advocated for the "development of efficient regional giant power systems from all sources," which encompassed oil, coal, natural gas, and the soft brown coal known as lignite. Additionally, it promoted nuclear power as a low-cost solution for electricity generation. This stance contrasts sharply with current Democratic policies, which emphasize phasing out fossil fuels in favor of renewable energy. Banks have also begun to withhold financial support from fossil fuel industries.[7] Joe Biden campaigned on transitioning away from fossil fuels, and his policies on drilling and pipelines have contributed to higher gas prices. Nuclear power, a clean energy source, is often rejected by Liberals who fear potential radiation leaks or accidents. Modern Democratic energy policies reflect a more concerning undertone, which will be discussed in depth later.

3. Standing Strong Against Communism

To the rulers of the Communist World: We confidently accept your challenge to competition in every field of human effort.

We recognize this contest as one between two radically different approaches to the meaning of life—our open society, which places its highest value upon individual dignity, and your closed society, in which men's rights are sacrificed to the state.

We believe your Communist ideology to be sterile, unsound, and doomed to failure. We believe that your children will reject the intellectual prison in which you seek to confine them and that, ultimately, they will choose the eternal principles of freedom.

We reaffirm our pledge of determined opposition to the present admission of Communist China to the United Nations.[8]

Communism has been responsible for millions of deaths and widespread poverty, as seen in Russia and China. However, instead of valuing individual dignity, contemporary Democrats often view people as victims and group them accordingly. They seem more focused on empowering China than addressing its threats. China is buying American farmland, stealing technologies, planting spies on college campuses, and sending spy balloons across the country, with little consequence.

A July 2018 Rasmussen poll showed that many Democrats would welcome some form of communism. Baxter Dmitry of News Punch reported that former President Obama suggested embracing certain communist ideas, like universal basic income.

Today's Democrats show less opposition to China, even with its atrocious human rights record, and are more inclined to accept centralized power. Some Liberals even consider communism an attractive economic system.

In a remarkable turn, the Communist Party in America endorsed Democrat Joe Biden in the 2020 election, and the Democratic Party did not denounce the endorsement. Sixty years ago, Democrats staunchly opposed communism; now they've accepted an endorsement from communists for their presidential candidate.

The 1960 Democratic Platform is notable for what it excluded as well. There is no mention of abortion or LGBTQ+ issues, as neither party advocated for these matters in 1960. Now, these issues are integral to the Democratic Party's values. Anyone not supporting these positions is unlikely to be considered a viable Democratic candidate.

Radical on Social Behavior

Leftist Democrats often support late-term abortions, with some even endorsing the denial of medical attention for infants who survive botched abortions. This stance is inhumane and unconstitutional. Modern Democrats' radical devotion to abortion extends to infanticide, disregarding the rights of legal American citizens in favor of appeasing the pro-choice lobby.

Leftist often label Christians as homophobic, bigoted, and hateful. However, Christians object to homosexuality not because they harbor hatred for gay individuals but because the Bible condemns it as sexual immorality. Christians adhere to biblical standards for sexual behavior, which prescribe a monogamous relationship between a married man and a woman. 1 Corinthians 6: 9-11 states:

> 9Do not be deceived: Neither the sexually immoral nor idolaters nor adulterers nor men who have sex with men, 10nor thieves nor the greedy nor drunkards nor slanderers nor swindlers will inherit the kingdom of God.

Paul even acknowledges that some who were now serving God were at one time living in such sin then he writes in the next verse:

> 11 And that is what some of you were. But you were washed, you were sanctified, you were justified in the name of the Lord Jesus Christ and by the Spirit of our God.

Christians maintain their moral stance based on their religious beliefs. Meanwhile, Liberals support the National Education Association (NEA), which endorses aggressive actions by the LGBTQ+ community in classrooms. Exposing children to such information isn't intended for educational purposes but rather to recruit them to become gay.[12] This approach is inappropriate; taxpayer-funded public schools should not allow the LGBTQ+ community to recruit in their classrooms.

The "T" in LGBTQ+ stands for transgender, a movement that poses significant dangers to children. The term "evil" can be applied to the harm it causes. Democrats and Republicans should agree on the safety of minor-age children. Transgender advocates support drug therapy and invasive surgeries on children's genitalia, which can have irreversible consequences and cause immense trauma.[13] Liberals want to allow minors to make life-altering decisions they may regret later. Many children who undergo gender transition do so due to aggressive promotion from the transgender community, peer pressure, or manipulation from authority figures in the education system. Minors have not fully developed their minds and need protection from actions that can lead to lifelong physical and emotional damage. Some states view these actions as child abuse, but radical Democrats use the issue to appease their base. A later chapter will focus on the transgender issue.

Attack on the Family and Safety

Historically, the nuclear family has been the stabilizing force for society's well-being. However, Liberals no longer hold this belief. Parents who protested the content taught in public schools were labeled "domestic terrorists" by the Democrat-run Department of Justice. The National School Boards Association sent a letter to President Joe Biden on September 29, 2021, seeking to undermine these parents' actions. John Malcolm, Vice President of the Institute for Constitutional Government, commented on the letter and the Federal Government's actions:

Citing a few examples of disturbances at school board meetings by individuals who were upset about mask mandates and critical race theory curricula—all of which were, presumably, ably handled by state and local authorities or by the school boards themselves—and stating that such incidents were "impacting the delivery of educational services to students and families," the letter implored Biden to deploy the Justice Department, the FBI (including its national Security Branch and Counterterrorism Division), the Department of Homeland Security, and the U.S. Secret Service (including its National Threat Assessment Center) to combat this supposed scourge.

Without providing evidence, the letter claimed that "extremist hate organizations" attended school board meetings and that these protests should be considered "equivalent to a form of domestic terrorism and hate crimes."[14]

Today's Liberals consider it acceptable to involve the FBI in targeting concerned parents as terrorists. The National School Boards Association later apologized, indicating they had misjudged the climate for making such an outrageous accusation. However, they might still find a more suitable opportunity in the future.

One extremely radical idea promoted by the Left is *defunding the police.* In areas where this has occurred, crime has surged. Law enforcement efforts are hindered, and criminals often receive preferential treatment. Some cities, like New York, have instituted no-bail laws, leading to many offenders being released after arrest with disastrous consequences. A man released without bail on an attempted murder charge proceeded to shoot three people.[15] Most Democrats support defunding the police and allowing early release of prisoners, which is a recipe for disaster. While many Democrats believe these policies will appeal to a specific segment of their voter base, it comes at a high cost for law-abiding citizens.

It has been revealed through Elon Musk's work that Democrats conspired with the FBI to pressure Twitter into suppressing damaging information about Hunter Biden's laptop during the 2020 presidential election. Additionally, reports have surfaced indicating a higher percentage of Republican campaign emails were sent to spam folders compared to Democratic emails, allegedly due to intentionally designed algorithms.

Prominent founding figures such as Thomas Jefferson, Benjamin Franklin, John Adams, and George Washington are still revered by Americans today. However, Liberal Democrats have turned their attention to the teachings of Saul Alinsky. His influential work, *Rules for Radicals*, teaches people how to become community organizers. Alinsky, a Left-wing radical revolutionary, aimed to overthrow the existing system. Although he didn't join the Communist Party, he shared many of their ideas and admired Lenin. David Horowitz's book, *Barack Obama's Rules for Revolution: The Alinsky Model, unveils Alinsky's extreme ideology.*

Alinsky's advice can be summed up in the following way. Even though you are at war with the system, don't confront it as an opposing army; join it and undermine it as a fifth column from within. To achieve this infiltration, you must work inside the system for now. Alinsky spells out exactly what this means. "Any revolutionary change must be preceded by a passive, affirmation, non-challenging attitude toward change among the mass of our people." In other words, it is first necessary to sell the people on change, the "audacity of hope," and "yes we can."

You do this by proposing moderate changes which open the door to your radical agendas: "Remember: once you organize people around something as commonly agreed upon as pollution, then an organized people is on the move. From there, it's a short and natural step to political pollution.[16]

Alinsky's radical objective was to dismantle our capitalist economy, republican government, and national moral values rooted in our Judeo-Christian heritage. He advocated for an internal war against America, which is evident in the actions of prominent Democrats like Obama and Biden. Obama severely damaged a functioning healthcare system, and Hillary Clinton, his potential successor, would have likely completed its destruction. Biden is now undermining the economy and weakening law enforcement. The implementation of the Alinsky model is well underway.

Conservatives aim to improve our system through practical, lawful changes, while Leftists seek to dismantle and transform our nation. Such a transformation is unlikely to benefit our republican form of government. Historically, these transformations result in a wealthy ruling class and widespread poverty. Venezuela and Cuba serve as prime examples. Liberal radicalization targets various aspects of society, including voting procedures, drug policies, social media, and immigration. Our nation doesn't need transformation; instead, many lives could benefit from the transformative power of Jesus Christ.

This chapter began with a quote from former Democratic Congresswoman Tulsi Gabbard. In closing, we cite her statement upon announcing her departure from the Democratic Party:

I believe in a government that is of the people, by the people, and for the people. Unfortunately, today's Democrat Party does not. Instead, it stands for a government that is of, by, and for the powerful elite.

I'm calling on my fellow commonsense, independent-minded Democrats to join me in leaving the Democrat Party. If you can no longer stomach the direction that so-called woke Democratic Party ideologies are taking our country, I invite you to join me.[17]

Chapter 4

No Longer One Nation Under God

*America increasingly produces and distributes
propaganda for every perversion and obscenity
imaginable. If many of us accept the assumptions on
which this is based, and many do, then we are well
on our way to an obscene culture.[1]
– Robert H. Bork*

The Prophet Jeremiah spoke to his nation of their great sin that offended God. They are appropriate words for our country today (Jeremiah 2:5-13).

₅ This is what the Lord says: "What fault did your ancestors find in me, that they strayed so far from me? They followed worthless idols and became worthless themselves. ₆ They did not ask, 'Where is the Lord, who brought us up out of Egypt and led us through the barren wilderness, through a land of deserts and ravines, a land of drought and utter darkness, a land where no one travels, and no one lives?' ₇ I brought you into a fertile land to eat its fruit and rich produce. But you came and defiled my land and made my inheritance detestable. ₈ The priests did not ask, 'Where is the Lord?' Those who dealt with the law did not know me; the leaders rebelled against me. The prophets prophesied by Baal by following worthless idols.

[9] "Therefore I bring charges against you again," declares the Lord. "And I will bring charges against your children's children. [10] Cross over to the coasts of Cyprus and look, [11] **Has a nation ever changed its gods?** (Yet they are not gods at all.) But my people have exchanged their glorious God for worthless idols. [12] Be appalled at this, you heavens, and shudder with great horror," declares the Lord. [13] **"My people have committed two sins: They have forsaken me, the spring of living water, and have dug their own cisterns, broken cisterns that cannot hold water.** (Bold print by authors)

Giving God the Boot

On September 9, 2012, The Baltimore Sun featured an editorial by Bob Harper titled "Democrats kicked God off the platform." The article quoted an unnamed DNC spokesperson who said some of their delegates were offended by including God in their plans for America. They reinserted God into their platform by a voice vote in which the nays clearly outnumbered the yeas, but the chair ruled that the motion to reinsert God passed. This occurred at the 2012 Democratic National Convention held in Charlotte, North Carolina.

Harper stated in his article, "After much bad publicity about giving God the boot, a vote was taken. Even though the voice vote reflected that the majority wanted God left out, the DNC allowed God back on their convention bus, but only as a passenger, not the driver.[2]" That thwarted attempt to remove God from their party platform revealed how committed the Liberal Left is to making America a secular nation without any Christian influence.

We could cite many examples, but when a major party of a nation treats the God who granted them their fundamental human rights as "persona non grata," that nation is in real trouble.

Christianity is seen as an enemy to most Liberal Democrats because they know studies have shown that the more devoted a person is to the Christian faith, the more likely they are to vote for conservative candidates found in the Republican Party. The Left desires the seats of power, and Christianity is seen as restricting that goal. America was founded on the concept that our rights come from God, not the government. The Liberal statist, who sees government as all-powerful, must regard the Christian faith and the God it worships as competition to be neutralized, not a national foundation stone to respect.

The Founding Fathers clearly stated in the *Declaration of Independence* that our rights come from the hand of God. All men are equal. They were all equal under God, having the same rights, and none were above the law to show favoritism in administering justice. It was not an equality of economic status which was to be gained through one's efforts, but the opportunity to do so was granted freely to all. Liberals today, through their secularization and socialism, seek to reverse this. They want all to be equal in economic status but not rights because they believe the government should dispense those as it sees fit. The Christian faith is a friend of freedom but an enemy of tyranny.

As we acknowledged in our previous chapter, there has been a steady and determined effort to erode our Christian foundations over the past 100 years. The nation is reeling upon becoming one without God and a positive moral direction. In this chapter, we will reveal how the once-secure foundation of our country is now being destroyed chip by chip. The Psalmist (Psalms 11:3) raises this profound question: *"When the foundations are being destroyed, what can the righteous do?"* Know this fact: Christians cannot lose unless they quit. We push forward despite the odds because we innately know God is real and has assured us ultimate victory!

Arrival of Humanism

There are only two sources of knowledge in the world: That which flows by revelation from God and that which comes from the Evil One. Man's wisdom divorced from God is called Secular Humanism, and it now permeates our intellectual elites and their devotees. God's wisdom is revealed in the Bible, His Holy Word, and the Holy Spirit gives it to anyone who humbly seeks it. In the second chapter of Proverbs, wise Solomon writes:

> ...3 if you call out for insight and cry aloud for understanding, 4 and if you look for it as for silver and search for it as for hidden treasure's then you will understand the fear of the Lord and find the knowledge of God. 6 For the Lord gives wisdom; from his mouth comes knowledge and understanding. 7 He holds success in store for the upright; he is a shield to those whose walk is blameless.

Man's knowledge, severed from God's revealed truth, is found in our halls of education, media, entertainment, and government. In their book *Mind Siege*, Tim LaHaye and David Noble point out that "Humanism is a very old religion. It rests its case on the side of the serpent in the Garden of Eden, who said to Eve, 'You will not surely die. For God knows that in that day your eyes will be opened, and you will be like God, knowing good and evil.'"[3]

Having rejected God's revealed truth and wisdom, secularists become their own god believing their knowledge is superior to the Bible. They see no need or purpose in studying the Bible, equating it to a book of unscientific myths written for superstitious and ignorant people. They use terms designed to fool Christians, especially Christian parents who think they understand what their children are studying when often the opposite is true. For instance, in the Humanist Manifesto, the term *"scientific naturalism"* leads many to think they are referring to science when it is another way of describing atheism.

A core value of humanists, impacting everything they do, is their belief there is no heaven, so they must create their heaven on Earth. All devoted humanists, and there are millions in the United States, are working toward a one-world government. They seek to use a centralized government's power to bring imposed peace on Earth. The end they seek is worth any means they use to achieve it. Christian author and activist Bill Murray refers to them as "Utopians," aiming for a state in which everything is perfect. Unfortunately, imperfect humans with a sinful nature cannot create an ideal world. This plan will ultimately end in disarray.

The Bible speaks of an Armageddon that must and will come because Jesus has told us to watch for the signs of his return and the end of this age. But we are not to sit back and let the world destroy itself. We have a ministry of reconciliation. We hold tightly to one promise our Lord said would happen before his return and the end of this world; Matthew 24:14 states: "14 *And this gospel of the kingdom will be preached in the whole world as a testimony to all nations, and then the end will come."*

That has yet to happen, but technology is making it more attainable. Dedicated people are taking the *Jesus Film* via portable generators and projectors to remote areas that have never heard the gospel. As we write this book, we pray and work for a Third Great Awakening that will bring tens of thousands of people to a first-time or renewed relationship with Jesus Christ. America is the place where an awakening can begin. We have a remnant of dedicated Christian leaders to make it happen. The Asbury University outpouring of God's spirit, which captured national attention in the winter of 2023, is a positive sign. A great awakening can happen again if Christian pastors, leaders, and church members will meet the conditions of *humility* and *agonizing prayer* called for in the often referred to revival verse of 2 Chronicles 7:14.

Trying to Make a Secular Nation

People say President Joe Biden is incompetent and making wrong policy decisions, but one can take a different view of his actions. Maybe he is doing precisely what he aimed to do. His mental competency aside, he could be considered one of the most accomplished presidents in our history when considering that he is achieving his goals. Tragically, he ran to transform the America we know into a secular nation, merging into a world community that denies God. Secularization means to remove the influence or value of God.

When Barack Hussein Obama ran for the Presidency in 2008, I (Rick) was writing a book entitled, *Enough is Enough*. I researched this newcomer to national politics and discovered he was a disciple of Saul Alinsky, whose book, *Rules for Radicals*, dedicated to Lucifer, had shaped his political views much as it did Hillary Clinton, his chief rival for the Democratic presidential nomination in 2008. She would become his Secretary of State and be the party's presidential nominee in 2016. The more I studied Obama's background and read his speeches and writings, the more dangerous I believed he would be to our country. In the initial months of his Presidency, he confirmed my suspicions. He appointed "Czars" for newly funded positions who did not have to face confirmation hearings. Many would never have been confirmed due to their extremist positions. These "Czars" numbered 28 according to PolitiFact, though Judicial Watch put the number at 45.[4] They were accountable to President Obama alone, and took the nation in a radically Liberal Left direction.

The Wall Street Journal, in an opinion piece by Karl Rove, entitled "The President's Apology Tour," reported; President Barack Obama has finished the second leg of his international confession tour. In less than 100 days, he has apologized on three continents for what he views as the sins of America and his predecessors.[5] When President Obama was asked if he believed in *American Exceptionalism,* he said he did, in the same way, "the Brits believe in British Exceptionalism and the Greeks in Greek Exceptionalism."[6] That's another way of saying, "No." His answer may seem fine for many who have never been taught what American Exceptionalism is, but it fails to carry the term's true meaning: America is more of an idea than a piece of real estate. Ours is the only nation on Earth primarily comprised of people who left other places to embrace a set of ideals articulated in the opening lines of our *Declaration of Independence* that *all men are created equal, that they are endowed by their Creator with certain unalienable Rights, that among these are Life, Liberty and the pursuit of Happiness.*

There is a reason why the courts are attacking Christianity. The Left long ago realized that they could accomplish their goals of secularization by using the courts rather than going the legislative route. As previously stated in Chapter Two, Americans' deeply rooted religious nature was considered too influential on lawmakers Alexis de Tocqueville was a French aristocrat, diplomat, and historian. He is best known for his works *Democracy in America* (appearing in two volumes, 1835 and 1840). It was published after Tocqueville traveled in the United States and is considered an early work of sociology and political science.

He said, "America is great because America is good. If America ever ceases to be good, America will cease to be great."[7] Andrew Reed and James Matheson, two British ministers who visited sister churches in the United States in 1834 to promote peace and friendship, wrote about their travels. In their 1835 book, they wrote: *"America will be great if America is good. If not, her greatness will vanish away like a morning cloud."* [8]

On Flag Day, June 14, 1954, President Eisenhower signed a bill into law adding the words "One nation under God" to our Pledge of Allegiance to our flag. This was a positive affirmation of our Christian heritage. The Left has made this a target phrase in its attempt to turn America into a secular country. The Supreme Court dealt with a case in 2004, *Elk Grove Unified School District v. Newdow*, where a California father, an atheist, claimed the words violated his daughter's rights under the First Amendment Free Exercise Cause. The case was not ruled on because the father did not have full custody of his daughter, therefore no proper standing. Chief Justice William Rehnquist and Justices Sandra Day O'Connor and Clarence Thomas wrote separate concurrences, requiring teachers to lead the Pledge, even with the words "under God," was constitutional.[9] Other Left attempts to remove these cherished words have also failed in the courts. However, the attacks on Christianity have remained strong in other legal battles.

Court Cases With Anti-Christian Content

The following cases reveal how Liberals have used the courts to target Christianity and speed the nation's secularization.

Engle v Vitale 1962

The Supreme Court ruled that prayer in public schools

violated the First Amendment Establishment Clause and that a nondenominational prayer in New York was illegal. Interestingly, the prayer itself was so innocuous that it is difficult to see what harm it could do to those praying the prayer. Take a look:

> "Almighty God, we acknowledge our dependence upon Thee, and we beg Thy blessings upon (1) us, (2) our parents, (3) our teachers and (4) our Country."

In another chapter, we will go into greater detail on the depth of degradation our nation has slid in education. Still, a simple look at what the children were forbidden to pray for reveals how steadfast the Left is in undermining the Christian faith and the wisdom of God.

"We beg thy blessings on "us," they recited each morning. Consider the state of childhood in 1962 compared to today. In schools today, children face bullying and even acts of violence. The suicide rate among teens is astonishing. Many turn to illegal drugs to cope with the stress and pain of modern life, and some meet an untimely death in the process. The pure secular education they receive, which has been more indoctrination than education, has denied them the required skills to have a productive life, and many are unprepared for the workplace. You cannot say this is a blessed life.

In 1962, divorce was uncommon, and most children lived in two-parent homes, with one parent providing the necessities of life and one parent devoted to making their house a home 24/7, providing care and security for their offspring. Today, divorce is widespread, and many children live in a single-parent home which is a significant disadvantage for them financially and emotionally.

Today divorce is declining slightly after rising every year since 1962. Still, the decline is because this generation is discarding marriage altogether, opting to live together without marriage, leading to other serious social issues. When the children were forbidden to have their morning prayer at schools across the country, a much larger audience was watching, and the consequences have devastated our nation. Clearly, God is not blessing the "us" in that prayer deemed a violation of the Separation of Church and State.

The second phase of that prayer, *"our parents,"* was a request for God's blessings upon their parents, but then everything changed as if God quit blessing the parents of the children in 1962. Those parents had witnessed more change than any generation. Some endured the Great Depression and fought in an overseas war. However, their government never accused them of being domestic terrorists just because they wanted to have a say in their kids' education.

Church attendance was at an all-time high in 1962, climbing to over 63 percent of the population. Billy Graham was at the height of his ministry as he packed the largest venues in America with people seeking to know Christ. By 2021, the percentage who claimed to attend weekly dropped to 22 percent. The "Greatest Generation" was replaced with the "Consumer Generation," which consumed everything, including themselves. Company / employee loyalty began a long slow, painful death as profits became the issue in boardrooms. The Consumer Generation of the sixties started experimenting with every drug imaginable as if personal pleasure and comfort were the sole objectives of living. That generation became the most self-destructive of any previous generation, with suicide and mental breakdowns becoming all too common. God was no longer being asked to "Bless our parents" daily as before. The prayer was gone, and so were the blessings.

Children had been taught to pray for their teachers. In previous decades, back to one-room schools, teaching was an honorable profession in which people invested years of preparation, knowing they would be underpaid but greatly respected and appreciated for their sacrifice. There was no more esteemed profession in America than being an educator. A satisfying reward for them was seeing their students succeed in life.

Schools and churches in communities used to partner together for the good of children. Besides having a commencement, every graduation class also had a cap and gown baccalaureate service, which featured a pastor giving a sermon. The authors of this book have each been a part of these services, but the event is no longer held. It has become a casualty of the Separation of Church and State mob. Schools used to not schedule events on Wednesday evenings, allowing people to attend mid-week church services and activities. That is now passé.

The teachers' unions control education today. They are not Christian-friendly. The National Education Association contributes tens of millions of dollars of teachers' dues to Liberal politicians, who reciprocate by passing legislation resulting in higher teacher salaries, tenure (guaranteed job security), and less classroom responsibility. When test scores decline, Liberal politicians lower the standards making it easier for teachers.[10] Many schools across America resemble a combat zone more than a place of learning. There are some inner-city schools where teachers risk their lives teaching due to classroom violence. God was removed from the school, and Satan quickly moved in with his deception and disruption.

An American Psychological Association Task Force on Violence recently made the following discovery, released on March 19, 2022:

> Overall, 59% of teachers, 58% of administrators, 48% of support staff, and 38% of school psychologists and social workers reported being victimized in some way while at work.

Regarding physical violence, support staff – like school resource officers, aides, and bus drivers – were the most likely to report physical aggression. **More than 99% of the aggressors were students.**[11]

The Bible is filled with admonishment to pray. A few of the best known are: *"Rejoice always, pray without ceasing, give thanks in all circumstances; for this is the will of God in Christ Jesus for you"* (1 Thessalonians 5:16-18) *"If my people, who are called by my name, will humble themselves and pray and seek my face and turn from their wicked ways, then I will hear from heaven, and I will forgive their sin and will heal their land."* (**2** Chronicles 7:14)

Murray v. Curlett 1963 and Abington School District v. Schempp 1963

David Horowitz refers to Madalyn Murray O'Hair as a "world-class provocateur," in his book, *Dark Agenda.*[12] In this case, she declared her son, Bill, was an atheist who was being forced to participate in a religious exercise by the state against his will. This raised the profile of O'Hair to national prominence as she fought to end any form of religious expression in the public square, primarily in public schools. Horowitz referred to this case as the "Ft. Sumter" of the war over religious liberty in America.[13]

It was combined with a similar case, and the Justices ruled in Murray's favor by a margin of 8-1. The sole dissent was by Justice Stewart, who correctly argued the Establishment Clause was only meant to prohibit the establishment of a state-sponsored church, such as the Church of England, and not restrict all types of government involvement with religion. In particular, he found that the nondenominational nature of the prayer and the "absentee" provision removed constitutional challenges. He went on to state in his minority opinion that rather than the Court remaining neutral in the matter of religion, they instead imposed a state religion and that the one religion left protected was the religion of secularism. The Wall Street Journal agreed, stating that atheism was now "the one belief to which the state's power will extend its protection."[14] The Schempp case made mandated Bible reading and reciting the Lord's Prayer unconstitutional.

Should they disagree, this matter should have been left to each state to decide through their duly elected representatives, leaving citizens some recourse. But in typical Leftist tyrannical fashion, they bypassed the citizens. They found eight unelected Justices willing to overturn lower Court rulings and impose their religious bias on the nation with the stroke of a pen. Murray, meanwhile, found fame and fortune in her new role, dubbed the "Most hated woman in America." Life Magazine did a cover story on her. The American Civil Liberties Union picked up her legal bills, as atheists worldwide had a new heroine. She became an instant celebrity by hating God and was noted on The Today Show when they celebrated her birthday in their segment, Great People Born Today.

I (Rick) have known and worked on projects with her son, Bill, for over thirty years. After his mother was murdered by one of her devotees, Bill came to know Christ and has had a wonderful ministry for more than three decades, helping refugees in the Middle East and speaking and writing in the U. S.

This ruling forbade the Bible to be read in school, in direct conflict with many passages in Scripture, but none more forthright in promises and warning than Psalm 1:1-6:

> [1] Blessed is the man who does not walk in the counsel of the wicked or stand in the way of sinners or sit in the seat of mockers. [2] But his delight is in the law of the LORD, and on his law he meditates day and

night. [3] He is like a tree planted by streams of water, which yields its fruit in season and whose leaf does not wither. Whatever he does prospers. [4] Not so the wicked! They are like chaff that the wind blows away. [5] Therefore, the wicked will not stand in the judgment, nor sinners in the assembly of the righteous. [6] For the LORD watches over the way of the righteous, but the way of the wicked will perish.

Stone v. Graham (1980)

The foundation of all moral law is the Ten Commandments, and our Founders built our entire legal system around the Ten Commandments. In 1980 in the Supreme Court case (Stone v. Graham), the Supremes struck down a Kentucky law requiring that a copy of the Ten Commandments be posted in every public school classroom, the Court saying:

"The preeminent purpose for posting the Ten Commandments on schoolroom walls is plainly religious in nature. The Ten Commandments are undeniably a sacred text in the Jewish and Christian faiths, and no legislative recitation of a supposed secular purpose can close our eyes to that fact. The Commandments do not confine themselves to arguably secular matters, such as honoring one's parents, killing or murder, adultery, stealing, false witness, and covetousness. Rather, the first part of the Commandments concerns the religious duties of believers: worshiping the Lord God alone, avoiding idolatry, not using the Lord's name in vain, and observing the Sabbath Day."

With the stroke of a pen, nine unelected Justices slapped God in the face. They said, your laws can no longer be posted in our schools because the Majority Opinion stated: *If the posted copies of the Ten Commandments are to have any effect at all, it will be to induce the schoolchildren to read, meditate upon, perhaps to venerate and obey, the Commandments.*

Here's a look into the Liberal mindset. Reading and meditating on the Ten Commandments might lead children to obey them. What could be worse than children obeying such laws as Thou shalt not steal, Thou shalt not kill, and Thou shalt not lie? Now we have school shootings, child trafficking, and attacks on schoolteachers, but the Liberal Court has protected the child from getting soiled by religion while at school.

Wallace v. Jaffree (1985)

In another case involving prayer, the Supreme Court examined whether an Alabama law authorizing a period of silence for "meditation or voluntary prayer" violated the Establishment Clause of the First Amendment. The Alabama law was an effort to thread the increasingly narrow needle to allow their students time to pray if they so desired. In a 6-3 decision, the Court struck down the law as violating the Establishment Clause because it had no secular purpose and because the addition of "and voluntary prayer" to the wording of an almost identical earlier statute "indicated that the State intended to characterize prayer as a favored practice, effectively endorsing a religion."

I (Rick) lived in Mobile, Alabama, between 1983-1988 and served on a church staff for part of that time. My role was to oversee all evangelistic outreach and train laypeople on how to share their faith. One afternoon, I took one of our leading laymen to a local mall to share our faith with a stranger. I saw a gentleman standing alone and approached him and asked if I could speak to him briefly about the most crucial subject he would ever discuss. My friend watched in amazement. I assumed it was because I was speaking to a stranger. However only after the gentleman courteously listened and rejected my offer to accept Christ did my friend tell me I was talking to Ishmael Jaffree, the plaintiff in a prayer case pending before the Supreme Court. I have often wondered if he ever thought more about our brief encounter. Christianity is an adventure when practiced in our daily lives.

This ruling struck down Alabama's effort to allow children to pray silently. Courts, ignorant of our Christian heritage, have a propensity to attack prayer. They sure work hard to stop it, even in a child's mind. Romans 1:22 applies: *Professing themselves to be wise, they became fools...*

Lawrence v. Texas (2002)

This landmark case, in which the Supreme Court of the United States, in a 6-3 decision, invalidated sodomy laws across the United States, making same-sex sexual activity legal in every state and United States territory. The majority opinion in this case, written by Justice Kennedy, overturned the previous ruling of the Supreme Court on the same issue. This ruling shouted at God, "Your moral law and the wisdom upon which it was given have no place in America."

In his scathing dissent, Justice Antonin Scalia, who was joined by Chief Justice William H. Rehnquist and Justice Clarence Thomas, wrote: "Today's opinion is the product of a Court, which is the product of a law-profession culture, that has largely signed on to the so-called homosexual agenda by which I mean the agenda promoted by some homosexual activists directed at eliminating the moral opprobrium that has traditionally attached to homosexual conduct. ... The Court has taken sides in the culture war, departing from its role of assuring, as a neutral observer, that the democratic rules of engagement are observed."

With this ruling, the Supreme Court escalated its war on religion. By striking down Texas's law prohibiting sodomy, they opened the nation to abhorrent behaviors and new strains of diseases associated with homosexual behavior. We now have a growing population of homosexuals, lesbians, bisexuals, transsexuals, drag queens, transgender surgeries, hormone treatment for those claiming to be "born in the wrong body," and all the attending confusion that comes with those mentioned above. Homosexuality, once thought to be associated with a mental disorder, is now celebrated with parades, with local and Federal Government sponsorship.

Historians of the future may compare America to the words of the Apostle Paul:

22 Although they claimed to be wise, they became fools 23 and exchanged the glory of the immortal God for images made to look like a mortal human beings and birds and animals and reptiles.

24 Therefore, God gave them over in the sinful desires of their hearts to sexual impurity for the degrading of their bodies with one another. 25 They exchanged the truth about God for a lie and worshiped and served created things rather than the Creator—who is forever praised. Amen.

26 Because of this, God gave them over to shameful lusts. Even their women exchanged natural sexual relations for unnatural ones. 27 In the same way, the men also abandoned natural relations with women and were inflamed with lust for one another. Men committed shameful acts with other men and received in themselves the due penalty for their error.

28 Furthermore, just as they did not think it worthwhile to retain the knowledge of God, so God

gave them over to a depraved mind so that they do what ought not to be done. [29] They have become filled with every kind of wickedness, evil, greed, and depravity. They are full of envy, murder, strife, deceit and malice. They are gossips, [30] slanderers, God-haters, insolent, arrogant and boastful; they invent ways of doing evil; they disobey their parents; [31] they have no understanding, no fidelity, no love, no mercy. [32] Although they know God's righteous decree that those who do such things deserve death, they not only continue to do these very things but also approve of those who practice them (Romans 1:22-33).

Obergefell v. Hodges (2015)

On June 26, 2015, the United States Supreme Court ruled in a landmark decision that the 14th Amendment required all states to license marriages between same-sex couples and to recognize all marriages that a Court lawfully performed out of state. This law, decided by a 5-4 majority, overturned thirty state constitutions defining marriage as a union between one man and one woman. It also rendered God's laws and definition of marriage as mute and unenforceable in the United States, even though most citizens support the biblical standard of the sanctity of marriage between one man and one woman.

By the thinnest margin, the Court acknowledged the states were dealing with this issue legislatively, but the time required was damaging same-sex couples. Therefore, the Court took the authority of both judge and jury and ruled that most Americans could not be trusted to handle this matter correctly. Never mind that the Supreme Court has a shady history of poor judgments impacting multitudes of people over time. Several times in history, the Supreme Court was forced, as a matter of law, to overturn previous

NO LONGER ONE NATION UNDER GOD

Court rulings and correct wrong decisions. An example is the Dread Scott case (7-2) which legalized slavery in 1857. The Court has work to do in the future.

This case stands against God's sanctity of marriage between one man and one woman, which was proclaimed by Jesus in Mark 10: 7-8, "[7]for this reason a man will leave his father and mother and be united to his wife, [8]and the two will become one flesh. So they are no longer two but one flesh."

Cultural War Battles

Each case above further secularized our nation, as each decision attacked some truth revealed in God's holy Scripture and rendered it mute and meaningless in America. As the forces on the Left have relentlessly pushed secularization in the country, schools have been target number one. They have used the courts as a special weapon. In their efforts to make "one nation under God" to be "one nation without God," radicals on the Left have put their imprint on other institutions and in numerous places in the culture.

One such institution is the military. On September 12, 1782, the Congress of the United States approved Philadelphia publisher, Robert Aitken, to print a Bible for the soldiers. It became known as the Aitken Bible or the Bible of the Revolution.[15] there would be little chance of Congress authorizing a Bible today. Hate groups on the Left have the military in their crosshairs. A group called "Military Religious Freedom Foundation" sounds harmless enough, but the group is anything but. Its goal is the complete secularization of the military with no reference to God in any fashion. Its leader, Michael Weinstein, describes his opponents as "incredibly well-funded gangs of fundamentalist Christian monsters who terrorize their fellow Americans by forcing their weaponized and twisted version of Christianity upon their helpless subordinates in our nation's armed forces."[16] His organization calls for the end of chaplains in the military.

Movies are one of the most influential items that shape a person's worldview. The Left has taken control of Hollywood for the advancement of its agenda. A positive view of Christianity is rare on the big screen, but film producers welcome anything degrading to Christianity. Given what we see in movies today, it is hard to believe that films were once subject to censorship to protect moral standards beneficial to the nation. The Supreme Court even decided on cases related to the issue. In the 1915 case of *Mutual Film Corp. V. Industrial Commission of Ohio*, the Court ruled movies were "business, pure and simple," no different from the pharmaceutical or banking industry, both of which were subject to federal regulation.[17] Hollywood once operated under the *Hays Code*. The Code was written by a Catholic priest, with filmmakers giving their approval so more restrictive legislation would not be placed on them since the public was calling for such from Congress. The Code resulted in many films being denied a showing or adjusted to fit the Code. The Code was only 19 pages long and had the following three principles:

No picture shall be produced which will lower the moral standards of those who see it. Hence, the audience's sympathy shall never be thrown to the side of crime, wrongdoing, evil, or sin.

Correct standards of life, subject only to the requirements of drama and entertainment, shall be presented.

Law, natural or human, shall not be ridiculed, nor shall sympathy be created for its violation.[18]

The Code no longer exists today. A Supreme Court rendering in 1952 ruled movies are to be regarded as free speech, and the *Hays Code* was thus canceled. From that time on, Leftists have been dedicated to the death of decency in films. Television has not fared any better. The Federal Communications Commission (FCC) regulates shows broadcasted over the airwaves. Cable does not go over the airwaves, so it does not come under the jurisdiction of the FCC. That is why "R" rated material can appear there. More people today have cable than those who had TVs when the FCC was first established. Broadcast networks pushed the envelope to keep from losing viewers to cable, releasing programs like *Will and Grace,* which put homosexuality in a positive light to hasten its acceptance. Many other sitcoms and dramas have promoted sexual immorality.

Music is another medium the Left has captured in the cultural war. The fun, wholesome lyrics of the sixties folk music and the soothing tones of John Denver and the Carpenters have been replaced by the likes of Beyoncé singing about oral sex in a limo, rap songs about raping 15-year-olds and killing cops. Contemporary Christian music is relegated to its radio stations because the Left can't have it influence the general public in the central marketplace. Once in a while, we can get one to slip through and climb the charts in the Country genre, like Carrie Underwood's *Jesus, Take the Wheel.* Don't ever expect such a song to come from the vocal cords of Madonna or Lady Gaga. Danny Goldberg, a Liberal music industry executive, who thinks the Democrat Party is not Liberal enough, testified in front of the Senate with these words:

> Angry weird songs often make adolescents feel less lonely and more connected to other kids. Millions of these teens and young adults feel ostracized when politicians and academics who have no accurate understanding of their culture make sweeping generalizations about their entertainment,

81

conveniently overlooking the fact that literally every generation has embraced entertainment with sexual and violent themes. Gangsta rap is the direct descendant of the gangster movies of the thirties and forties, the TV westerns of the fifties, and critically acclaimed films like *The Godfather*.[19]

These sound like nice words, but Mr. Goldberg needs to address the real issues. The Gangsta movies of the thirties and forties and the westerns of the fifties showed the bad guys losing in the end. Goldberg defends music that blatantly makes evil people the heroes who serve as the new role models for a misguided generation.

Many states have historical villages constructed to replicate the founding era establishment. They have actors who play roles of pioneers interacting with the visitors who pass through. These are great places to take children to learn about history. One such village, aimed as a replica of the early 1800s, had a church. Most every small town in America in the 1800s did have a church. It was the social center of the community. This imitation village had a lady who played the role of the minister's wife. Every morning when she came on the set, she would go to the church's altar and pray, a common and appropriate thing to do in a church. But Leftists could not tolerate this true depiction and forced the lady to stop praying because it might offend some visitors who were not of the Christian faith.[20] Woke Liberals revised history, in a setting designed to teach it, to protect non-Christians. The Left does not worry about Christians being offended by a Gay Pride Parade promoting lewdness, drag queens in public schools, or some risqué billboard advertisement pitching a product with sexual innuendo.

Removing God from the life and culture of America is a primary goal of Leftist Democrats, as evidenced by the actions of Barack Obama. No other president had

Christianity higher on his hit list than Obama. David Horowitz listed several things in his book *Dark Agenda* that Obama did when he was in office which were purposely detrimental to Christians. We present four of them below:

April 2009 – When speaking at Georgetown University, Obama ordered that a monogram symbolizing Jesus' name be covered when he made his speech.[21]

April 2011- For the first time in American history, Obama urges passage of a non-discrimination law that does not contain hiring protections for religious groups, forcing religious organizations to hire according to federal mandates without regard to the dictates of their faith, thus eliminating conscience protection in hiring.[22]

November 2011 – President Obama opposed the inclusion of President Franklin Roosevelt's D-Day Prayer in the WWII Memorial.[23] (Authors' note: This memorial is now completed. It was a project started by my (Steve) friend, Chris Long, the president of The Ohio Christian Alliance. It is the only prayer memorialized on the National Mall. I was privileged to be at the dedication of it on Veterans Day 2022.)

February 2012 – The Obama administration forgives student loans in exchange for public services but announces it will no longer forgive student loans if the public service is related to religion.[24]

Social Media is another means the Left has become skilled at weaponizing for the country's secularization. Social media is used to present the agenda of the Left and the philosophy of Humanism. The Internet and Google allow people worldwide to access information from various sources, many of which are unreliable or purposely designed to misinform. An online searcher can also easily access pornography. Some porn magazines have gone out of business because pornography is accessed easily at no charge on the Net. Teens can stream a porn video on their phones in 30 seconds. They can also tune into a Christian sermon or song the same way, but given the cultural trend of our day, which do you think they are most likely to choose?

In discussing the topic of secularization, we would be amiss not to mention "Blue Laws." These laws were restrictions to prevent businesses from operating on Sunday, again underscoring that America indeed has a Christian Heritage. These laws were in place to protect Sunday as a Sabbath day for Christian worship. In my late teens, I (Steve) remember my dad telling me to have gas in my car at the start of the weekend because it was hard to find a service station open on Sundays. Blue laws are no more, and Sunday is just another day.

John Witherspoon was the only minister to sign the *Declaration of Independence* and also was the president of what is now Princeton University. He wrote a somber charge to all Leftist politicians and their radical humanistic supporters:

> He is the best friend to American liberty, most sincere and active in promoting true and undefiled religion. He sets himself with the greatest firmness to bear down on profanity and immorality of every kind. Whoever is an avowed enemy of God, I scruple [hesitate] not to call him an enemy to his country.[25]

As pointed out earlier, the Communist Party in America endorsed Joe Biden for president in 2020. This Marxist-inspired organization opposes the Christian faith, as are all who embrace Humanism. If the words of Witherspoon are accurate, there are many enemies within our nation's political realm, and many support the Democrat Party.

President Ronald Reagan said at an Ecumenical Prayer Breakfast in Dallas in 1984, "If we ever forget that we're one nation under God, then we will be a nation gone under."[26] We must do all we can to live and speak our faith in God so we don't go under. The future of our children depends on this.

Part Two

The Issues That Divide America

Chapter 5

Race and Poverty,
A New Perspective

*What Progressives are doing, they have hijacked the
legacy of the Civil Rights Movement and used it as
a bludgeon against the values of this nation.*[1]
– Robert Woodson

Identity politics plays a significant role in the political
strategy of Liberal Democrats, with a particular emphasis
on highlighting racism, which becomes even more potent
when intertwined with poverty. Democrats position
themselves as the saviors who emerge every election cycle
to rescue those affected by these societal problems, which
they often attribute to their conservative Republican
opponents. However, upon closer examination, it becomes
evident that these issues bear the fingerprints and DNA of
Liberal policies more than any other source. For example, in
the 1950s, Democrats in the Deep South were responsible
for creating and enforcing Jim Crow laws to uphold racial
discrimination. Similarly, President Lyndon Johnson's War
on Poverty in the 1960s significantly failed to reduce poverty
rates in subsequent decades. Despite their lack of
effectiveness, these policies have allowed Liberals to
maintain two voting blocs that contribute to their electoral
victories. A closer scrutiny of these issues reveals some
surprising facts.

As someone who has closely observed the political
landscape, I (Steve) have noticed the recent surge in
popularity of the term "systemic racism." This term implies
that racism is deeply ingrained in the functioning of our
country. However, I find it challenging to accept this claim
considering recent history. We have elected a black president
twice, black senators (including one who won by a landslide
in South Carolina), and one of the wealthiest women in the
country is a black TV talk show host. Black professionals in
various fields, such as entertainment, law, medicine,
education, and literature, have also achieved significant
success. Additionally, 70% of our professional sports teams
are black athletes earning multimillion-dollar salaries. If
systemic racism indeed characterized our nation, we would
be doing an abysmal job of it.

Meeting the Old Deep South

My personal experiences (Steve) have further solidified my
skepticism toward the concept of systemic racism. When I
was around 12 or 13 years old in the late 1950s, my father
taught me a crucial lesson about racism during a trip to
Florida. While visiting a Civil War attraction in Tennessee, I
unknowingly drank from a water fountain designated for
black people, and my father promptly corrected me,
explaining why it was wrong. He believed that public
facilities should not be segregated based on race, and he
wanted me to understand the stark differences between the
South and our home state of Ohio. He didn't want me to
face potential hostility from the locals, who might interpret
my actions as provocative or borne out of ignorance. The
segregation laws, commonly known as "Jim Crow," were a
product of the Democratic Party, which controlled the state
capitols in the South at that time.

When I began writing my first major book, I recognized

the need for a co-author with a larger platform to amplify our impact. Thankfully, I teamed up with Dr. Carol Swain, a black Christian conservative who was then a Law and Political Science professor at Vanderbilt University. Based on my personal experiences and collaborations, I find it difficult to buy into the prevailing narrative of systemic racism that is currently sweeping the nation.

In 1956, Georgia Tech was scheduled to play against the University of Pittsburgh in the Sugar Bowl. The game was almost canceled because Pittsburgh had a black player on its team. Some individuals in Georgia, including the Democratic governor, believed Tech should refuse to participate if the black player was allowed to play. However, the Sugar Bowl proceeded as planned, and the black player did participate in the game.[2]

Let's fast-forward to 1990 when Georgia Tech won the National Championship in college football, led by their black quarterback, Shawn Jones, who threw to black receivers. The fans at Georgia Tech were ecstatic. If systemic racism was truly prevalent, how could this success story unfold?

The Black Lives Matter Issue

The Liberal Left has a penchant for playing semantic games and inventing terms to pin on their opponents. One such term currently making the rounds is "white privilege." It aims to make white individuals feel guilty for their skin color, suggesting they have easier access to success denied to minorities. While segregation and prejudice were once prevalent in the South and the North, providing advantages for whites over blacks in various spheres, significant progress has been made due to legislation, education, and the common sense of the vast majority of people from all political persuasions. Unfortunately, biased media coverage

91

often fails to highlight these improvements. Democrats, lacking the wisdom to embrace a new virtuous cause, continue pulling the scabs off healing wounds for party loyalty.

Today, privilege is more closely tied to economic status than skin color. Michael Jordan's children, for example, may have a greater chance at financial success than many white children from middle-class homes simply because they have more economic resources to pursue their aspirations. In America, there is no nobility class. Individuals from the lowest economic strata can work hard and ascend to the top of their chosen profession, regardless of race. The inspiring stories of individuals like Dr. Carol Swain, who rose from severe poverty to become a tenured professor at the prestigious Vanderbilt University, or Dr. Ben Carson and Barack Obama, regardless of their political preferences, demonstrate the potential for upward mobility.

No person should bear guilt merely for being white. That is how God created them, and His Word explicitly states that we should not consider anyone inferior due to their unique characteristics (Romans 2:11). There is a phrase on the back of some athletic team members' t-shirts at a small liberal arts college that reads, "EARNED NOT GIVEN." It serves as a reminder that success in sports, as in life, requires dedication, sacrifice, and effort to enhance one's skills and achieve team goals.

The phrase "Black Lives Matter" emerged in our culture and became a movement many politicians and corporations embraced. However, it is vital to recognize the organization itself leans towards Marxism and promotes a reprehensible and hateful agenda fueled by violence. One of its leaders, Shaun King, has even called for the destruction of statues of Jesus Christ and stained-glass windows depicting a white Madonna and Child. These actions reveal a disregard for the civil rights of all individuals.

Christian denominations and other institutions that value decency should denounce the Black Lives Matter movement as it stands against American ideals and could rightly be considered a domestic enemy. How can they be seen otherwise when they march through the streets chanting, "What do we want? Dead cops! When do we want them? Right now!" or "Pigs in a blanket, fry them like bacon!"[3] Why is this not considered hate speech? How can a group that uses funds raised for its cause allow its founders to purchase million-dollar mansions maintain any credibility? Any organization that advocates for the death of another group of people should not be granted legitimacy. Unfortunately, this is not a concern for Leftist politicians within the Democratic Party.

Despite its name, the Black Lives Matter movement does a disservice to law-abiding and hard-working black individuals who value decency and promote positive relationships with people of all races. Injustice is wrong, regardless of whether it is racially motivated or not. It was wrong when George Floyd suffered at the hands of bad police officers on the streets of Minneapolis. It was also wrong when Michael Flynn was targeted by unscrupulous FBI agents and other individuals with ulterior motives during his service in the Trump Administration.

Consider the case of John Arntz, a white man who had diligently worked in charge of elections for 20 years in San Francisco. He was unjustly fired, receiving an email stating that his dismissal had nothing to do with his job performance. Instead, it resulted from the city's employment equity policy, which required creating more positions for minorities. Such an action violated John Arntz's constitutional rights as he was being dismissed solely based on the color of his skin.[4] The outcry across America was so strong that the action was rescinded.

Recognizing that injustice should be condemned regardless of the circumstances is essential. The Black Lives Matter movement's divisive rhetoric and questionable allocation of funds undermine its credibility and hinder genuine progress toward equality and justice.

African Americans in America owe their freedom to the sacrifices made by white men. These courageous individuals wore blue coat uniforms during the Civil War, gathering around campfires and singing the *Battle Hymn of the Republic*, passionately proclaiming the words, "...as He died to make men holy, let us die to make men free."[5] Civil War cemeteries stand as solemn reminders, housing the graves of countless brave men who sang those very words and gave their lives so that enslaved people could experience true freedom. Some of these heroes never even reached their 20th birthday, yet they were willing to lay down their lives for the cause of emancipation.

Regrettably, the Black Lives Matter movement tarnishes the memory of the ultimate sacrifice these thousands of brave individuals made by destroying monuments dedicated to Union soldiers. These actions are rationalized by Democratic political leaders, which only further undermines the significance of those sacrifices.

Some Facts to Ponder

If Democrats believe racial discord will grant them a political advantage, they will continue fostering it. They will point fingers at Republicans as the culprits, amplifying their narrative through their deceitful media allies who have forsaken the pursuit of truth to advance a Liberal agenda. Let us take a moment to examine some historical facts about the relationship between black people and the Democratic Party:

94

- Only Democrats enslaved people. The Republican Party was formed with its central plank to prevent the spread of slavery to new territories. A Republican president freed the enslaved people.[6]

- Democrats created the Jim Crow laws in the South and perpetuated segregation.[7]

- The KKK was an organization created by people aligned with the Democrats.[8.]

- A higher percentage of Republicans voted to pass the Civil Rights Act than did Democrats.[9]

- The War on Poverty, which benefited black people, has been a total failure as the same percentage remains in poverty, and the Black nuclear family has been devastated by these policies.[10]

- Schools in the inner cities run by Democrats are failing black students; many do not graduate 50% of those who enter high school. President Obama ended the school choice voucher program for black students in DC when he came into office. It was more important to appease the NEA teachers' union to ensure its campaign donations than help improve the lives of black children.[11]

- Planned Parenthood, strongly supported by Democrats, has a history of desiring the genocide of the black race. The founder, Margret Sanger, referred to Blacks as "weeds."[12]

- The majority of Planned Parenthood Clinics are located in minority neighborhoods.

Search for "Black Lives Matter Curriculum" on Google. You will discover that some schools are considering incorporating a curriculum that aligns with the radical Left agenda of the Black Lives Matter movement. This agenda includes calls for violence against police officers, and unfortunately, your

AMERICA IN THE BALANCE

tax dollars may fund such initiatives. The Democratic Party has a poor track record for serving and improving the lives of the black community. Democratic mayors struggle to maintain law and order and protect black citizens and property as crime rates skyrocket.

Dr. Martin Luther King Jr. famously stated, "I have a dream that my four little children will one day live in a nation where they will not be judged by the color of their skin but by the content of their character."[13] Many millions of Americans, including us, wholeheartedly agree with this sentiment. However, the Black Lives Matter movement seems to reject this vision. For them, skin color is a means to raise funds and an excuse to engage in rioting, looting, terrorizing the police, and disregarding the law. They ignore the importance of character, showing disdain for decency and the rights of others.

Black Lives Matter supporters take offense when they hear the phrase "All Lives Matter." However, all humans, regardless of race, are created in God's image, and Jesus Christ sacrificed himself on the cross to save all people from their sins if they turn to him in repentance. Ultimately, what truly matters is "Eternal Life." In the end, that will be the only thing that truly matters. We believe that black and white Christians can lead the way toward healing. As all races draw closer to Jesus, they will draw closer to one another and discover that the love of Christ is the true foundation for a genuine solution. We must not give our allegiance and trust to hate merchants from anarchist mobs, dishonest politicians, or the deceitful media.

The notion of systemic racism is a significant falsehood perpetuated by progressive Democrats. It is misinformation. Poverty levels in the country were lower under President Trump than under President Obama. Black individuals excel in all areas of life without oppression. While individuals from all races may hold racist views, systemic racism does not exist in America. Conservatives want black people to experience the American dream through assistance and support, not handouts. If America indeed suffers from systemic racism, why are so many people of color seeking to come here, and why do some risk their lives to do so illegally? If Leftists are willing to lie about systemic racism, what else might they be dishonest about?

What about the Poor?

Certain Left-leaning evangelicals justify their support for the Left by citing their concern for individuals experiencing poverty. However, it is essential to examine this perspective critically. When President Obama first assumed office in 2008, the poverty rate was 14.3 percent. By 2011 it had risen to 15%, the highest on record.[14]

According to this narrative, electing Liberal politicians is the solution, regardless of any other policies they may hold. However, during the initial two years of the Obama Administration, when Democrats held the majority in the House and had a supermajority in the Senate (60 members that prevented a filibuster by Republicans), they were in a position of considerable power. Despite this advantage, why did they not effectively address poverty or the immigration problem?

Perhaps, the Democrats deliberately avoided resolving these issues because they were politically advantageous for them. Poverty and immigration remained persistent campaign topics for them. Every presidential and midterm election followed the same playbook: Democrats expressed their desire to help the poor and disadvantaged while accusing their opponents of indifference to these groups.

During the Obama Administration, when the Democrats held significant power, there was no comprehensive immigration reform that included amnesty for undocumented immigrants. Implementing such reform required securing the borders and resolving the immigration issue. Similarly, if poverty were genuinely addressed and resolved, it would no longer serve as a political talking point. People experiencing poverty often form a loyal voting bloc for the Democrats, and reducing poverty would diminish their reliance on big government. The Democrats prefer to maintain or expand this voting bloc, as more individuals dependent on the government translates to more support for their party. By utilizing taxpayer money for benefit programs targeting low-income individuals, the Democrats secure the continued support of this voting bloc.

Open borders also provide the Democratic Party with more potential new voters at the expense of law-abiding taxpayers, including white and black citizens. Unbeknownst to Republicans, their tax contributions indirectly fund Democratic campaigns.

As someone who worked as a Jobs Consultant in the Department of Welfare in Indiana, I (Steve) have gained insights into poverty firsthand. Our department aimed to assist welfare recipients by providing training and helping them find jobs with discretionary income. We experienced some success in assisting individuals to escape poverty. However, I also observed that those lacking a strong work ethic often fell into poverty due to their personal choices. Some individuals end up impoverished because they drop out of school or lose their low-income jobs by not showing up for work as scheduled. Ultimately, their decisions, rather than the actions of corporate CEOs or a group accused of "white privilege," contribute to their state of poverty.

In my observation (Steve), I have witnessed individuals completely transform their lives by adopting a solid work ethic and lifting themselves out of poverty. Their transformation stemmed from embracing the presence of Jesus Christ in their lives, leading to a profound shift in their values. As a result, self-centeredness dissipated, paving the way for prosperity. The critical factor in their success was aligning their lives with the teachings of the Word of God rather than relying on government programs.

It is worth acknowledging that in some instances, having children outside of marriage can result in increased welfare support for the mother, while the father may find it more financially advantageous to rely on unemployment benefits rather than seeking employment. The Democratic Party knows this dynamic and has expanded its voter base by providing Liberal welfare benefits. Unfortunately, this approach hinders the black community rather than providing genuine assistance. High school graduation rates are alarmingly low in some metropolitan regions, often below 50 percent. Combining a lack of work ethic with the absence of a diploma frequently leads to poverty.

Interestingly, these metropolitan school districts are predominantly governed by Liberal officials who have held mayoral offices for decades. The school administrators and most teachers, supported by the National Education Association (NEA), the influential teachers' union, are staunch Liberals. Regrettably, they opposed school vouchers and choice. They even closed schools after the pandemic subsided, which, according to scientific evidence, harmed students further, perpetuating the plight of children trapped in public schools.

Why haven't proactive initiatives been implemented to keep children in classrooms, enabling them to acquire essential reading, writing, and mathematics skills, rather than being subjected to a Liberal reinterpretation of history aimed at indoctrinating their minds for future support of Liberal candidates? Present-day children can select their pronouns and engage in discussions about sex in elementary school, yet many are struggling with basic literacy.

Undoubtedly, there is a genuine need to assist those living in poverty. However, some individuals exploit the system, squandering taxpayer dollars. As long as poverty benefits the Left's pursuit of power, it will persist, as they have no interest in resolving the issue when it provides them with a political advantage.

During the decline of the poverty rate to approximately 12.5 percent in 2019 (nearly 2.5 points lower than the peak rate during the Obama administration), NPR attributed the improvement to a robust economy. It is important to note that this period coincided with Donald Trump's presidency. Trump implemented measures to bolster the economy, resulting in historically low unemployment rates for blacks and other minority groups. Like Democratic President John F. Kennedy, he achieved this by reducing taxes for individuals and businesses, which, paradoxically, led to increased tax revenues for the Federal Government due to more people contributing to the system, despite lower tax rates. Trump also focused on achieving energy independence, maintaining affordable prices, and curbing inflation. His policies incentivized manufacturing companies to remain in the country, creating more job opportunities for Americans and increasing wages due to increased employee competition.

The key to lifting people out of poverty is providing them with employment that offers discretionary income. The Trump administration's economic policies were instrumental in facilitating this. Unfortunately, these policies are now being dismantled by the Democratic Party. Considering these circumstances, it becomes clear that the Democrats are not genuinely aiding in reducing the poverty rate. Although they present themselves as champions of the cause, their actions tend to exploit people in poverty for political gain rather than providing genuine assistance.

The impact of printing more money for government handouts ultimately leads to inflation, which negatively impacts everyone. However, individuals with low incomes bear the brunt of this economic consequence. Although handouts may appear compassionate, they do not improve one's work ethic or help one get a job.

Asking the Right Question

Countless hours of seminars and meetings have been dedicated to the question, "What causes poverty?" To find a solution to this persistent problem that plagues society, many have searched for a magical cure, to no avail. However, a tweet by Per Bylund on Twitter offers a refreshing change in perspective. Bylund suggests that poverty is the original state, the default, and the starting point and instead proposes that we should ask, "What causes prosperity?"[15] He correctly highlights that everyone enters this world with nothing, and we can escape poverty through our actions and choices. Doing nothing will keep us in a state of poverty. So, what brings about prosperity? Here are some contributing factors: completing high school, avoiding involvement in crime, waiting until marriage to have children and being able to provide for them, maintaining a solid work ethic, and taking personal responsibility.

Everyone I know who has followed these guidelines has managed to avoid poverty. As long as we continue to subsidize poverty, it will persist. If we want to see more of something, we must incentivize it, which is precisely what Democrats have been doing for decades. Given the job opportunities available in America today, unless someone is physically or mentally disabled, they have no reason to be poor. If someone finds themselves in poverty, it results from their choices. A high school diploma opens doors to opportunities such as military service, which provides future benefits that help individuals avoid poverty. The skilled trades also offer lucrative incomes, and alternative paths exist to acquire those skills without accumulating significant debt.

Following the COVID lockdown, companies actively sought employees, and the wages offered for many jobs far exceeded the minimum wage. These companies were not concerned about the color of a person's skin. Some didn't even require a high school diploma. They simply sought individuals with solid work ethics, reliability, and honesty. Unfortunately, too many people have bought into the Democrat-promoted "victim mentality." The reality is that they are victims of the Liberal agenda rather than pursuing their education and striving for the American dream. It is hard to identify corporations that actively seek to oppress people based on their race or economic background. I am unaware of any company encouraging kids to drop out of high school, get involved in drug addiction, or choose a life of crime. Some companies even provide college tuition assistance as a benefit. Conservatives and corporations are not the cause of poverty. It does not benefit them in any way. The only ones who benefit from poverty are Liberal candidates who rely on this voting bloc. Systemic racism does not exist in America; if one is in good health, one can pursue wealth. This country remains a land of opportunity. So, if you are unemployed, the next time you see a "help wanted" sign, walk in and apply.

Chapter 6

Climate Change –
Truth or Trojan Horse

*The basic problem is that the process for solar and
wind to generate reliable electricity requires so
many resources that it has never been cheap and
plentiful. In fact, modern solar and wind technology
do not produce reliable energy.[1]*
– Alex Epstein

For many Liberals, Climate Change is a sacred Cow. For those who bow, it is as essential to their existence as the Second Coming is to Christianity. There are several questions those of us who are sincerely searching for the truth must ask regarding climate change. Is it for real, a hoax, or a tactic? If it is real, is it the looming doom that many young people fear it is? If climate change is real, are human beings the primary cause, as the Liberal alarmists believe?

Since whole books have been and will be written on this subject, one chapter cannot cover all the details related to the debate on fossil fuels and climate change. We intend to write this chapter to inform you that the demonization of fossil fuels and the imminent disastrous effects predicted by present-day climate change alarmists are based on partial truths. Those loyal believers in climate change like to proclaim their position is based on solid science. However, this is not true. There is no consensus that climate change will bring about a world catastrophe in just a few years, as alarmists claim.

Those who worship the sacred cow of climate change have made the pseudo-scientific claims that man is causing climate change, and the notion of stopping it is their religion. The most devout devotees of this new religion are driven to cancel and cut off anyone who disagrees with their claims. Be encouraged, as millions have not embraced this false god. Still, we must work to stave off their wicked agenda, designed to reduce America into a third-world country and ultimately a part of the New World Order being planned by their elitist leaders.

The High Priests of this new cult-like worship of saving the planet is a group of elite men and women, many of whom flew their private jets to Davos, Switzerland, January 26-30th to discuss their plans to save the planet. Included in the Forum were founder Klaus Schwab, Bill Gates, Al Gore, U.S. Climate Czar John Kerry, Wall Street executives such as JP Morgan's Jamie Dimon, David Solomon from Goldman Sachs, and Morgan Stanley's James Gorman, Germany's Chancellor Olaf Scholz, the presidents of Spain, South Korea, Poland, and the Philippines were among 51 heads of state present. Another 56 finance ministers, 19 central bank governors, 30 trade ministers, and 35 foreign ministers, Idris Elba and Sabrina Dhowre Elba, cellist Yo-Yo Ma, Renee Fleming, rapper, and songwriter, will.i.am and social media star Nas Daly.

On August 28, 2022, 1200 scientists signed the *World Climate Declaration,* conveying no emergency related to climate change. The document admonished the climate change proponents as more politically motivated than scientifically based.[2] Science should be free of politics, but politics dominates the climate change debate. The COVID lockdowns and mask mandates should have opened every American's eyes to how the government when dominated by self-seeking politicians, can use the power of the government to impose its will on the people and, in the process, eliminate fundamental freedoms granted by the Constitution. Christians, some led by compromising pastors, should be ashamed of their willingness to comply with decrees that commanded them to deny Scriptural mandates to assemble for worship and encouragement. At the same time, they patronized Walmart, Lowes, and other big box stores, which politicians kept open because they needed them. Never mind the casinos and liquor stores that were allowed to also remain open.

Genesis 1:28 states: "And God blessed them, (Adam and Eve) and God said unto them, Be fruitful, and multiply, and replenish the earth, and subdue it." Those words implied a command to be good stewards of the world God gave Adam and Eve to manage. As is always the case, Godless leaders have distorted or ignored God's plan. "In the name of saving the planet," Liberal politicians want us to use fewer fossil fuels, raising the price of those we use until they are no longer affordable and taxing them to support those in government who run programs to keep climate change in check. The ultimate end, we believe, is something much more sinister and dangerous to America's freedom, and this agenda is being driven by some of our own elected officials and the High Priests of the Climate Change cult.

Four Reasons The Climate Change Experts Are Wrong

Number one, if it is so severe of a problem, why don't those who are its champions lead by example? If there were experts who discovered tomatoes were now deadly and would kill people within two years if eaten in any form, we are confident these experts would not only broadcast their concerns and sound a warning; they would also immediately stop consuming tomatoes themselves. If those experts went out and had pizza parties and spaghetti suppers every weekend, their actions would give you a reason to doubt their message. We could use many examples of elites who live hypocritically, ranging from entertainment celebrities to politicians. Because of space limitations, we only will focus on two prominent politicians. Former Vice President Al Gore is our first focus. In a CNN interview with Jake Tapper, Gore was exposed, and the climate change guru's hypocrisy became obvious. One of the big deals for climate change faithful is the "carbon footprint," which is how much energy you use to live your life. Another aspect is actions that offset the harm done by one's energy use. For example, if you take a plane trip, you plant a tree when you come home. Mr. Gore is the "Bigfoot" when it comes to a carbon footprint, and he is no Johnny Appleseed, and the concept of carbon offset is flawed. Investor's Business Daily provides the incriminating facts regarding Gore's carbon footprint:

> A new National Center for Public Policy Research analysis found that Gore's Tennessee home "guzzles more electricity in one year than the average American family uses in 21 years."

The report found that in one month last year, Gore's home consumed more electricity than the average family uses in 34 months. The electricity used to heat Gore's swimming pool would power *six homes* for a year.

And this is after Gore spent tens of thousands of dollars installing "green" upgrades, which he was embarrassed to do when his energy-hogging home first came to light a decade ago.

In fact, according to the NCPPR report, Gore's home used *more* electricity last year than it did in 2007 before he installed all those energy-reducing features.[3] Gore claimed he accounted for his high energy use by buying "carbon offsets" at $432 a month to a program formed to help fund renewable energy projects in Tennessee.[4] More on this dubious practice later.

Another climate change zealot is John Kerry, former senator, former presidential candidate, former secretary of state, and climate change czar for the Biden Administration. This multimillionaire received criticism for flying around in his jet to the extent he announced he would start going by commercial airlines except for his trip to the World Economic Forum Conference. At the World Economic Forum, Kerry said, "When you start to think about it, it's pretty extraordinary that we — select group of human beings because of whatever touched us at some point in our lives — can sit in a room and come together and actually talk about saving the planet."[5] John Kerry sees himself as the man to save the planet by stopping climate change with a bit of help from his international elitist friends.

John Kerry has a 12-million-dollar house on the island of Martha's Vineyard. Why such a location if you believe the sea levels will rise with destructive results[6] All toll Kerry and his wife own five houses worth around 30 million dollars. [7] With his yacht and private plane, John Kerry likely has a bigger carbon footprint than Al Gore, and Mr. Kerry keeps us from knowing if he is purchasing any offsets.

Secondly, why have the climate change experts been wrong about so many of their predictions? Here are some claims that climate change experts have made which have been proven false (Authors' comments in parenthesis):

Wisconsin Senator Gaylord Nelson, the father of Earth Day, said before the first Earth Day in 1970, "The secretary of the Smithsonian Institute believes that in 25 years, somewhere between 75 and 80 percent of all the species of living animals will be extinct."[8]
Stanford biologist Paul Ehrlich, the celebrated author of *The Climate Bomb*, wrote in 1971, "By the year 2000, the United Kingdom will be simply a

small group of impoverished islands, inhabited by some 70 million hungry people ... If I were a gambler, I would take even money that England will not exist in the year 2000."[9] (England hosted the 2012 Olympics, evidently existing past 2000.)

In 1986, NASA scientist James Hansen testified before Congress that "global temperatures should be nearly 2 degrees higher in 20 years, 'which is about the warmest the earth has been in the last 100,000 years.'"[10] (This has yet to happen.)

Two years later, Dr. Hansen told an interviewer that in 20 years, the area below his New York City office would be completely changed, most notably that "the West Side Highway [which runs along the Hudson River] will be under water." [11] today, this highway is not underwater.

Dr. Michael Oppenheimer of the Environmental Defense Fund wrote: By 1995, the greenhouse effect would be desolating North America's and Eurasia's heartlands with horrific drought, causing crop failures and food riots...."(By 1996) The Platte River of Nebraska would be dry, while a continent-wide black prairie topsoil blizzard would stop interstate traffic, strip paint from houses, and shut down computers...The Mexican police will round up illegal American migrants surging into Mexico seeking work as field hands.[12] There was no wave of illegal American migrants seeking field work south of the border in 1996 or any year after.

As recently as the last decade, both Dr. Hansen and Peter Wadhams, the head of the Polar Ocean Physics Group at the University of Cambridge, believe "that the Arctic is likely to become ice-free... as early as 2015." [13] (Last checked in 2022. The Arctic ice is still with us.)

No one with good sense would continue doing business with a store that keeps giving them false product information. That is, however, what the so-called climate change experts want us to do. Why should we believe the High Priests of climate change predictions when they have been so wrong?

Thirdly, why aren't the big polluters of China and India targeted to clean up their countries? Seeing the United States voluntarily taking the brunt of the climate change animosity is perplexing. China is the worst polluter in the world, and India ranks high. Still, you never see Alexandria Ocasio-Cortez (AOC) and her faithful fanatics protesting in front of the Chinese or Indian embassies in Washington, DC. Byford Tsang, a senior policy advisor for the London-based E3G, an independent think tank focusing on strategies to reduce carbon emissions, said, "China and India are among the world's biggest emitters, so without them, it will be impossible to achieve the Paris Agreement."[14] If the existence of the planet at stake, then giving a pass to China and India does not make sense.

Lastly, why are so many climate change advocates profiting off the cause? Al Gore's practice of buying offsets is very controversial. It may ease someone's guilt, but proving that a genuine offset occurs isn't easy. Some offset exchanges are legit, but many are fraudulent, and their schemes are hard to detect.[15] Kevin Anderson, deputy director of the Tyndall Centre for Climate Change Research at the University of Manchester, England, argued that offsets were "worse than doing nothing."[16] That old saying, "Follow the money," can provide interesting facts, valid with climate change. Climate change has become big business, especially for those who follow the Left's viewpoint. Take note of this information from a report by the U.S. Government Accountability Office:

Federal funding for climate change research, technology, international assistance, and adaptation has increased from $2.4 billion in 1993 to $11.6 billion in 2014, with an additional $26.1 billion for climate change programs and activities provided by the American Recovery and Reinvestment Act in 2009.[17]But that was fourteen years ago. The "Inflation Reduction Act of 2022," provided $369 billion for climate and clean energy provisions…[18]

We have handed out hundreds of billions of dollars from all the investments and giveaways made. With money like this, our Federal Government has to borrow from foreign investors like China due to Congress's inability to pass a balanced budget.

The fact the government is giving out lucrative grants for climate change research motivates one to deliver information that supports climate change is taking place. Stephen Moore of the Heritage Foundation explains this in greater detail:

How dare I impugn the integrity of scientists and Left-wing think tanks by suggesting that hundreds of billions of dollars of taxpayer handouts pervert their research findings. The irony of this resentment is that any academic whose research dares question the "settled science" of the climate change complex is instantly accused of being a shill for the oil and gas industry or the Koch brothers[19].

During President Obama's first term, Forbes Magazine reported that the federal budget estimated about $150 billion in spending on climate change and green energy subsidies. This budget didn't include the tax subsidies, which provide a 30 percent tax credit for wind and solar power. Adding those numbers estimates comes to about $8 billion to $10 billion annually. Then you can add billions more in costs attributable to the 29 states with renewable energy mandates, which require utilities to buy expensive "green" energy.[20] The real hit comes when we learn from "experts" all the trillions of dollars spent have not altered the fast-approaching doomsday. To this, Steve Moore writes:

> Has there ever been such a massive government expenditure that has had such minuscule returns on investment? After three decades of "research," the only "solution" is for the world to stop using fossil fuels, which is like saying that we should stop growing food.[21]

If we eliminate fossil fuels, which Joe Biden said he wanted during the 2020 presidential campaign, we would awaken to a world of chaos. Millions would be forced into poverty. Famine would be common worldwide, and life expectancy would plummet. Liberals want all of us to drive electric cars. What do we use to produce electricity? As of November 2022, fossil fuels generated 61 percent of our electricity. Coal was responsible for 21.9 percent, and natural gas was 38.4.[22] Can you imagine how much you will have to pay for a kilowatt of electricity if fossil fuels are banned?

Speaking of fossil fuels, here are a few items made from petroleum (with the more intriguing ones in **bold**) listed below:[23.]

> Solvents, Diesel Fuel, Motor Oil, Bearing Grease, Ink, Floor Wax, Ballpoint Pens, Upholstery, Sweaters, Boats, Insecticides, Bicycle Tires, Sport Car Bodies, **Nail Polish**, **Fishing Lures**, Dresses, Tires, Golf Bags, Golf Balls, **Perfumes**, Dishwasher Parts, Tool Boxes, Shoe Polish, Motorcycle Helmet, Caulking, Petroleum Jelly, Transparent Tape, CD Player, C.D.s

& DVDs, Faucet Washers, **Antiseptics**, Curtains, Food Preservatives, Soap, Basketballs, **Footballs**, Football Helmets, Refrigerant, Putty, Panty Hose, Dyes, Percolators, Life Jackets, Rubbing Alcohol, **Skis**, Rugs, T.V. Cabinets, Electrician's Tape, Tool Racks, Car Battery Cases, Cell Phone Cases, Telephones, Epoxy, Paint, Paint Brushes, Paint Rollers, Insect Repellent, Mops, Slacks, Oil Filters, Umbrellas, Fertilizers, **Yarn**, **Hair Coloring**, Roofing, Toilet Seats, Fishing Rods, **Lipstick**, Denture Adhesive, Linoleum, Ice Cube Trays, Synthetic Rubber, Glycerin, Rubber Boots, Electric Blankets, **Plastic Wood**, Speakers, Tennis Rackets, Rubber Cement, Nylon Rope, Candles, Trash Bags, Water Pipes, Hand Lotion, Roller Skates, **Surf Boards**, **Shampoo**, Wheels, Shower Curtains, Guitar Strings, Luggage, Aspirin, Safety Glasses, Eyeglasses, Sun Glasses, Antifreeze, Awnings, Toothbrushes, **Toothpaste**, Clothes, Ice Chests, Detergents, Combs, Vaporizers, Balloons, Heart Valves, Tents, Crayons, Parachutes, Enamel, Pillows, Dishes, Cameras, **Anesthetics**, Artificial Turf, Artificial Limbs, Bandages, Dentures, Folding Doors, Hair Curlers, **Cold Cream**, Movie Film, Soft Contact Lenses, Drinking Cups, Fan Belts, **Shaving Cream**, Ammonia, Refrigerators, and of course Gasoline.

Still want to end the use of fossil fuels? Think of all the jobs these products represent, including all things made of plastic that were not listed. Imagine how different your life would be if they were not available to you, and remember, at one time in our nation's history, they were not available because we did not know oil existed. Maybe AOC will change her mind about the New Green Deal if she learns she has to give up her lipstick.

There is a dark side to climate change which aims to destroy and not save. Christiana Figueres, who was the Executive Secretary of the U.N.'s Framework Convention on Climate Change in February 2015, at a press conference in Brussels, said, "This is the first time in human history that we are setting ourselves the task of intentionally changing [getting rid of] the economic development model that has reigned since the Industrial Revolution."[24] The economic development model is none other than capitalism. A year earlier, this woman complained that America's two-party constitutional system hindered the U.N.'s climate objectives. She favored the one-party approach of Communism, as found in China, as a better choice for America if environmental goals were to be achieved[25]. Climate change is the Trojan horse for advancing Communism in America, and it is alarming how many are falling for it.

Figueres is not alone in her thinking. Dr. Ottmar Edenhofer, a senior U.N. official and co-chair of the U.N. IPCC's Working Group III, leaves no doubt about the fundamental goal of climate change. In an interview with a Swiss newspaper on November 14, 2010, he said: "One must free oneself from the illusion that international climate policy is environmental policy. [What we're doing] does almost nothing with the climate. We must state clearly that we use climate policy to redistribute de facto the world's wealth."[26.] How come the media is silent on the words of Dr. Ottmar Edenhofer? This is not an opponent of climate change making this statement, but an avid supporter of it. If you are having trouble getting your head around this, look at another of his admissions: "Climate policy has almost nothing to do anymore with protecting the environment. The next world climate summit in Cancun is actually an economy summit during which distribution of the world's resources will be negotiated."[27.]

The high-ranking U.N. official admits that climate change has no real connection to the environment but is merely a cover for advancing the communistic idea of redistribution of wealth. It is time we introduce the statements of Mr. Edenhofer to America's college students. Climate change is not about saving the planet. It is about ending capitalism and ruling the planet by globalists.

What is an absolute tragedy is most Liberal Democrats support the intent of the climate agenda 100 percent. If you want to destroy America, wreck its economy. There is no better way to do that than to attack its energy industry. The following words by John Eidson should be a wakeup call to every American:

> No intelligent person can fail to recognize that the modern Democratic Party is using "climate change" as a ruse to fundamentally transform the United States of America into a socialist-cum-communist nation. But because the human ego is reluctant to admit when it's been duped, many patriotic Liberals will continue allowing themselves to be led like sheep into the closing noose of the hammer and sickle. By the time they realize what happened, it will be too late.[28]

The University of Pennsylvania geologist Robert Giegengack stated: "None of the strategies that have been offered by the U.S. government or by the EPA or by anybody else has be the remotest chance of altering climate if in fact climate is controlled by carbon dioxide."[29] The Apostle Paul warned the Thessalonians, "Don't let anyone deceive you in any way..." (2 Thessalonians 2:3). He directed his words to spiritual matters. Still, they are also relevant for us today regarding political issues. The Left is protective of its deceptive narrative. It does not like formidable opposition with sound scientific research supporting it regardless of the issue, be it abortion, COVID, transgender fluidity, or climate change.

Simply put, it is designed by men like those who have attended the multiple World Economic Forums conducted annually in Devos, who agree to carry out what Von Klaus Schwab has written in his two books, The Great Reset, Volumes I and II, co-authored with Thierry Malleret. He and his co-author saw the COVID lockdowns as a template to control masses of people and create a global society with a single-party rule and centralized government made up of elitist men and women who think they know what is best for humankind.

Those of us who are Christians know such schemes are born with evil intent. To accomplish their plans, Christianity must be eliminated. The COVID lockdowns allowed power-centered leaders to observe how compliant most pastors and churches are willing to be to stay in favor of the government. Now, more than ever, the true church of the living God must stand up for truth. Our country was founded by men who believed that if they stood up for God, He would stand up for them. 1 Samuel 2:30 states: "Those who honor me I will honor, but those who despise me will be disdained."

But be warned; any denial of climate change will bring the wrath of the Left upon you. New York Times writer Paul Krugman recently wrote in a column to those of us who dare question the religious dogma of Climate worship: "May you be punished in the afterlife for doing so [deny Climate Change]."[30] He called it the "almost inconceivable sin.[31]Vogue Magazine called having a baby in 2021 "pure environmental vandalism."[32] Al Gore recently stated that "Fertility Management" was needed to reduce the number of Africans to help control unusual weather due to the climate effect of too many people.[33] Had any conservative made such a comment, they would have been immediately labeled a racist, but the Left protects their own.

Konstantin Kisin, a Russian-British comedian, spoke at a debate at the Oxford Union Society, which got five million hits on various platforms. He believes young people are being brainwashed by the Woke on the issue of climate change. Kisin stated:

We can only do one thing in this country to stop climate change: make scientific and technological breakthroughs that will create clean and cheap energy. The only thing wokeness has to offer in exchange is to brainwash bright young minds like you to believe that you are victims, to believe that you have no agency, to think that what you must do to improve the world is to complain, is to protest, is to throw soup on paintings. [34]

Kisin's emphasis on "scientific and technological breakthroughs" is the correct approach to solving climate change problems. Several sources have reported temperatures have increased from 1880 by around 1.5 F degrees. The earth may be warming, but not at a rate deserving a panic. More efforts should be put into research to find solutions instead of brainwashing school kids for political gain. One thing is certain: climate change will not cease to be a problem by having the masses suck rocks and pay higher prices for those rocks while the elite jet set around the world and enjoy their yacht parties. If you live in abject poverty in a developing nation, you are not worried about the world ending eight years from now due to climate change when trying to stay alive today.

We should return to the energy independence achieved under President Trump, where we also exported oil and natural gas to other nations. God blessed us with these natural resources, which we can use for good to enhance people's lives in our own country and elsewhere. This independence makes energy available at a lower price, benefiting poor people and impoverished nations. At the same time, we should encourage innovation in new energy sources, solar, wind, safe nuclear, and other references that have yet to be discovered. We can learn from past mistakes and even improve our conservation of energy sources while practicing sensible ways to protect the environment.

Chapter 7

The Fight for Life

We cannot diminish the value of one category
of human life — the unborn — without
diminishing the value of all human life.[1]
- Ronald Reagan

Abortion is a highly controversial topic in American politics and national culture. That wasn't always true. There was a time when neither political party advocated for it, and every state had laws against it by 1900. However, things changed in the 1960s when certain groups voiced their concerns. In 1969 Norma McCorvey sought an abortion, but Texas law did not allow it.[2] She was introduced to Linda Coffee and Sarah Weddington, who were determined to challenge abortion laws. This challenge led to McCorvey becoming Jane Roe in the landmark 1973 Supreme Court case of *Roe v. Wade*.[3] Despite this, McCorvey ultimately decided to have the child.

She became an activist for abortion, working in an abortion center in Dallas. Pro-life activist, Pastor Flip Benham of Operation Rescue, talked to her about the love of Christ, and one day, she listened intently, resulting in surrendering her life to Christ.[4] She later became an activist for the pro-life movement. She was one of four employees of abortion clinics that Pastor Benham led to Christ in his ministry. His persistent witnessing prevented over 5,000 abortions as potential candidates for abortion had a change of heart. Flip is an example to all of us of our power in Christ to accomplish great things.

A Bad Court Decision

The decision to legalize abortion in the Roe v. Wade ruling was not close, with a vote of 7 to 2. Interestingly, this is the same margin as the infamous Dred Scott decision that upheld slavery back in 1857. The justices who ruled in favor of legalizing abortion in 1973 based their decision on the Fourteenth Amendment, which they argued gave women a constitutional right to terminate their pregnancy. While this interpretation may seem like a stretch, it was ultimately the basis for the landmark ruling. To give you an idea of what the Fourteenth Amendment entails, here is Section 1 of the Amendment:

> All persons born or naturalized in the United States and subject to its jurisdiction are citizens of the United States and the state wherein they reside. No state shall make or enforce any law which shall abridge the privileges or immunities of citizens of the United States; nor shall any state deprive any person of life, liberty, or property, without due process of law; nor deny to any person within its jurisdiction the equal protection of the laws.

This Amendment was ratified on July 9, 1868, to assure rights for the newly freed slaves. There was no intent for abortion to be encompassed by those who drafted it. It was presented and approved to protect the rights of formerly enslaved people. It prevented states from passing laws that would infringe on those rights. It says, "nor shall any state deprive any person of life, liberty, or property, without due process of law; nor deny to any person within its jurisdiction the equal protection of the laws." According to the Constitution's Fourteenth Amendment, a person cannot be denied life, yet an unborn child is denied life in an abortion.

The "due process of law" was what the Court used to somehow give a woman the right to have an abortion. They claimed this clause carried the "right to privacy," which allowed a woman to abort a fetus. The "right to privacy" does not appear in the Fourteenth Amendment. The ruling was a stretch indeed of the Amendment's meaning. The result was to legalize the taking of over sixty million innocent unborn children. There is no way to comprehend the damage this has done to our country. The Left defends open borders saying we need the workers to pay the taxes that fund Medicare, Medicaid, Social Security, etc. Perhaps, had we not aborted over sixty-four million of our unborn children, this need would not exist? We are compounding our sins as a nation with more sin.

The Issue of Personhood

The crux of the argument for abortion is when does a person become a person? Those who favor abortion adamantly believe personhood begins when one is born or draws first breath. Pro-lifers believe that life begins at conception, and that is when personhood begins, which means the Fourteenth Amendment would safeguard the unborn child. Justice Harry Blackmun wrote the majority opinion of the *Roe v. Wade* case and made a critical point about abortion in the years following the ruling. He wrote:

> The *appellee* and certain *amici* argue that the fetus is a "person" within the language and meaning of the Fourteenth Amendment. In support of this, they outline at length and in detail the well-known facts of fetal development. If this suggestion of personhood is established, the appellant's case collapses, for the fetus's right to life would then be guaranteed expressly by the Amendment. The appellant conceded as much on the reargument.[5]

121

The appellant, in this case, was the party wanting to make abortion legal. The justice says a fetus would have a right to life if determined to be a person. Since the 1973 Court decision, advancements in medical science have given us tremendous insight into the development of an unborn child. Ultrasounds are now available, allowing a pregnant woman to see the form of the child she is carrying, and it does look like a child even at only 12 weeks. At 20 weeks, an ultrasound can reveal the gender of a male or female. You can hear his or her heartbeat as early as eight weeks.

Medical Doctors' Views

Medical doctors have gone on record to say life begins at conception. Below are comments from a few:

> **Dr. Alfred M. Bongioanni**, professor of pediatrics and obstetrics at the University of Pennsylvania: I have learned from my earliest medical education that human life begins at conception…. I submit that human life is present throughout this entire sequence from conception to adulthood and that any interruption at any point constitutes a termination of human life….
>
> I am no more prepared to say that these early stages [of development in the womb] represent an incomplete human being than I would be to say that the child before the dramatic effects of puberty…is not a human being. This is human life at every stage.

> **Professor Hymie Gordon, Mayo Clinic**: "By all the criteria of modern molecular biology, life is present from the moment of conception."

> **Professor Micheline Matthews-Roth, Harvard University Medical School**: "It is incorrect to say

that biological data cannot be decisive.... It is scientifically correct to say that an individual human life begins at conception.... Our laws, one function of which is to help preserve the lives of our people, should be based on accurate scientific data."

Dr. Watson A. Bowes, University of Colorado Medical School: "The beginning of a single human life is from a biological point of view a simple and straightforward matter—the beginning is conception. This straightforward biological fact should not be distorted to serve sociological, political, or economic goals."[6]

Dr. Bernard Nathanson co-founded the National Abortion Rights Action League (NARAL). This internationally known OBGYN owned and operated the largest abortion clinic in the western hemisphere during his practice. When he began to use ultrasound and observe the child's development in the womb, it dramatically impacted him. He wrote in the New England Journal of Medicine that he was deeply troubled by the fact he had presided over more than 60,000 deaths.[7]

Nathanson did a film called *The Silent Scream*. In it, he said, "Modern technologies have convinced us that beyond question the unborn child is simply another human being, another member of the human community, indistinguishable in every way from any of us."[8] Dr. Nathanson is an atheist, so his findings were not based on some religious experience or faith encounter. They were solely based on biological facts.

Dr. Landrum Shettles served 27 years as the attending OBGYN physician at Columbia-Presbyterian Medical Center in New York. His intrauterine photographs of preborn children appear in more than fifty medical textbooks. He states:

I oppose abortion. I do so because I accept what is biologically manifest—that human life commences at conception—and because I believe taking innocent human life under any circumstances is wrong. My position is scientific, pragmatic, and humanitarian.[9]

Ultrasounds have saved the lives of many babies. There have been numerous expectant mothers contemplating abortion who have changed their minds after viewing their babies in an ultrasound. There is a 4D ultrasound which generates detailed images as if a camera were in the womb. When this ultrasound is done in the third semester of pregnancy, the distinct features of the baby can clearly be seen. Technological advances have significantly weakened the claims by abortion advocates that only a mass or glob of tissue makes up the fetus in its early stages. Whenever a law is proposed that a woman considering an abortion must view an ultrasound before the procedure, it is always opposed by Liberals. Why? Because they fear it might dissuade the mother from having an abortion.

Being a Victim

At least 38 states make the death of a fetus a homicide when a pregnant woman is assaulted. This means that in these states, the unborn child is considered a victim of a crime.[10] If the unborn child can become a victim of a crime, why is it not considered a person? Does it not seem odd that someone can target a criminal act on a pregnant woman resulting in the death of the child inside her, and be charged with a crime, yet the woman can walk into an abortion clinic and have a doctor assault the child in her womb resulting in the unborn child's death, and it is all perfectly legal?

One of the most noted cases of the homicide of an unborn child was the Laci Peterson murder case. She went missing on December 24, 2002, in Modesto, California, when she was eight months pregnant. Her body and that of her son Connor, who was named but not yet born, washed up on the California coast on April 2003. Laci's husband, Scott Peterson, was charged and convicted for the first-degree murder of Laci and the second-degree murder of Connor, who died when his mother was murdered.[11] California has some of the most Liberal abortion laws in the nation, so, interestingly, it has a strong law making it clear that killing a fetus is a criminal act. When they realized their daughter and unborn grandson were murdered, Laci's parent's pain must have been excruciating. They never got to see or hold this grandchild.

Being a Patient

Perhaps the most compelling argument against abortion is the advances that have transpired in surgeries on preborn children. In 1997 at Vanderbilt University Medical Center, an extraordinary surgery took place. It was performed on a 22-week-old fetus that had spina bifida. The surgery was successful. After birth, the child was able to walk and live an ordinary life. A photo of the surgery stunned the world as the tiny hand of the fetus touched the finger of Dr. Joseph Bruner. This photo can be seen at the website URL address provided in the endnote related to this information.[12] Many other surgeries on unborn children have taken place at Vanderbilt, and other medical centers in the nation are now doing these surgeries.

If an unborn child can have corrective surgery while in the womb, they should be regarded as a person and, therefore, as Justice Blackmun indicated, would have all the protection granted by the Fourteenth Amendment. If the fetus can be a person at 22 weeks, then why not at 21, or at 15, or at 10, or at five, or not even at conception? Once personhood is recognized for an unborn child in the womb, it is logical that it would be the status for all the time in the womb. How could it be otherwise? Who has the right to designate at what moment in the womb "tissue mass" went to personhood? When conception takes place, human life begins. It is all that this new human life can be at that moment. The same can be said eight weeks later, 22 weeks later, and until birth. At every stage of development, it is all that he or she can be at that point of the development process. After a child is born, development still takes place. Every newborn has a soft spot at the center top of their head, which goes away as the skull grows to full cover. This allows for the crown to be easily molded during the time in the womb.

Biblical Evidence

We have substantiated in an earlier chapter that America has a Christian heritage related to its founding. Therefore, no apology is made for including Scriptures pertaining to life's sanctity, even in the womb. David's Psalm 139:13-16 (NIV) provides excellent insight regarding God and the child in the womb:

[13] For you created my inmost being; you knit me together in my mother's womb.
[14] I praise you because I am fearfully and wonderfully made;
your works are wonderful,
I know that full well.
[15] My frame was not hidden from you
when I was made in the secret place,
when I was woven together in the depths of
the earth.

¹⁶ Your eyes saw my unformed body;
   all the days ordained for me were written in
your book
   before one of them came to be.

The biblical text states that God is involved in developing every child in the womb. Every pregnant woman is in a partnership with God, whether she knows it or not, in forming a new human being. During an abortion, a doctor must enter the womb and tell God to stand down. He now dares to undo what God has done and is still in the process of doing. The Prophet Isaiah stated in Chapter 49, verses 1 and 5:

¹ Listen to me, you islands; hear this, you distant nations: Before I was born, the Lord called me; from my mother's womb, he has spoken my name.
   ⁵ And now the Lord says—he who formed me in the womb to be his servant to bring Jacob back to him and gather Israel to himself, for I am honored in the eyes of the Lord and my God has been my strength—

These verses claim God knew Isaiah when he was in his mother's womb and was involved in his formation. The unborn John the Baptist, whom scripture records, "leaped in his mother's womb when Elizabeth entered the room where Mary and the unborn Jesus resided" (Luke 1:41). This is evidence God sees the unborn as a person. Anyone who even remotely connects to the Christian or Jewish faith should stand opposed to abortion based on the Word of God, as seen in these verses from the Bible. Many Christians have been maligned for their pro-life position. It is said they are too insensitive to a woman's plight of an unwanted pregnancy; they disregard a woman's reproductive rights of her body and her choice. Christians are pro-life because of one thing – the Word of God. God is pro-life based on His Word and expects those who believe in him to be the same.

The "My body, my choice" claim is not factual. During a pregnancy, two bodies are involved, the mother's and the unborn child's. The unborn child is not an extension of the mother's body. The mother hosts the body of a separate person during the early development stages. This unborn child can have a different blood type from the mother. As the baby develops in the womb, it can reach a stage where it feels pain, can react to light, and even learn to recognize the mother's voice.[13] The unborn child has a right to be seen as a person and should be provided all the protection that the Constitution grants people in America.

The Unholy Alliance

The Liberal Democrat Party is a pro-abortion party. To learn why they hold such a position, "follow the money." After the Supreme Court made abortion legal in its *Roe v. Wade* decision, abortion clinics became lucrative businesses. Planned Parenthood emerged as the leader of the pack. Democrats have an unholy alliance with Planned Parenthood, which pays them well. In the name of women's health benefits, Democrats in Congress have made it possible for Planned Parenthood to receive around $500 million a year from U.S. taxpayers. Planned Parenthood would be quick to say that none of these funds go to operate the abortion segment of its services. This means it is spent on salaries, operational expenses, etc., freeing up all the money private donors give to the organization's 501 (c)(4) can/will be used for various causes, including campaign contributions, overwhelmingly given to pro-abortion candidates who favor abortion. Planned Parenthood charges a healthy sum for its abortion services, generating a significant profit.

It is enlightening to examine Planned Parenthood by the numbers. Planned Parenthood does 40% of all abortions in the nation annually. Fifty-one percent of all its revenue comes from abortions. In 2012, this amounted to $164,154,000. It performs 329,445 abortions per year. This works out to be close to $500 per abortion. Total income from clinic services is around $320,000,000 with an additional $224,000,000 by donations, and then there is that $500,000,000 contribution by the American taxpayer courtesy of the government.[14]

Liberal Democrats protect Planned Parenthood and the whole abortion industry because it pays them to do so. In the election year of 2014, the Planned Parenthood PAC was busy. It spent $1,854,476 for Democrats to $13,390 for Republicans. It did not spend one dollar against a Democrat candidate, but it did manage to shell out $2,873,201 against Republicans.[15] The cozy relationship the Democrats have with this organization is ironic since the party likes to be thought of as the champions of social justice to end racism when Planned Parenthood has a very dubious history of being racist. Margret Sanger, the founder of Planned Parenthood, oversaw "The Negro Project," which aimed to exterminate African Americans using birth control and abortion. Sanger wrote a letter to Dr. C.J. Gamble, a supporter, in 1939 in which she stated, "**We do not want word to go out that we want to exterminate the Negro population...**"[16] Eighty percent of Planned Parenthood abortion facilities are in minority neighborhoods.[17] The partnership of Planned Parenthood and the Democrat Party is exploiting the black community. Why would either want to change the poverty situation of these neighborhoods when each is cashing in on them?

National Review's headline on an article by Michael J. New on September 11, 2022, was "Planned Parenthood's Annual Report: Abortion Increases, Health Service Declines." He reported that Planned Parenthood performed

129

a record 383,460 abortions in 2021, even while medical science continues to reveal more and more about the development of the child in the womb.[18] If we can apply the same calculus of 2012 to 2021, it becomes clear that Planned Parenthood is a cash cow for politicians who vote "death to the fetus." In his latest book, *The Return of the Gods*, Jonathan Cahn refers to this slaughter of preborn children as the worship of the ancient deity Molech.[19] God help us.

Pro-life pregnancy centers do not receive funding from the Federal Government, yet they provide needed services to women. With the reversal of abortion on demand nationwide as many states place significant restrictions, funding for Planned Parenthood should end since the issue is now at the state level. If Planned Parenthood gets tax dollars, it should come from the state, not the Federal Government. Some women seek help regarding unwanted pregnancy; others seek counseling after an abortion or help with items to help care for their infant. When a woman seeks the services of a pro-life pregnancy center, she is referred to as a client. If she comes in with an unwanted pregnancy, she is told she has three choices: abortion, delivery of the baby and parenting, or adoption.

A counselor will educate them on whether abortion is legal or not in their state and, if so, what restrictions are in place. If the client is set on abortion, the counselor informs her that the center's services do not include abortions. The counselor will ask if the client would like to have the process of an abortion explained, much like a medical provider would do to anyone facing a knee or other kind of surgery. The client must know that abortion is a surgical procedure with risks like other surgeries. There have been deaths associated with abortions and reports of women being unable to conceive again. These cases may be rare, but the client needs to know about them. The client can refuse this information and leave but will be told that she may return for free post-abortive counseling if she feels the need.

Most clinics offer free ultrasounds if the client chooses to deliver the baby. She is offered regular times for counseling and prenatal care. She can take advantage of baby supplies and clothing at the center's store at no cost or a low price. The center also offers counseling for the child's father if he wants to participate.

If the client chooses adoption, the counselor educates the client about the process. A family desiring to adopt will frequently pay all medical and legal bills involved in the process.

It is healthier for a woman to carry the baby to full term than to have an abortion. The birth mother is not responsible for caring for the child. Many families cannot have children and are more than willing to cover all expenses. In "open adoptions," the adopting couple allows the birth mother to have a role in her child's life.

Studies reveal many women who had an abortion regretted it severely. There is guilt, shame, and depression. For many women, abortion is just trading one set of problems for another set of problems.[20]

Liberals have taken abortion to radical extremes. Some even campaigned in the 2022 midterm election that they favored abortion up to the day of birth. This should not be surprising when considering the Born-Alive Infant Protection Act of 2018, which guaranteed medical care for an infant who accidentally survived an abortion. To abort in late-term and when an unborn child is viable for life outside the womb, the woman must undergo an abortion procedure known as "Dilation and Extraction." The infant's body is pulled out feet first in a breech position except for the head. The spinal cord is cut at the brain stem, and the brain tissue is vacuumed out. There have been incidents when the baby slipped all the way out and thus was born. One would think that the Fourteenth Amendment would be in play for this new arrival, and he or she would be given medical attention. On January 19, 2018, 183 Democratic congressional representatives voted against Born-Alive Abortion Survivors Protection Act. They favored the infant being denied care so he or she would die. This is pure evil. The Fourteenth Amendment does not make exceptions for those born due to a botched abortion.

Since *Roe* became law, over 64,000,000 unborn children have been terminated. This number is equal to the entire population of California and Florida. Can we truly call ourselves a civilized society when this is allowed? People are getting rich and gaining political power from it. The only parallel in American history to such an atrocity is slavery.

Death by Choice

This chapter is titled "The Fight for Life" because it highlights the broader scope of the battle for preserving life beyond the issue of abortion. It delves into the increasing support for euthanasia, also known as "painless termination," for individuals suffering from terminal illnesses. This presents a complex ethical dilemma, and it poses a slippery slope. The belief that human beings are created in the image of God, as stated in the Bible, has historically deemed life as sacred. Consequently, this belief has led to the protection of both the unborn and those nearing the end of life.

Advocates of assisted suicide argue that granting the terminally ill the right to end their suffering by choosing to end their own lives is a compassionate choice. However, there are concerns that this perspective may be driven by financial considerations, such as the potential cost savings associated with older adults receiving Social Security and Medicare benefits.

Canada has already legalized euthanasia nationally,

even promoting it through commercials. An example was reported by Laura Ingram of Fox News involving a disabled female military veteran, Christine Gauthier, who represented Canada and won a gold medal in powerlifting at the Paralympic Games. Despite her achievements, she faced difficulties obtaining government assistance for a wheelchair ramp and a lift for her stairs. Shockingly, she received a letter from a Canadian VA official offering her the option of assisted suicide due to her struggles: "I have a letter saying that if you're so desperate, madam, we can offer you MAID, medical assistance in dying."

In the United States, several states, including Oregon, Montana, Washington, Vermont, Hawaii, California, Colorado, and Washington D.C., have passed legislation legalizing assisted suicide. The sanctity of life is grounded in the understanding that humans possess eternal souls. The transition from this life to the next should remain within the hands of God, the Creator of life. Government should not assume the role of playing God with our final breath. Christians, who find solace in their faith, have been powerful witnesses to their beliefs even amidst painful terminal illnesses. Many maintain a vibrant prayer life for others during their time of suffering. Although they endure hardship, God continues to work through them, using their last days for His glory. Those who adhere to the Christian faith should oppose euthanasia and fight to protect and preserve life.

AMERICA IN THE BALANCE

CHAPTER 8

There's Nothing Gay
About Homosexuality

God is the Creator and the judge of the universe; his
character is the law of the universe, and when he tells us
a thing is wrong, it is wrong[1]
– Francis Schaeffer.

In recent years, the United States has witnessed a notable surge in the prevalence of sexual content across a wide range of media platforms. Avoiding encounters with sexualization or explicit sexual content has become increasingly challenging, whether it's while watching television, going to the movies, or simply driving through bustling streets adorned with billboard advertisements. It is worth acknowledging that in 1996, the proportion of individuals identifying as homosexuals within the general population was less than one percent.

Making Homosexuality Acceptable

Today, 20 percent of millennials declare themselves as LGBTQ+, according to NBC. In an article released on March 31, 2017, Catalina Gonella asked the president of GLAAD, the world's largest Lesbian, Gay, Bisexual, Transgender, and Queer (LGBTQ+) media advocacy organization, Sarah Kate Ellis, in an email if this trend would continue. Her answer:

"More young people identifying outside of binaries means that we are at a place in our culture where youth today feel free and open to living their lives as their *authentic* selves... It is "heartening" to see the future of this country loosen the shackles of traditional identities and unapologetically embrace who they are."[2]

Perhaps even more disturbing is the report that 12 percent of millennials identify as transgender or gender nonconforming. When asked whether Gonella expects the percentage of people who identify as LGBTQ+ to continue to rise in future generations, Ellis said, "absolutely."[3] That was in 2017, over five years ago. The Church is clearly losing the culture war and appears to be in full retreat, with many churches going "Woke."

Ten years ago, no one in mainstream America discussed transgender identity or gender fluidity. Today, it is considered a normal occurrence in academia, medicine, and public schools. This concept defies biology, but anyone who challenges such fake science is regarded as a homophobic bigot who causes those struggling with gender confusion to consider suicide. The Bible is not confused over such matters: Genesis 1:27 states, "So, God created mankind in His image, in the image of God He created them; male and female He created them."

Paul, addressing the Corinthian Church, which had allowed the surrounding culture to penetrate the Church rather than the Church penetrating the culture with the gospel, writes... "or do you not know that wrongdoers will not inherit the kingdom of God? Do not be deceived: Neither the sexually immoral nor idolaters nor adulterers nor men who have sex with men" (1 Cor. 6:9). Those words must be heeded as the culture overwhelms the Church in America.

Perhaps you have never heard of or read *The Gay Manifesto*. Rest assured, it does exist. Michael Swift wrote an article entitled "Gay Revolutionary" in the *Gay Community*

News. It reveals the deplorable intentions of the militants in the Gay community, and it also appeared in *The Congressional Record of the United States Congress.* Please note how much of it has come to pass since Swift released it in 1987. If the Church doesn't awaken fast, America as we know it will be no more. God will not remain silent forever. This essay is an outrage, an eruption of inner rage on how the oppressed desperately dream of being the oppressor. Swift's shocking words are below:

> We shall sodomize your sons, emblems of your feeble masculinity, shallow dreams, and vulgar lies. We shall seduce them in your schools, in your dormitories, in your gymnasiums, in your locker rooms, in your sports arenas, in your seminaries, in your youth groups, in your movie theater bathrooms, in your army bunkhouses, in your truck stops, in your all-male clubs, in your houses of Congress, wherever men are with men together. Your sons shall become our minions and do our bidding. They will be recast in our image. They will come to crave and adore us.
>
> Women, you cry for freedom. You say you are no longer satisfied with men; they make you unhappy. We, connoisseurs of the masculine face and physique, shall take your men from you then. We will amuse them, instruct them; we will embrace them when they weep. Women, you say you wish to live with each other instead of with men. Then go and be with each other. We shall give your men pleasures they have never known because we are foremost men too, and only one man knows how to truly please another man; only one man can understand the depth and feeling, the mind and body of another man.
>
> All laws banning homosexual activity will be

revoked. Instead, legislation shall be passed which engenders love between men. All homosexuals must stand together as brothers; we must be united artistically, philosophically, socially, politically, and financially. We will triumph only when we present a common face to the vicious heterosexual enemy.

If you dare to cry faggot, fairy, queer, at us, we will stab you in your cowardly hearts and defile your dead, puny bodies.

We shall write poems of the love between men; we shall stage plays in which man openly caresses man; we shall make films about the love between heroic men, which will replace the cheap, superficial, sentimental, insipid, juvenile, heterosexual infatuations presently dominating your cinema screens. We shall sculpt statues of beautiful young men and bold athletes, which will be placed in your parks, squares, and plazas. The world's museums will be filled only with paintings of graceful, naked lads.

Our writers and artists will make love between men fashionable and de rigueur, and we will succeed because we are adept at setting styles. We will eliminate heterosexual liaisons through the usage of the devices of wit and ridicule, devices which we are skilled in employing.

We will unmask the powerful homosexuals who masquerade as heterosexuals. You will be shocked and frightened when you find that your presidents and their sons, your industrialists, your senators, your mayors, your generals, your athletes, your film stars, your television personalities, your civic leaders, and your priests are not the safe, familiar, bourgeois, heterosexual figures you assumed them to be. We are everywhere; we have infiltrated your ranks. Be careful when you speak of homosexuals because we are always among you; we may be sitting across the desk from you or sleeping in the same bed with you.

There will be no compromises. We are not middle-class weaklings. We are brilliant, natural aristocrats of the human race, and steely-minded aristocrats never settle for less. Those who oppose us will be exiled. As Mishima did, we shall raise vast private armies to defeat you. We shall conquer the world because warriors inspired by and banded together by homosexual love and honor are invincible, as were the ancient Greek soldiers.

The family unit-spawning ground of lies, betrayals, mediocrity, hypocrisy, and violence–will be abolished. The family unit must be eliminated, dampening imagination and curbing free will. Perfect boys will be conceived and grown in the genetic laboratory. They will be bonded together in a communal setting, under the control and instruction of homosexual savants.

All churches that condemn us will be closed. Our only gods are handsome young men. We adhere to a cult of beauty, morality, and esthetics. All that is ugly and vulgar and banal will be annihilated. Since we are alienated from middle-class heterosexual conventions, we are free to live according to the dictates of the pure imagination. For us, too much is not enough.

An elite group of gay poets will govern the exquisite society to emerge. One of the major requirements for a position of power in the new culture of homoeroticism will be indulgence in Greek passion. Any man contaminated with heterosexual lust will be automatically barred from a place of influence. All males who insist on remaining stupidly heterosexual will be tried in homosexual courts of justice and will become invisible men.

We shall rewrite history filled and debased with your heterosexual lies and distortions. We shall portray the homosexuality of the great leaders and thinkers who have shaped the world. We will demonstrate that homosexuality, intelligence, and imagination are inextricably linked and that homosexuality is a requirement for true nobility and true beauty in a man.

We shall be victorious because we are fueled with the ferocious bitterness of the oppressed who have been forced to play seemingly bit parts in your dumb, heterosexual shows throughout the ages. We, too, are capable of firing guns and manning the barricades of the ultimate revolution.

Tremble, hetero swine, when we appear before you without our masks.[4]

Time Magazine once agreed with my position on homosexuality:

Even in purely nonreligious terms, homosexuality represents a misuse of the sexual faculty and, in the words of one educator of "human construction," … It deserves no encouragement, no glamorization, no rationalization, no fake status as a minority martyrdom…[5]

A Biblical Warning

The generation of the mid-sixties was not confused about this subject. Our views were reinforced in our churches, schools, and media sources, like *Time Magazine*. Isaiah the prophet wrote in Isaiah 3:9 (NIV) over 2700 years ago that … "The look on their faces testifies against them; …they parade their sin as Sodom; they do not hide it. Woe to them! They have brought disaster upon themselves." According to Isaiah, homosexuals boldly parading their sin are a sign that a nation is heading to disaster.

Homosexuals are getting bolder and bolder now. They make no secret what their intentions are; for example, the renowned San Francisco Gay Men's Choir recorded and released a song entitled *We'll Convert Your Children*, released July 1, 2021, which contained the following lyrics:

> *If you think we will corrupt your kids,*
> *If our agenda goes unchecked,*
> *Hey, just this once, you're correct!*
> *We'll convert your children; it happens bit by bit;*
> *Quietly and suddenly, and you won't even notice it.*
>
> *You can keep them from discos,*
> *Warn them about San Francisco.*
> *Make them wear pleated pants,*
> *We don't care!*
> *We'll make them tolerant and fair.*
>
> *We'll convert your children,*
> *Someone's got to teach them not to hate.*
> *We're coming for them.*[6]

This song received such a backlash that they released a statement that they were kidding, being sarcastic. Still, the proof this was no accident is evident when you see how professionally it was created and then look at the curriculum being developed for pre-K through elementary age, teaching them through drawings that wrong is right and right is wrong. There is a critical phrase we must not overlook in the song. *We will corrupt your kids if our agenda goes unchecked.*

In Isaiah 5, he records God's warning to Israel for their betrayal of all that He had done for them, and it sounds as if written to America:

> I will sing for the one I love
>   a song about his vineyard:
> 1 My loved one had a vineyard
>   on a fertile hillside.
> 2 He dug it up and cleared it of stones
>   and planted it with the choicest vines.
> He built a watchtower in it
>   and cut out a winepress as well.
> Then he looked for a crop of good grapes,
>   but it yielded only bad fruit.
> 3 "Now you dwellers in Jerusalem [Washington] and
> people of Judah [United States],
>   judge between me and my vineyard.
> 4 What more could have been done for my vineyard
>   than I have done for it?
> When I looked for good grapes,
>   why did it yield only bad?
> 5 Now I will tell you
>   what I am going to do to my vineyard:
> **I will take away its hedge,**
>   **and it will be destroyed;**
> **I will break down its wall,**
>   **and it will be trampled.**
> 6 I will make it a wasteland,
>   neither pruned nor cultivated,
>   and briers and thorns will grow there.
> I will command the clouds
>   not to rain on it."

God's commands are never broken. You may choose to disobey them, but you cannot break them. Sooner or later, they always break those who seek to defy them. Homosexuality was the central sin cited in Isaiah Chapter 3, and then in Chapter 5, Isaiah announces the hedge will be removed. That should cause every alarm to go off among Christians who love America, for God is consistent. What He did to His beloved Israel, He must do to America if we do not recognize that homosexuality is a sin and will never cease to be a sin.

Nowhere is that more confirmed than what is happening right now to millions of homosexuals who are demanding that our culture believe that their same-sex attractions are a natural result of biology (God's design) and deserve not only acceptance but affirmation and even celebration. Pride month in America brings parades that feature drag queens, advocates for child-adult sex, bare-breasted women, and both male and female nudity. At the same time, adults and children line the streets of our major cities, looking on with amazement and often shock. But that's the whole point and their desired intent! They want to normalize the abnormal and immoral. The more often you see something, the more normal it becomes. Rainbow flags are flown by public and private businesses, including many public schools, with more yearly celebrations.

There is no equivalency here for the opposite side. No month is set aside as a National Celebration for Americans committed to God's design for marriage and wholesome families. Each year America grows a little more accustomed to the abnormal and immoral becoming normalized.

The Dark Side of a Sin

I (Rick) have witnessed first-hand the slow and painful death of a cousin whom I loved dearly, who died of AIDS; at the time, it was called GRIDS (**G**ay **R**elated **I**mmune **D**eficiency **S**yndrome). Most everyone reading this text has a similar story of someone close who is dying or has died of AIDS. We must guard our hearts, not redefine God's laws to fit our circumstances. Pastors with children caught up in this shameful lifestyle have difficulty preaching it is wrong. In the same way, parents of children who have been caught up in this lifestyle find it hard to receive the biblical Truth about it and often get offended at the pastor if he addresses the subject. We must all be reminded that Jesus is the Truth, and when you know the Truth, the Truth will set you free (John 14:6; 8:32).

This country had a singular view that homosexuality was unnatural and wrong until a shift began in the seventies. Homosexuals who refused to turn from their sin and align with God's word began demanding the Church to align with their behavior, endorsing and accepting it or suffering the consequences of a movement which the Bible identifies as a group, [18]who suppress the Truth by their wickedness... and then warns those who oppose them that they[30]"invent ways of doing evil; they disobey their parents; [31] they have no understanding, no fidelity, no love, no mercy" (Rom. 1: 18-31).

It's that "no mercy" phrase that silences many Pastors and Christians, which in effect, becomes an endorsement of their behavior and robs them of a chance for redemption. Every follower of Christ must be reminded that perfect love casts out fear. We must tell the Truth in love to anyone living outside God's law, fearing God more than man. If you doubt that homosexuals face severe judgment from God, read Paul in verse 1 Corinthians 6:9: "Or do you not know that wrongdoers will not inherit the kingdom of God? Do not be deceived: Neither the sexually immoral nor idolaters nor adulterers nor men who have sex with men ...will inherit the kingdom of God." Any sexually immoral person who reads those words must realize that homosexuality is no different in God's eyes than adultery, fornication, or pornography.

During the eighties, ACT UP was born: *AIDS Coalition To Unleash Power* and became a tool for terrorizing many. In the summer of 1985, Mike Petrelis, an openly homosexual man in New York City, was living the dream life of a gay man. He lived in an apartment not far from the homosexual (un)holy land of Greenwich Village.

One day Petrelis discovered a blotch on his arm that caused him to see a doctor. After a few tests, the doctor told Petrelis that he had AIDS, which in 1985 was a death sentence. On that day, everything changed for Petrelis. He was 26 years old with two choices: Repent of his homosexual lifestyle with all of its forbidden pleasure and ask God for guidance and help. Or double down in his rebellion and focus on creating havoc for others. He chose the latter. As he discovered how little was being done to fight AIDS, often called GRIDS or the Gay Related disease, he grew outraged and decided to spend the remainder of his shortened life fighting to change the status quo, with no regard for God or His Word.

It is interesting how Satan's methods are always the opposite of God's. Satan inspired young Petrelis to form a protest movement that would use rage and anger to fuel the movement.[7] How different from the love of God that has driven so many to find miraculous cures for the misfortunate of the world or the missionaries who have suffered a significant loss to spread the gospel of love.

His anger was focused on how little was being done to find cures and how few of his dying and living homosexual friends were fighting back against the system. Ultimately this movement died due to the division it caused in the homosexual community, but not before thousands joined his efforts and started terrorizing pastors and Christians as they worshiped.

The **Stop the Church** protest was held on December 10, 1989, at St. Patrick's Cathedral in New York City.

145

The idea originated with ACT UP members Vincent Gagliostro and Victor Mendolia. Cardinal John O'Connor was celebrating a Mass attended by Mayor Ed Koch and other political leaders. Koch and the other dignitaries attended as a sign of support for O'Connor.

The protesters had indicated in advance that they planned to protest. While pretending to be church ushers; some handed out flyers explaining why they would disrupt the service to those entering the cathedral. The crowd outside grew to 4,500 people. The demonstrators stood outside the cathedral shouting and raising placards that read "Eternal life to Cardinal O'Connor now," "Know your scumbags," "Curb your dogma," "Papal Bull," and the like. Some tried to "storm" the Church, but police stopped those who were obvious protesters from entering. Plainclothes police officers, expecting trouble, were sitting in the pews during Mass.

At the outset of Mass, O'Connor said he knew several protesters were in attendance but asked for a friendly service. Initially, the plan was a silent protest with a "die-in" during the exposition of the Scripture portion of the Mass. When the protest appeared to have little effect on O'Connor, who continued with Mass, Michael Petrelis stood on a pew and shouted, "You bigot O'Connor, you're killing us!" The cathedral then descended into "pandemonium." A few dozen activists interrupted Mass, chanted slogans, blew whistles, "kept up a banshee screech," chained themselves to pews, threw condoms in the air, waved their fists, and lay down in the aisles to stage a "die-in.[8]

ACT UP accomplished several of its goals, but any movement that begins with the premise that God's way is the wrong way raises the question: "Is there any possibility of God revealing the right way? When all things are made known after this dispensation, eternity will reveal what God could have done to impact the AIDS epidemic had he been sought. Scripture teaches this in several passages: Luke 8:17 says, "For there is nothing hidden that will not be disclosed, and nothing concealed that will not be known or brought out into the open." Jeremiah 33:3 promises: "Call to Me, and I will answer you, and I will tell you great and mighty things, which you do not know." And in Daniel 2:28, Daniel confirms to King Nebuchadnezzar. "However, there is a God in heaven who reveals mysteries…" ACT UP quickly made its name known nationally with unapologetically confrontational tactics, says David France, the author of a history of AIDS activism called How to Survive a Plague, as well as a 2012 documentary by the same name.[9]

The New Yorker carried a story by Michael Spector on June 7, 2021, entitled: *How ACT UP Changed America*, in which he began with the following sentence illustrating the methods of this radical group: "One day in June, 1990, at the height of the aids epidemic, I sat in the auditorium of San Francisco's Moscone Center and watched as hundreds of activists pelted Louis W. Sullivan, the Secretary of Health, and Human Services, with condoms."[10]

Ultimately they were accredited for forcing the government and the scientific community to fundamentally change the way medical research is conducted — paving the way for the discovery of a treatment that today keeps alive an estimated half-million HIV-positive Americans and millions more worldwide. They also allowed untold numbers of homosexual men to continue with sexual immorality in the Gay lifestyle and survive on a host of medical concoctions at the expense of millions of God-fearing Americans who pay taxes and indemnify insurance companies who must ultimately make a profit or go out of business.

Homosexuals often hold a seething rage inside for anyone who dares say what they are doing is wrong. But we say it because we genuinely love them and want them to be free from such rage. You do not really love someone when you hold the Truth from them, especially when that Truth has eternal consequences. The following declarations appear in the *Humanist Manifesto* regarding human sexuality:

In the area of sexuality, we believe that intolerant attitudes, often cultivated by orthodox religions and puritanical cultures, unduly repress sexual conduct. We...do not wish to prohibit, by law or social sanction, sexual behavior between consenting adults. The many varieties of sexual exploration should not in themselves be considered "evil" ... individuals should be permitted to express their sexual proclivities and pursue lifestyles as they desire ...moral education for children and adults is an important way of developing awareness and sexual maturity.[11]

An Absurd Agenda

Let's explore further what humanists are advocating in their *Humanist Manifesto*. Quotes from the document appear in italics, and the rebuttal is in parenthesis:

1. *In the area of sexuality, we believe that intolerant attitudes, often cultivated by orthodox religions and puritanical cultures, unduly repress sexual conduct.* (God and God's word forbids any sex outside the marriage bond between a man and a woman.)

2. *We...do not wish to prohibit, by law or social sanction, sexual behavior between consenting adults.* (Laws in America have historically been based on God's law, the Ten

148

Commandments being the foundation of all moral law. They have served us well for over 240 years. Humanists want to discard these laws and open the door to relative morality with all its social and physical consequences, of which there are many.)

3. *...individuals should be permitted to express their sexual proclivities and pursue lifestyles as they desire.* (Either they are open to rapists and child molesters pursuing their *"proclivities,"* or they are not serious about laws and social sanctions.)

4. *The wide varieties of sexual exploration should not in themselves be considered "evil."* (This includes multiple partners, drag queens, adultery, pedophilia, bestiality, bathhouses, sodomy, rimming, and fisting, et al.)

5. *... moral education for children and adults is an important way of developing awareness and sexual maturity.*[12] (Evil people always tell you what they intend to do.)

We are now a generation into the LGBTQ+ propaganda that portrays those who pursue a homosexual lifestyle as poor victims of a puritanical culture driven by narrow-minded Christians. The issue goes far beyond a simple moral judgment and the ultimate Truth of God's eternal judgment, which will follow. There are now enough results and information for the world to observe the physical consequences of ignoring God's laws. The diseases unique to the homosexual community are staggering and often fatal. As a society, we choose to ignore them and continue to protect the right of homosexuals to practice dangerous activities, knowing disease among some will be spread to others and some will die.

When my (Rick) mother, who was 88, contracted the Corona Virus contributing to her death, her family was prevented by the hospital staff from being in her room until her last few hours, and then only if we wore protective coverings. How differently do we treat homosexuals carrying diseases just as deadly, unique to their lifestyle? They can continue to patronize bathhouses and have anonymous sex with others without notifying their sexual partners of the known virus they carry. To require this notification would make them the "victims" of the self-righteous crowd. Clearly, their propaganda is succeeding in making them victims, and holding society accountable for their victimhood, rather than making them take responsibility for their choices.

We have discovered first-hand, through churches and friends, that decent people who fervently practice their Christian faith and try to live by the moral code it provides do not want to hear or read a frank discussion of the sexual practices and lifestyles of homosexuals. The "normal" sexual practices of homosexuals are so repulsive to some Christians that they prefer not knowing about it, helping them to avoid any responsibility of taking action against it.

This is sad and dangerous. When addressing the issue of homosexuality, Paul, in Romans Chapter 1, candidly states:

> [24] Therefore, God gave them over in the sinful desires of their hearts to sexual impurity for the degrading of their bodies with one another [25] They exchanged the Truth about God for a lie and worshiped and served created things rather than the Creator—who is forever praised. Amen. [26] Because of this, God gave them over to shameful lusts. Even their women exchanged natural sexual relations for unnatural ones. [27] In the same way, the men also abandoned natural relations with women and were inflamed with lust for one another. Men committed shameful acts with other men and received in themselves the

due penalty for their error. [28] Furthermore, just as they did not think it worthwhile to retain the knowledge of God, so God gave them over to a depraved mind so that they do what ought not to be done. [29] They have become filled with every kind of wickedness, evil, greed and depravity.

It can be disheartening when certain believers close themselves off from even discussing the experiences and lives of homosexual individuals. Sometimes, preachers have been guilty of letting their emotions guide them to say more than necessary when addressing homosexual behavior. This is often done with the intention of encouraging Christians to actively engage in efforts to protect our nation and embody the true essence of the Church as intended by God. However, we can find guidance in Paul's example, which teaches us important lessons. Can any of us honestly believe that we care more about the Church and the issue of homosexuality than Paul himself?

Choosing Comfort over Truth

How did we arrive at this point? The answer can be traced to a simple fact: many pastors have lost their initial enthusiasm or compromised their faith. At the beginning of their journeys, during their time in college, Bible college, or seminary, these pastors deeply loved Jesus. They made significant sacrifices to pursue their calling. Some even faced financial hardships and lived in substandard conditions, all in the pursuit of preparing themselves for Christ's ministry.

However, as the years passed by, some pastors veered off the path of true faith. The challenges of leading a church, and increasing financial burdens and family responsibilities have led certain ministers to compromise their principles and spiritual integrity. It's important to remember that churches are made up of people, and all people possess a sinful nature, as Romans 3:23 reminds us.

Many young preachers have encountered conflicts with church members over matters of biblical principles. Unfortunately, when the member in question had more allies within the Church and wielded significant influence, the pastor found himself dismissed. In my personal experience, it was an issue of racism. I (Rick) sought to baptize two black students who had experienced salvation during a revival. However, I faced opposition from certain church members. Although most of the Church supported me, the two black students ultimately decided to attend a local black congregation instead. I left shortly after that. Thankfully, most young preachers move on with their integrity intact and often find themselves in better church environments. However, the desire to stabilize their families by establishing roots in a desired town makes it increasingly difficult to confront serious issues. Regrettably, many preachers choose comfort over conviction, transforming into "hirelings" rather than the called men of God they once were. When danger approaches, these hirelings inevitably flee like sheep in the presence of a wolf.

Tragically, compromising ministers often fare better within the Church than those who stand firm and remain true to their faith. This compromise is not limited to individual churches but extends to parachurch organizations as well. For example, one prominent Christian adoption agency has modified its policy to allow homosexual couples to adopt children. Additionally, certain evangelical colleges have relaxed their policies regarding the acceptance of gay students. This battle is far from over. Satan's objective of normalizing homosexuality within our culture was never his endgame. He has returned with the atrocity of transgender fluidity. His appetite for pushing boundaries knows no bounds, but we must continue to fight for the heritage and values of our nation. The transgender movement and our culture's normalization and acceptance of drag queens represent a fierce assault on our precious children. The upcoming chapter will explore these topics further, shedding light on the absurdities surrounding them.

As Christians, we must demonstrate love and compassion towards homosexuals, with the ultimate aim of leading them to find forgiveness in Christ for their sexual immorality. The familiar phrase "hate the sin and love the sinner" is relevant in this situation and represents the appropriate Christian response. Unfortunately, certain denominations are deviating from the biblical standards regarding homosexuality. One such example is the United Methodist Church, which now ordains homosexuals, accepts them as members, and performs same-sex marriages. This has resulted in a division within the denomination, with thousands of churches departing to join the Global Methodist Church, which upholds the biblical doctrines established by the founder of Methodism, John Wesley.

Some argue that embracing homosexuals within the Church and granting them leadership roles reflects genuine Christian love. However, we hold a different viewpoint. We believe that withholding the Truth, which holds eternal implications for their lives, does not demonstrate love toward them. Irrespective of the specific sexual immorality a person may be engaged in, it is our responsibility to compassionately convey the Truth, hoping that they will recognize the biblical Truth that denounces their sin and encourages them to pursue liberation and forgiveness through Jesus Christ.

CHAPTER 9

Puppies & Dolls to Drag Queens & Gender Mutilation

Gender identity and gender roles are part of God's plan
for creation, not a result of the fall. Any deviation from
this plan is a result of the fall and therefore
a violation of God's design and order.[1]
– Paul Smith, Vice President of the
SBC Pastors' Conference

In 2016, after two decades of leading a grassroots organization that mobilized pastors and their congregations to vote based on their values during elections, I (Rick) started feeling a strong desire to return to the pastoral role. At that time, my dear friend Dr. Jim Garlow, who served as the Senior Pastor of Skyline Church in La Mesa, California, offered me an incredible opportunity. He was seeking someone to become the Skyline DC Pastor, a role where I would directly report to Jim as a member of the Skyline Church staff. My task was to initiate multiple Bible studies with government workers in Washington, DC, mainly targeting members of Congress, the State Department, high-ranking employees, Pentagon staff, and World Bank personnel. It was the perfect way to conclude my ministry career.

My wife and I relocated to a condo provided by the church, conveniently situated across from the Supreme Court. God graciously blessed the ministry as I developed meaningful relationships with members of Congress, the State Department, and various others that will endure a lifetime. I encountered some of the most dedicated and devout Christians I have ever known and individuals who displayed negative qualities. Practically everyone in DC identifies with a religious affiliation; however, many do not allow it to impact their actions. Christians who sincerely prioritize their faith are often met with hatred.

In 2018, something pivotal occurred that changed everything. Senator Ted Cruz of Texas came close to losing his seat to a relatively new figure in national politics, Beto O'Rourke, with a narrow three-percentage-point margin. Subsequently, friends and supporters of my work with pastors urged me to return to Texas and reinvigorate pastors' involvement to maintain a conservative stance within the state. It was crucial to ensure that individuals like Senator Cruz, whose father was a committed Christian pastor that had fled Cuba after enduring time in Castro's prison, continued representing us in the Senate. After a season of prayer, I decided to resign from my position with Jim Garlow, and my wife and I returned to our Texas home.

We established offices in Houston and assembled a small team as we prepared for the 2020 elections. During this process, one of my staff members mentioned that there were elections taking place in Houston and the surrounding counties in 2019. Upon further inquiry, I discovered that these elections pertained to school boards. During this time, I began to learn about Drag Queens, pronoun usage, gender fluidity, and the issue of gender confusion. I became aware of the LGBTQ+ agenda and their efforts to influence and convert children to their cause.

Targeting the Schools

The Houston Independent School Board faced a crucial election in November, with five out of nine seats up for grabs. By August, time was running out. With over 200,000 students, the HISD stood as the largest school district in Texas. Another significant district, CyFair, located in a Houston suburb, had approximately 160,000 students and ranked as the state's third-largest district. In CyFair, three seats were open for re-election, occupied by incumbents with more than 15 years of service.

Motivated to take action, I (Rick) organized gatherings at my home, hosting over 25 pastors for back-to-back dinners. The purpose was to discuss the upcoming races and devise a plan to mobilize churches effectively to secure as many seats as possible with qualified Christian candidates. During one of these gatherings, a pastor expressed doubt, boldly declaring, "It cannot be done." Curious about his perspective, I inquired further. He explained, "Pastors don't prioritize school board elections." Although I respected his opinion, his statement only fueled my determination to try.

As we became more involved, I began hearing disturbing accounts about the state of our local schools. Our children's faith was being challenged and, in many cases, eroded by Liberal professors in college. When our brightest students entered the college environment, their faith came under attack, and without the guidance of their parents, they succumbed to the allure of sex, alcohol, and drugs. Even more alarming was discovering that the assault on our children's values started as early as pre-K and intensified throughout elementary school. By the time they reached middle school, shame and morality were replaced by a distorted "new normal," which they were encouraged not to discuss with their parents.

Ironically, one positive outcome of the COVID lockdowns and school closures was that many parents awakened to the curriculum their children were exposed to. We discovered that the same issues that made national headlines in Loudin County, Virginia, were prevalent in

Houston and its surrounding schools. We began organizing public meetings and hosting smaller gatherings to raise awareness about what was happening in our community. The more we uncovered and shared with parents and the public, the greater their outrage became. Eventually, we succeeded by replacing all three incumbents in Cy-Fair with conservative candidates and securing the election of two conservatives as Trustees in HISD for the first time in over a decade. It demonstrated the power of Christian participation at the polls.

One particularly unsettling revelation was the extent of the LGBTQ+ agenda's influence in our public schools. While Christians had been focused on their churches and personal lives, the radicals within the LGBTQ+ movement, with support from teachers' unions and organizations like AFSCME (representing librarians and library workers nationwide), had been designing and implementing materials that aimed to indoctrinate our children within the public school system.

We came across a collection of books containing explicit depictions of sexual acts and illustrations that would be deemed pornographic in any other context. Some of the content was too disgusting even to mention here. When we made these books available to parents in Houston Area schools, they were appalled to discover that such materials were in their children's school libraries.

In the past, it was common for some girls to excel in sports more than some boys of the same age. We referred to them as "tomboys." Similarly, some boys displayed less interest in athletics and preferred different activities. This has been a societal norm for years, without anyone suggesting that these children might be trapped in the wrong gender. However, today, children can access books in their school libraries that teach them explicit details about various sexual practices with anyone they choose. They are being taught at school that what they learned at home and in their churches is wrong. Regrettably, the manner in which our children are being educated about sex is concerning. Some individuals who adhere to the teachings of Albert Kinsey have taken on the role of imparting sexual knowledge to our youth. As a result, we have observed an increase in the percentage of individuals identifying as bisexual or homosexual. It is disheartening to see that the LGBTQ+ community has taken over the responsibility of educating our children about sexuality, a role traditionally fulfilled by parents. This trend will only continue if the church does not rise and voice its concerns. It is worth noting that homosexual individuals cannot reproduce naturally, so they often adopt and influence the next generation to be more open-minded about sexuality, aligning with their cause.

In addition, Drag Queens have become prominent figures in promoting their agenda, receiving unexpected support from individuals outside the LGBTQ+ community. Drag Queens, typically homosexual men, dress in feminine attire and engage in performances involving dancing, gestures, and actions of a sexual nature. Unfortunately, these displays are accessible to individuals of all ages. *OUT Magazine* reports:

RuPaul is taking over the mother-tucking world as she expands the Drag Race universe. Still, there are also numerous drag performers not attached to the franchise who are ruling the globe when it comes to their social media following: "Whether they work as musicians, actors, comedians, models, or digital influencers, certain drag performers are truly taking this artform into mainstream media and pushing the boundaries for LGBTQ+ content. What's more, these queer artists are becoming legitimate celebrities with as many followers as their straight peers –

which used to be unthinkable for out LGBTQ+ artists in the public eye."[2]

Drag Queen Story Time is becoming increasingly popular in public libraries aimed at children and often allows children to sit on their laps or lay down with them.

Not surprisingly, Reporter Lauren Talarico, on March 15, 2019, filed the following news story about Drag Queen Story Time:

> HOUSTON — A registered child sex offender has been reading to children at Houston Public Library as part of its Drag Queen Storytime. A group called Mass Resistance, which had been trying to end the program, contacted KHOU TV about the child sex offender. Mass Resistance claims it had been asking the City of Houston for months to disclose information about the drag queens, and when requests went unanswered, it did its own digging and made the shocking link.[3]

Drag Queens should not be in the presence of children. Christians must be vigilant about what their children see and experience while attending local schools. One topic that may surprise and concern parents is "Transgenderism and Pronouns," which represents the latest aspect of the gender battle affecting our children.

The Need to Protect Our Children

It is pretty common for children to explore dressing as the opposite sex out of curiosity, but for most, it remains a fleeting moment of experimentation. They quickly return to their usual activities, such as baseball, basketball, or football for boys. As a child, I (Rick) may have appeared in pictures or home movies dressed differently, but I ultimately excelled in the sports for which I received a full college scholarship. Similarly, as a nine-year-old, I (Steve) dressed as a girl to participate in my older cousin's trampoline show at community fairs. After a few flips and some laughter from the crowd, I discarded the feminine attire and resumed my routine with an all-boy look. Neither Rick nor I experienced confusion about our true gender or felt the need to change our physical characteristics.

No school should engage in activities or distribute materials related to gender change. Administering puberty blockers or hormone treatments without parental knowledge should be deemed unlawful. Children naturally seek the affirmation of adults, and those raised in Christian households are taught to respect their elders appropriately.

School teachers, coaches, and other individuals who spend significant time with our children during the week overstep their authority when they attempt to influence a child's sexual orientation and encourage them to engage in immoral acts. Teaching is a noble profession aimed at helping children succeed in life. The majority of teachers and coaches demonstrate professional integrity and are a credit to their field. However, some exploit their positions to fulfill their indecent fantasies at the expense of our children. We must demand that schools focus on core subjects such as reading, writing, math, spelling, and accurate history education. The decline in student proficiency, particularly in math, as a result of COVID-related disruptions should serve as a wake-up call for schools to prioritize academic excellence rather than spending time on sexual orientation and transgender issues.[4]

While COVID may no longer be classified as a pandemic in schools, the widespread prevalence of transgender fluidity within the public education system seems like an epidemic. Shockingly, some schools have initiated a child's gender transition without their parent's knowledge. In Coeur d'Alene, Idaho, school administrators influenced an 11-year-old girl to believe she was a boy and should undergo gender transition surgery. The school counselor convinced the child of this identity and even instructed her on how to inform her parents about her new gender identity. Phone recordings between the counselor and parent revealed that the principal and other school officials were aware of the situation but deliberately kept the parents uninformed.[5]

In another case, a mother took legal action against the Spreckels Union School District in California. She accused two teachers who ran the LGBTQ+ club at the school of coercing her 11-year-old daughter into changing her gender identity without informing the parent. The mother confronted the teachers in a meeting, but no satisfactory resolution was reached. The school did place the teachers on leave pending an investigation. It is worth noting that California law allows teachers to approach students about joining LGBTQ+ clubs. It prohibits teachers from discussing students' LGBTQ+ identities with parents without the child's permission. This restriction on informing parents about their child's sexual orientation or identity is outrageous and undermines parental authority. Schools potentially cause children significant emotional and physical harm by deliberately withholding this information from parents. No parent should have to send their child to school for an education and witness them being targeted for devious sexualization, protected by state laws.[6]

The transgender process can be a risky proposition. The Washington University Transgender Center at St Louis Children's Hospital in Missouri has come under scrutiny, as have other hospitals regarding hormonal therapy and transgender surgeries on minors. Jamie Reed, who was a supporter of transgender activity, was appalled at what she saw when she worked at the St Louis Children's Hospital.

She has become a brave whistleblower on the questionable practices she observed firsthand. She states:

> During my time at the Center, I witnessed Center healthcare providers lie to the public and parents of patients about the treatment, or lack of treatment, and the effects of treatment provided to children at the Center.
>
> I witnessed children experience shocking injuries from the medication the Center prescribed. And I saw the Center make no attempt to track the adverse outcomes of patients after they left the Center.[7]

Reed said she raised concerns for years, but doctors at the Center told her to stop giving her opinion. She also testified she saw doctors continue to prescribe puberty blockers to children, even if their parents no longer gave consent, and that the doctors lied in public statements regarding performing gender transition surgeries on minors.[8] Some states have started to draft and pass legislation prohibiting gender-altering treatments for minors due to similar concerns. Alabama, Arizona, and Arkansas, along with the Florida Boards of Medicine and Osteopathic Medicine, have forbidden such treatment on minors.[9]

Stop the Insanity

Dr. Paul R. McHugh, former psychiatrist-in-chief for John Hopkins Hospital and current Distinguished Service Professor of Psychiatry, has presented a scientific perspective on gender. He describes transgenderism as a "mental disorder" that requires treatment and asserts that sex change is biologically impossible. Dr. McHugh suggests that those who advocate for sexual reassignment surgery are promoting and collaborating with a mental disorder.[10]

163

The current transgender movement has introduced a disruptive trend concerning the use of pronouns. It is no longer appropriate to assume that individuals prefer the specific pronouns associated with their birth gender solely based on appearance. This has led to confusion in various settings, such as workplaces, the military, and educational institutions. Some argue that individuals should disclose their preferred pronouns upon first meeting, while others believe it is essential to ask sensitively. However, remembering everyone's preferred pronouns can be challenging, especially in larger gatherings. Dr. Leor Sapir, a new adjunct fellow at the Manhattan Institute, asserts that complying with demands to use pronouns contrary to biological reality is tantamount to surrendering to a new, artificial, and unscientific gender ideology. It is wrong to be compelled to speak falsehoods that we know to be untrue.[11]

The practice of transgender identification poses absurdity and significant dangers, particularly for girls and women. Extremist views on the Left suggest that anyone identifying with a specific gender can freely use restrooms and locker rooms, regardless of biological sex. This has resulted in instances of sexual assault, such as a male student raping a girl in a school restroom.[12] Furthermore, it undermines the progress made in female sports programs.

The extreme and obnoxious behavior of the transgender movement has led some within the LGBTQ+ community to consider removing the "T." Emily Zinos, the Project Coordinator for *Ask Me First MN* of the Minnesota Family Council. She reports the following enlightening information:

> The GLAAD [Gay & Lesbian Alliance Against Defamation] needs to wake up to the fact that buyer's remorse has set in for many of those who once supported the LGBT movement. All that time, money, and effort spent on injecting society and the

law with transgender ideas only serves to erode support for their actions as young people realize that LGBT ideas come with severe consequences.[13]

While some argue that the Bible is more vocal about homosexuality than transgender issues, it is incorrect to assume that transgender actions are not biblically condemned. As mentioned by Dr. Paul R. McHugh, sex change is not medically possible, despite physical alterations that can be made. Most transgender individuals engage in homosexual activities. Additionally, there are biblical verses denouncing cross-dressing, indicating that pursuing transgenderism would be similarly regarded. The transgender movement represents a direct rebellion against God and a defiant act against His design. We are fearfully and wonderfully made by God, as stated in Psalms 139:14. Although some may question the presence of deformities in individuals, we must acknowledge that we live in a fallen world where abnormalities occur but are not the norm.

The fact is God made us, and that includes our gender. It is morally wrong for deviant individuals to exploit and groom children for gender change at school. States have laws regarding sexual consent, recognizing that minors lack the mental capacity to make informed decisions with potentially detrimental consequences.[14] Therefore, it is reasonable and necessary for states to pass laws protecting minors from gender change therapy and surgeries. Christians should actively advocate for the passage of such laws in their respective states if they are not already in place.

Chapter 10

The Battle for the Classroom

*Religion, morality, and knowledge being necessary to
good government and the happiness of mankind, schools
and the meads of education shall forever be encouraged.[1]
- The Northwest Ordinance, July 23, 1787*

T he above quote, originating from an act passed by
Congress under the Articles of Confederation, is not
widely known to most individuals today. However, it holds
great significance as it outlines the framework for the
establishment and future statehood of Ohio, Michigan,
Indiana, Illinois, and Wisconsin. Within this document, we
find words pertaining to education that offer valuable
insights into the principles cherished by our nation's
Founders and their deep belief in the pivotal role of
education for the country's future success. By examining
these lines, we can clearly understand their educational
philosophy.

Opposing Viewpoints

Education of the nation's youth was necessary for good
government and personal happiness. It required attention
given to religion and morality. For years this concept of

education was followed, and our nation thrived. Unfortunately, that has changed. Founding Father Noah Webster not only distinguished himself as the author of a dictionary but he was also considered "Schoolmaster of the Republic," as we noted earlier. His view of education was strongly tied to the Christian faith, as evidenced by the following quotes:

> In my view, the Christian religion is the most important and one of the first things in which all children, under a free government, ought to be instructed.[2]

> Education is useless without the Bible. The Bible was America's basic textbook in all fields. God's Word, contained in the Bible, has furnished all necessary rules to direct our conduct.[3]

Webster's view of education was followed in America's public education system for hundreds of years. The Bible was indeed used as a textbook. That all changed mainly due to two events. One was the arrival of John Dewey, who was considered by many the "Father of Modern Education." There were those enamored with John Dewey who devoted his life to progressive education. He was one of the founders of a theory called instrumentalism, also called pragmatism, believing the child should be the center of education, not the curriculum.

Dewey was a humanist and a signer of the *Humanist Manifesto* in 1933.[4] He was also an avowed atheist. This shaped his view of education, which is now more influential on American public education than Noah Webster's. Dewey once said, "There is no God and no soul. Hence, there are no needs for the props of traditional religion. With dogma and creed excluded, then immutable (unchangeable) truth is also dead and buried. No room exists for fixed, natural law, or permanent moral absolutes."[5]

To our great misfortune, these words from Dewey are what our public education system is being built on today, and it is a far cry from what the Founding Fathers intended for our nation. Dewey says, "immutable (unchangeable) truth is also dead and buried." This is a bit laughable because the truth he is referring to does not die. The truth in the Bible, which Webster held in the highest regard, does not die because it is true from the living God, the Creator of life. One may disagree with this truth, deny its existence and ignore it, but no one can kill or bury it. The enemies of Jesus found this to be a reality on the first Easter morning. The truth established by God in His Word and His Son will not die; it will prevail. The public education institutions of today embrace the Dewey philosophy with humanism as their guidance system. Just how is that working out for our nation and culture? According to news headlines and current events, it could be better.

The second adverse event to education in America occurred ten years after Dewey's death, and had he been alive, he would have rejoiced. We have previously given attention to the Supreme Court ruling in *Engel v. Vitale* on June 25, 1962, that prayer was unconstitutional in public schools. There is more to know about it. In this case, the "Separation of Church and State" advocates launched one of their most fierce volleys in the cultural war. God was officially expelled from the classroom. The vote was 6-1 with two justices not taking part. Christians began to realize the culture was becoming unfriendly to their faith, which was once a vital part of America's life and culture. Religion and morality are no longer seen as necessary by the Left for good government. Therefore, it should be taught outside of schools as was called for in the Northwest Ordinance.

Religion is now ridiculed in schools today, and instructions in morality are being replaced by promiscuous sex education and drag queen storytime. Those justices who ruled prayer unconstitutional cited the Establishment Clause of the First Amendment as their reason for making this decision.

The recent ruling has sparked a significant disconnect. The justices argued that it is unconstitutional for school systems funded by taxpayer dollars to support any religious activities. However, two main objections arise from this decision. The first objection is that the restriction in the First Amendment was applied to the Federal Government, not to the states. Secondly, why are national educational institutions exempted if they apply to the Federal Government? One might wonder about the federal educational institutions referred to here, which include our well-known military academies: the Army at West Point, Navy at Annapolis, and Air Force at Colorado Springs. These academies are federally operated colleges specializing in military service training. All their students receive full scholarships funded by taxpayers, and they are required to serve six years in military service following graduation.

Interestingly, these academies all have chaplains who conduct religious service on their grounds. The Air Force has a stunning architectural chapel which was started in 1959 and completed in September of 1962, three months after the Court decision on prayer in schools. State universities make great efforts to ensure the separation of church and state doctrine is followed. Why do these three historically unique federal institutions get to have religious facilities and staff financed by federal tax revenue?

The best answer is tradition and precedence. The U. S. Military Academy at West Point was established in 1802, some 14 years after the Constitution was ratified. The men who drafted the esteemed document would have still been alive. The first military chaplain was appointed In 1791, and many followed. Some chaplains served at West Point from its founding. All this is evidence the framers of the Constitution saw no conflict between religion in federally run academies and the First Amendment. Left-leaning judges ignored years of precedence to advance their political agenda, and our children are paying the price in classrooms today. If federally supported academies can have a welcome religious presence on their campuses, every school in America should have the same privilege. Recent Supreme Court rulings are acknowledging this Constitutional fact.

The Liberal Influence

As a rule, godly children are reared by godly parents. Godliness is not the result of constantly studying the Bible or memorizing Scripture, though that is undoubtedly important.

Godliness is more caught than taught. God knew that when He inspired Moses to write in Deuteronomy 6 the following words:

> [4] Hear, O Israel: The Lord our God, the Lord is one. [5] Love the Lord your God with all your heart and with all your soul and with all your strength. [6] These commandments that I give you today are to be on your hearts. [7] Impress them on your children. *Talk about them when you sit at home and when you walk along the road, when you lie down, and when you get up.*

Those words are the secret to rearing children who respect authority and honor their parents throughout life.

First, Moses writes: *Parents, you are to love the Lord, your God, with all your heart and with all your soul and with all your strength.* Parents are always instructed to keep the Lord's commands in their hearts. Only then can they impress them upon their children when they are sitting in their homes (Bible studies and readings). Your religion must be firsthand, for children learn more from what they see than hear.

Secondly, they are to discuss and apply Bible reading and studies as they walk along the way.

Thirdly, when the child goes to bed, the parent is to spend a few minutes with the child and discuss the day's activities, applying God's teachings to those events. Then pray for the child and his perceived needs.

Finally, when the family awakens, start the day off right by talking about the Lord.

God gave Moses the secret for rearing the next generation to love God and uphold the nation. However, how many parents are doing these simple yet necessary things to impart grace, truth, and knowledge of our Lord to their children today? With so many single-parent families or two working parents scrambling to get their children off to school and get to work on time, comparatively few follow these simple and proven instructions. Our nation is increasingly suffering the consequences.

God never intended education to be handed over to the government and left unmonitored, but that is what is happening in America. Fortunately, for most of our history, a Judeo-Christian worldview provided a common thread that kept the country on the right track. America and her educational institutions were the world's envy until radicals, inspired by godless humanism, took God's instructions out and then went to work to impart evil to our children.

The Scripture assures us that *"if we train up a child in the way he should go, when he is old he will not depart from it."* (Proverbs 22.6). We used to believe it was normal for young men or women to question everything they were taught as they matured and developed. Still, if trained correctly and biblically, they would eventually return to their faith. That was the common pattern until the radical sixties and seventies when everything changed.

What caused this significant change of attitude in the nation's adolescents were the new Liberal and socialistic teachings in high school and college classrooms. David T. Koyzis, a professor of political science at Redeemer University College in Ontario, Canada, believes the cultural shifts in the 1960s focused on the emphasis moving from material opportunities through state intervention to expanding the human capacity to choose.[6] It was a pure rebellion against authority, which was in harmony with the tenets of emerging Liberalism on the American political scene.

Colleges and universities became the hotbeds of radicalizing our children. In the sixties, the finished product came out swinging. This new breed of brainwashed radicals rebelled on everything that had made this a great nation. The church, parents, clergy, police, the military, and governmental leaders (unless they were radicals as well); all felt the wrath of their vicious rebellion. Our motto, *E Pluribus Unum*, stamped on our currency, which is Latin for "Out of many...One," was being questioned and rejected.

America changed from being a land of law, order, and opportunity to the world's chief purveyor of pornography and immorality, exporting our sins across the globe. The new generation didn't pledge allegiance to anything but themselves. The classroom Liberalism of the sixties produced people who loved themselves much more than they did their country. Liberal universities filled with Leftists and often communist-leaning professors led the next generation to question everything they knew about America. Many of the students embraced the lies they heard about America. They became ashamed of America and pursued careers enabling them to "make a harmful difference."

173

Some admired Robert Baldwin, who founded the American Civil Liberties Union and pursued careers that would enable them to further secularize the nation through philosophy, law, and the courts. Every moral pillar that undergirded America since her founding started to fall, aided by rulings of the Supreme Court. Prayer in our schools was ruled unconstitutional and therefore forbidden, as was Bible reading, the posting of the Ten Commandments, protection from infanticide for innocent unborn children, sodomy laws, and the Biblical definition of marriage. All have been removed by lawyers in black robes on the Supreme Court. Most of those cases were initiated and won by the ACLU.[7]

Some align with the work of Dr. Alfred Charles Kinsey, the so-called "father of sexuality in America," and entered medicine, psychology, education, sex counseling, and other counseling specialties that allowed them to advance the Liberal sexology of the bi-sexual and polyamorous of Kinsey. He participated in and experimented with various sexually deviant activities with his "open marriage" wife. This is not the place to expose all of the godless sexual experimentations and studies that Kinsey performed, but he, more than any other sexologist, advanced pedophilia, homosexuality, polyamory, and transgender studies. For Kinsey, there were no boundaries. His admirers and students followed suit. He and his research have since been discredited. The Department of Justice, in its 1990 report, *Kinsey, Sex and Fraud: The Indoctrination of a People*, exposes in a report the disservice Kinsey did to the American people:

Kinsey reached three general conclusions about human sexuality: (1) the normal expression of human sexuality is bisexuality; (2) sexual contact would be a normal part of growing up for children in a less inhibited society; and (3) promiscuity and diversity of sexual expression correlate with sexual health. The authors produce evidence to demonstrate that much of Kinsey's research is unscientific and deliberately deceitful. They believe many of Kinsey's conclusions are false, even though his research has become the basis for many school sex education programs. The authors raise questions about the accuracy and reliability of Kinsey's data. For example, they believe one of the most seriously distorted aspects of Kinsey's sex research was that he sought out a population that would provide the data to support his preset agenda. The authors examine the nature of sexuality, the relation between heterosexuality and homosexuality, and the sexual development of children. They feel Kinsey is responsible for making the risks of promiscuity and sex seem less in an era when sexually transmitted diseases and AIDS are significant problems.[8]

Finally, some were enamored with John Dewey, who we have already mentioned. This progressive intellectual devoted his life to reshaping education. His belief that the child should be the center of education and not the curriculum paved the way to the common belief today among educators that anything advancing the child toward an agenda that the educational elites believe will help the child should be taught, even if it means traditional core curriculum must be discarded or minimized.[9] Hence, today, our children know what pronoun they want to be called, even if they cannot read or write proficiently. Dewey's work is thought to be controversial. In 2005, a team of scholars from Princeton University and *Human Events* news outlets were tasked to designate the most harmful books from the 19th and 20th centuries. Dewey's *Democracy and Education* rated at number five below *The Communist Manifesto"*, *Mein*

175

Kampf, Mao's Little Red Book, and Kinsey's *Sexual Behavior in the Human Male.*[10]

As a nation, we entrust our children to the state for six to eight hours a day, ten to twelve, if they play athletics or participate in after-school activities. We expect them to instill our values and love of our country in our children. For many years, that worked because the teachers, principals, and administrators went to church like us and shared our values.

Indoctrination Instead of Education

Beginning in pre-K, our children are indoctrinated and sexualized with pornographic materials that shock parents when they see them. Recover America has over a dozen books taken from local libraries or given to it by teachers fighting this assault on our children. A parent would be shocked and shamed by the images seen related to this new crusade in our public schools. There are entire novels of cartoon pictures of children indulging in every sex act imaginable, designed to teach children abhorrent and immoral acts with no regard for decency and a total disregard for the Bible or parental approval. Child-adult sex acts have made it to public schools, and our children are being groomed for pedophilia. One mom protested such degrading materials being introduced in her children's school, including a book entitled *Lawn Boy,* which is pro-pedophilia.[11] Already, men and women are lobbying members in Congress to lower the age of consent for minors so that pedophilia can become legal.

This form of indoctrination seeks to create a divide between children and their parents, fostering a sense of resentment towards parents for supposedly denying them pleasure. Children are being taught that they have the freedom to engage in any sexual activity they desire as long as all parties involved give consent. When children encounter differing views at home or in religious settings, they are told that their parents and the church are misinformed or even labeled as phobic and hate-driven, resulting in some individuals feeling so unwanted that they resort to suicide.

This entire agenda is often associated with classic Marxism, a belief system that thrives on division and destruction. If the church fails to recognize this, woke ideologies will lead to the downfall of America. It is crucial for pastors who follow biblical teachings to speak out against such immoral behavior and provide redemption and salvation through God's forgiveness. Unfortunately, entire Christian denominations and millions of individuals have embraced the new "Woke" philosophy, prioritizing emotions and feelings over facts and science. This philosophy demands that if a male declares himself as female, others must engage in his lie and ignore scientific evidence and proper language usage. Failing to comply could cause distress to the individual, and anyone who perceives them as their biological sex and uses corresponding pronouns is deemed offensive and non-woke.

This troubling trend needs to be rejected and eradicated from our culture; otherwise, we risk fragmentation and vulnerability to adversaries who seek to conquer our great land. While our military forces are being trained in "Woke" principles, our enemies observe our weaknesses as a nation entangled in these absurd concepts. It is high time for parents and pastors to join forces and reclaim our schools, where indoctrination has replaced true education, and children are being exposed to sexualization to an extent where nothing embarrasses or shames them. What was once considered abnormal and immoral is now being normalized, and anyone challenging this narrative is portrayed as an enemy standing in the way of personal gratification.

Left Extremism

Just how bad can it get in the classroom? San Francisco Bay area teacher Steven Williams knows how bad. He was a fifth-grade teacher who was prevented from distributing copies of the *Declaration of Independence* to his students because it referred to God. Williams sued the school, and his lawyer said, "It's a fact of American history that our Founding Fathers were religious men, and to hide this fact from young fifth-graders in the name of political correctness is outrageous and shameful."[12] We have reached an all-time low when history teachers are not allowed to use the actual founding documents written by our Founding Fathers because the students might be exposed to God.

Williams was also prevented from using George Washington's journal, John Adams' diary, "The Rights of the Colonists" by Samuel Adams, and William Penn's "The Frame of Government of Pennsylvania."[13] These items were denied because they refer to God. The school's policy was that students must be denied the historical truth if it deals with religion and God. In other words, the Leftist narrative was more important than the historical truth.

In Charleston, West Virginia, Mr. Liston was a father who was upset that his high school daughter had to read a book for an assignment, which was literary porn. He went to a school board meeting to complain about this. As he made his protest, he started reading from the book. What he read was graphically obscene, so much so that one of the board members asked him to stop reading. Another board member said that if an eleventh grader had to read these words as an assignment, then she, as an adult, should be able to hear them.[14] The Bible has been banned from school, but in the school where Mr. Liston's daughter attended, literary porn was acceptable.

In Amherst, Massachusetts, a high school made the

178

controversial decision to choose "The Vagina Monologues" as its school play. During the performance, teenage girls took the stage and openly discussed their female genitalia, using explicit language, including the four-letter "c" word. This occurred in the presence of fellow students, some as young as 13, as well as parents. It's worth noting that regardless of personal preferences, the taxpayers of Amherst financially supported the production of this play. In this situation, the views and desires of the Left prevailed, even if it was met with opposition from those who didn't agree.

Interestingly, while some individuals express concern over religious symbols potentially offending others, they appear to be less attentive to the possibility of causing offense when they display a fondness for vulgarity.[15]

One of the cruelest assaults made on the public classroom has been Critical Race Theory. Princeton University professor Allen C. Guelzo did a deep dive into CRT and found it a dangerous curriculum. He believes Critical Race Theory helped foster totalitarian ideologies in the 20th century, such as Marxism and Nazism, which promoted that all human relationships are relationships of power between an oppressor class and an oppressed class. For the Marxists, the bourgeoisie were the oppressors. And for the Nazis, the Jews were the oppressors. And today, in 21st century America, for promoters of Critical Race Theory, all whites are the oppressors.[16]

Critical Race Theory rejects reason, so it cannot be questioned. Guelzo says the only purpose of questions is to serve the interests of the oppressive class, and "any answer you come up with, which doesn't speak in terms of some hidden structure of oppression, can simply be dismissed as part of the structure of oppression."[17] If you question whether all White people are oppressors, "the questioning itself is an example of how you're in on the oppression."[18] It is atrocious that this insanity is forced on our kids at the expense of our tax dollars. It is clearly used by the Left to indoctrinate students and shape their political preference for the Leftist camp.

It is not just in public schools where tax dollars are being misused for the sake of the Left Wokeism. Lakeland Community College near Cleveland, Ohio, is supported by state tax dollars and decided to target a student. He was taking a class where the professor required the students to wear a pink triangle to symbolize homosexual "pride." The student refused to comply on the grounds that it was against his personal moral beliefs. He tried to work within the system and asked for an alternative assignment, but his request was denied. This honor student received an F grade in the class for his refusal to participate, even though to do so would require him to set aside his moral convictions. The student was even facing expulsion until the story was covered by local TV news and created such negative publicity that the college had to recant and make amends.[19]

Public-supported colleges are easily outmatched by private colleges when it comes to making the indecent acceptable. Pornography has been deemed an appropriate academic topic to explore at some colleges. Wesleyan University, in Middletown, Connecticut, named after John Wesley, the founder of the Methodist Church, offered a course entitled "Pornography: Writing of Prostitutes." Professor Hope Weissman gave an assignment where students were to produce a piece of pornography, and she gave no constraints. Some of the projects were despicable. "One student produced a video, training the camera's lens on a man's eyes while masturbating. Another turned in pictures of herself engaged in oral sex with her boyfriend."[20] Someone objected to this course, and the administration investigated it only to have outcries from students protesting their academic freedom was being hampered.

Four things that Christians in America should do:

1. Get your children out of public schools as quickly as possible. If you cannot afford private school, home school them, and if that is impractical, then join a co-op of others who share your concern for the public schools and learn how you can help each other and get the job done. No price is too high to save your children. Trust God to help you. This may not be a consideration for some singles with extremely difficult financial circumstances. If that is your situation, stay engaged in your child's education, know what they are being taught, and counter it by contesting anything you find illicit. Enlist a pastor or church leader who cares to assist you if necessary.

2. Pastors should consider starting a Christian school in their building immediately. We have beautiful facilities in every community that are empty Monday through Friday. Why not fill them with children and give them a chance at an education based on Christian principles?

3. Send mature Christian adults into the public school arena, running for School Boards as candidates. In the nineties, I (Rick) discovered that our high school-age children were being taught things that countered what they heard at church, and we got involved. We soon had four members of our church elected to the school board out of seven positions, and they made a difference. Please do not believe the lie that your school is different and that your children can handle anything that comes their way. Your school district needs mature Christian adults serving as teachers, administrators, principals, and board members. They can change the direction of your school.

4. Get involved in politics at the grassroots level, promoting legislation in your state that allows the tax money collected for education to be used for public or private instruction. School choice vouchers allow the money to follow the child and empower the parents to choose how their children are educated. It is foolish to pay for the corruption of our children.

The Separation of Church and State zealots have made the classroom their prime target. They have landed damaging direct hits creating a tragedy for the nation. God was forced out, and the guns came in. Morality is being replaced by permissive sexuality. Education is being replaced by indoctrination. If you do not think Liberal indoctrination is going on, then why do Democrats want the voting age lowered to 16? The Supreme Court sent the abortion issue back to the states when it overturned *Roe* in June of 2022. We must vigorously oppose the Liberal Left's war on the Christian faith in our schools. Step up and make your voices heard, your faces seen, and your votes counted in electing God-fearing conservatives to your school boards.

Oklahoma is OK

In February of 2023, Oklahoma passed a law allowing parents to send their children elsewhere than public schools. Regardless of income, all parents can receive $5,000 per child to be used at a private school. If the choice is home school, the amount is $2,500 per child.[21] You can be sure several concerned parents and conservative legislators worked hard to make this happen. If your state still needs to get something like this going, you can start it. Oklahomans are showing us that it is possible to win the battle of the classroom by getting children in a school where abstinence is taught in sex education, where CRT is not welcomed but encouragement for learning the Christian faith is.

CHAPTER 11

Crime and Justice - Wrong is Never Right

Equal and exact justice to all men, of whatever persuasion, Religious or political.[1]
— Thomas Jefferson

Injustice is common where there is tyranny. The Founders were painfully aware of this. Their suffering of injustice at the hand of the British crown was so unbearable it motivated them to a revolution and the forming of a new nation. Ensuring this new nation enacted justice for its citizens was a high priority. The Founders were believers in law administered equally to all citizens, and the king was not to be above it. There are passages in the Bible that instruct the Christian believer to respect the governing authorities. 1 Peter 2.13-17 and Romans 13 are examples. If rulers were respectful to the people and served and protected them, then this respect and submission would be merited. However, if the ruler was evil in governing, he gained the displeasure and judgment of God. Proverbs 29.2 (NKJV) states, "When the righteous are in authority, the people rejoice; But when a wicked man rules, the people groan." The Founders were suffering under the oppression of the British Crown. They no doubt felt that the British monarch was the living example of Isaiah 10.1, 2 (NIV): "Woe to those who make unjust laws, to those who issue oppressive decrees, to deprive the poor of their rights and withhold justice from the oppressed of my people..." The Founding Fathers believed that the Scriptures mandated that the people had the right to confront any form of government that levied evil oppression on those it ruled

God Loves Justice

God demands that those who rule do it justly. Exodus 23.6 (NIV) states: "Do not deny justice to your poor people in their lawsuits. Have nothing to do with a false charge, and do not put an innocent or honest person to death, for I will not acquit the guilty." The Founders did not believe the colonies were receiving justice from the British king's rule. Kings often misused their authority throughout history. James Madison wrote in *Federalist Number 51*, "Justice is the end of government. It is the end of civil society. It ever has been and ever will be pursued until it is obtained, or until liberty be lost in the pursuit."[2] It is little wonder that a *Declaration of Independence*, such as the one that created the United States of America, was written, approved, signed, and fought for.

Law is King

Many Christians are familiar with British ministers Wesley and Whitfield but not so much with Presbyterian Scottish minister Samuel Rutherford who lived from 1600 to 1661. Rutherford wrote the literary earthquake, *Lex Rex*. The translation from Latin is "Law is King." Pastor Samuel Rutherford did not take a neutral position on politics. Francis Schaeffer summarizes the essence of *Lex Rex*: "What is the concept of *Lex Rex*? Very simply: The law is king, and if the king and the government disobey the law, they are to be disobeyed. And the law is founded on the Law of God."[3]

Rutherford directly attacked the doctrine of the "Divine Right of Kings." In protecting the inalienable rights of men given by God, he proclaimed that kings had to become subject to the law. The law protected men's rights, and kings must also obey it. Clearly, this did not go over well with the royalty of the day. *Lex Rex* was banned in both Scotland and England. The Scottish parliament met to approve Rutherford's execution for his views, but he died before they could carry out this wicked deed.

Schaeffer provides further insight into Rutherford's thoughts on the matter of law and kings in relationship to Romans 13, where Paul instructs believers to submit to the existing government authorities. Rutherford wrote: "The state, however, is to be administered according to the principles of God's Law. Acts of the state which contradicted God's Law were illegitimate and acts of tyranny. Tyranny was defined as ruling without the sanction of God."[4]

American patriot Thomas Paine in his pamphlet, *Common Sense*, revealed the impact Rutherford's ideas had on the Founders:

> But where, says some, is the King of America? I'll tell you, Friend, he reigns above, and doth not make havoc of mankind like the Royal Brute of Britain … let it be brought forth placed on the divine law, the word of God; let a crown be placed thereon, by which the world may know, that so far as we approve of monarchy, that in America THE LAW IS KING.[5]

Checking the Bill of Rights

The Constitution reveals how serious the Founders were about justice being served by the law. Five of the *Bill of Rights* amendments directly relate to legal matters

185

concerning the nation's citizens. The content of these amendments and the spirit with which they were written shows the Founders desired justice and not biased oppression, which comes from the hand of tyranny. They knew that the strongest political forces would rule if justice did not prevail, evolving into tyranny. This concept rocked the political world like a major earthquake, as the rights of people were considered a higher priority than a ruler's power.

The Fourth Amendment protects us from search warrants without probable cause. Law enforcement could not appear at a person's house and barge in for a search, hoping to find evidence of wrongdoing. We have often heard of people pleading the "Fifth." When a person does this, they are exercising their right not to have to testify against themselves, which might incriminate them. Lois Lerner of the IRS found this Fifth Amendment very useful. This amendment also prevented trying someone again for the same crime once they had been acquitted, meaning an accused person could not face double jeopardy.

The sixth amendment gives a person accused of a crime a right to "a speedy trial, by an impartial jury, not common in monarchy rule. This was one oppression the Founders wanted to eradicate. The word "speedy" may perplex some today since it seems like a long time before a case does go to trial, but under the rule of kings, it might take years. It was done so purposely to add hardship to the accused, even if they were not guilty. The Seventh Amendment guarantees the right of trial by jury for "suits at common law," which were over $20. The Ninth Amendment prevented levying excessive bail on the accused.

The *Bill of Rights* gave the advantage to the accused, protecting their rights to due process. When the accused (defendant) came to trial, he or she stood innocent until proven guilty. This puts the burden of proof on law enforcement or the accuser (plaintiff). The concept of "innocent until proven guilty" is not found in the Constitution, but it has come to be regarded over time as a right one has when accused of a crime in court. This concept is rarely practiced in other countries.

It should be noted the Fourteenth Amendment gave the legal right to equal protection to the newly freed slaves and guaranteed them due process. Justice was a high priority for the Founders, and they tried to create a fair and effective system. It has turned out to be a good but imperfect system. We live in a fallen world, and perfection is often not attainable. There have been times when the guilty have gone free and the innocent have been convicted. Our system of appeals to a higher court is designed to safeguard against injustice, but we must remember judges and juries are composed of imperfect people. Our system might not be perfect, but it is one of the best, if not the best, in the world.

In the Words of the Founders

Since the Founders highly regarded the law, we must review some of their words about it. Samuel Adams said, "In the supposed state of nature, all men are equally bound by the laws of nature, or to speak more properly, the laws of the Creator."[6] The cousin of John Adams reveals the Founders regarded the laws of nature as the laws of God and that all men were bound by them, a concept no longer adhered to today. John Quincy Adams, son of John Adams and the nephew of Samuel Adams, stated, "The laws of nature and of nature's God . . . of course presupposes the existence of a God, the moral ruler of the universe, and a rule of right and wrong, of just and unjust, binding upon man, preceding all institutions of human society and of government.[7] The Founders accepted the existence of God and that his laws were binding on all men. The absolute moral standards of the

Bible became foundational to the laws created by this new nation. Alexander Hamilton also referred to the law of nature as God's law when he wrote, "This is what is called 'the law of nature,' which, being coeval with mankind, and dictated by God Himself, is, of course, superior in obligation to any other. It is binding globally, in all countries, and always. No human laws are of any validity if contrary to this."[8] He, like other Founders, regarded law made by man to have no validity if such laws were contrary to God's law. Sadly, many Congressmen and women do not see it this way today.

James Wilson, who was one of the first justices to be appointed by President George Washington, penned the words, "Human law must rest its authority ultimately upon the authority of that law which is Divine."[9]

George Mason, known for his significant influence on the Bill of Rights, reemphasizes law being tied to God, stating:

All acts of legislation apparently contrary to natural rights and justice ... must be considered void in the nature of things. The laws of nature are the laws of God, whose authority can be superseded by no power on earth. A legislature must not obstruct our obedience to him from whose punishments they cannot protect us. All human constitutions which contradict His laws we are in conscience bound to disobey. Such has been the adjudication of our courts.[10]

Mason conveys that no laws made were to contradict God's laws. If this principle were followed today, many of our problems as a nation would cease to exist.

Noah Webster, famous for writing a dictionary and having the Bible as a textbook in schools, favored the Bible being used as a guide to lawmaking when he wrote:

The moral principles and precepts contained in the scriptures ought to form the basis of all our civil constitutions and laws. All the miseries and evils which men suffer from, vice, crime, ambition, injustice, oppression, slavery, and war, proceed from their despising or neglecting the precepts contained in the Bible.[11]

The comments from these Founding Fathers leave no doubt America had a Christian foundation for its laws and moral standards of conduct. It is bewildering that forces in political parties and activist groups are working to end this godly influence on our nation.

Biblical Standard on Crime

Crime is a major concern in the country today, and the Bible effectively addresses this topic. In the March 2022 edition of *Decision Magazine*, Franklin Graham published an article entitled "Crime and No Punishment." In it, he documents the Left's interest in defunding police and their desire to show favoritism to the criminal over the victim. Franklin Graham writes the following disturbing words:

I believe the fundamental cause of this problem [high crime] – which I thought I would never see – is the absurd notion that crime and criminals don't deserve to be justly punished. The foundation of our justice system has always been a punishment that fits the crime, but apparently, it is now turning into crime and no punishment.[12]

Most of the people who committed violent acts during the protests of 2020 were not prosecuted. Many were out with little or no bail with no requirement to return and stand trial. Liberal states have released criminals from prison. COVID was used as the reason in some cases for the releases. Still, there is evidence that a lower prison population is a high priority of many Democratic leaders, pandemic or not. Alfred S. Regnery wrote:

> Liberals just don't think people should be punished. Crime, in their lexicon, is caused by social injustice. It's a symptom of all the wrongs of modern society. Instead of punishing wrongdoers, liberals believe we should cure them of the disease. Their only guilt is that they got caught up in some unfortunate circumstance not of their making, and therefore it is unfair to hold them accountable and punish them. In a telling move, just last week, the Obama Administration sent a directive to colleges telling them not to ask applicants if they have a criminal history – it might stigmatize them – but to refer to them only as "justice-involved individuals."[13]

Note that it is "justice-involved individuals," not "criminally involved individuals." Many Liberals want us to believe criminals are victims, which is why they became criminals, not exercising their free will. They just got caught up in "some unfortunate circumstance not of their making." I don't think those words would comfort parents at the graveside of their murdered teenager. The Apostle Paul writes in Romans 13.3 and 4 (NIV):

> 3For rulers are not a terror to good works, but to evil. Do you want to be unafraid of the authority? Do what is good, and you will have praise from the same. 4For he is God's minister to you for good. But if you do evil, be afraid; for he does not bear the

sword in vain; for he is God's minister, an avenger
to execute wrath on him who practices evil.

Our leaders fail to protect the people they serve when they
don't punish crime justly. There is a theory that this very
soft approach to crime is part of "identity politics" since a
higher percentage of the minority population is apprehended
for crimes. Blacks and Hispanics comprise 30 percent of the
population but 51 percent of those incarcerated.[14] Policies
that benefit the criminal are seen as social justice endeavors
by many liberal politicians, which they think plays well to
the large group of minorities in their base.[15]

Many liberals ignore the Bible when dealing with crime
and the administration of justice. Equal justice for all is a
long-gone concept. It does not enhance their political goals.
A past case in Bristol, Pennsylvania, reveals just how bad
the administration of justice has become. Terrence Dickerson
burglarized a house and made his exit through the garage.
The automatic garage door opener malfunctioned, and the
door into the house locked behind him. The house owners
were on vacation and did not return for eight days.
Dickerson had to live on a case of Pepsi and a large bag of
dry dog food. The hard-luck thief sued the family for mental
anguish, and a jury awarded him $500,000, which the
family's insurance company had to pay.[16] The blindfold
from Lady Justice's eyes has been pulled, and her tunic is
stained.

Helping the Criminals

A liberal philosophy on crime takes a more serious turn
than just supporting ridiculous lawsuits brought by those
caught in criminal acts. What is supported now is putting
lives in jeopardy. There are three policies promoted by the
Radical Left spelling a danger to Americans; defunding the

police, early release of prisoners convicted of serious crimes, and offenders released without posting any bail.

After the George Floyd killing by police in Minneapolis in 2020, many Liberals called for the defunding of police forces. Oddly, they never called for defunding the teachers' union or public schools when a teacher sexually abused a student. It does not take high intellect to see reducing the number of police while flooding the streets with experienced criminals is a formula for disaster, making it more unsafe for law-abiding citizens. Zaid Jilani of the National Review wrote an article entitled "The Deadly Consequences of 'Defund the Police.'" In it, he writes:

These cuts are coming at a time when many American cities have experienced a huge increase in homicides and shootings. Some locales, such as Wilmington, Del., saw a record number of homicides last year. St. Louis, Mo., long one of America's most violent spots, saw its highest rate of killing in 50 years.[17]

Many other cities could be added to the lists experiencing a record rise in crime because there are fewer police officers on the force. Law enforcement has become so frustrating and dangerous that fewer people seek to become police officers, and many are resigning to pursue other work.[18] In the 2022 midterm election, defunding the police was an important issue.

Releasing prisoners early, some of whom are violent offenders, is indeed perplexing. California is leading the way. The Golden State's early release from prison program will free around 76,000, including violent and repeat felons. There is no proof any have been rehabilitated, but only that they had a recent record of good behavior.[19] Thankfully, the proposed release plan ran into problems when the California Supreme Court unanimously ruled such could not be done for violent prisoners. Fewer police officers and more felons on the streets is hardly a wise policy for public safety.

A simple Google search reveals stories of people killed by early-release prisoners nationwide. The policy of release after arrest with no bail is not working. In California, a man was arrested three times in one day but released each time because of the new "no bail" policy. On his first arrest, he was driving a stolen vehicle with stolen property in it. He was given a citation and released. He was later arrested with more stolen property in his possession.[20]

The soft-on-crime policies are not working in New York City. Criminal acts by released violent offenders are up 50 percent.[21] The most important responsibility of the government is to keep its citizens safe. Darrell Brooks of Waukesha, Wisconsin, was charged with attacking his ex-girlfriend and obstructing an officer. He merited high-risk classification when evaluated but was released on $1000 bail, a meager amount because of bail reform. This allowed Brooks to drive his SUV at a Christmas parade on November 21, 2021, killing six people; some were children.[22]

When Government is the Criminal

Gregg Jarrett, a commentator from Fox News, extensively explored the allegations suggesting that candidate and President Donald Trump colluded with the Russians during the election and acted in their interests while in office. However, Trump was found innocent of any wrongdoing following an investigation led by Special Counsel Robert Mueller. In his book titled *The Russian Hoax* and other works, Jarrett exposes the involvement of FBI leadership in an attempt to construct a damaging case against Trump. Central to this effort was the notorious Steele Dossier, a document created by Christopher Steele, a former British intelligence officer. The dossier contained incriminating information about Donald Trump but was later revealed to be entirely fabricated. Furthermore, it was established that the Hillary Clinton campaign had contributed funds to the dossier research.[23]

The dossier served as the primary justification for obtaining a FISA warrant, allowing the FBI to secretly review communications within the Trump campaign. The Durham Report found that the FBI offered Christopher Steele, the dossier's author, one million dollars from taxpayers' funds to verify its contents. However, Steele was unable to substantiate the claims made in the dossier. Nonetheless, despite lacking evidence, the FBI treated it as if it were true.[24] This incident exemplifies how the world's premier law enforcement agency engaged in actions with no valid justification, aiming to influence the outcome of an election and remove a duly elected president.[25]

During the 2020 presidential election, the FBI found itself embroiled in another controversy. This time, the focus was on a laptop belonging to Hunter Biden, the son of Joe Biden, the Democratic candidate. Hunter, who has a history of drug addiction, left his laptop at a repair shop and failed to retrieve it. The laptop subsequently became the shop owner's property, who discovered files containing pornographic videos featuring Hunter, along with evidence of his involvement in questionable activities with corrupt Chinese and Ukrainian businessmen. Miranda Devine's book, *Laptop from Hell*, details Hunter Biden's wrongful behavior and the discussions and deals worth millions of dollars.[26]

The laptop also revealed evidence implicating Joe Biden, then the vice president, in benefiting from these deals, constituting corruption at the highest level of government. Representative James Comer, the Committee on Oversight and Accountability Chairman, disclosed this information during a press conference on May 10, 2023. Records showed that 10 million dollars were wired from foreign countries to 20 Biden family-owned LLCs.[27] Devine's book delves into Hunter Biden's deceitful actions. When the computer shop owner realized the significance of the contents, he made copies to protect himself and informed the FBI, who obtained the laptop in December 2019. Despite evidence of wrongdoing by Hunter Biden and incriminating ties to his father, the FBI chose not to take any action related to these matters. However, Hunter Biden was charged with two misdemeanors of failing to pay income tax and was allowed to execute a plea deal that likely would result in him serving no jail time. Other people have not been as fortunate and have served time in prison for this same offense. Hunter also was charged with committing a federal felony for lying on a firearm purchasing application, saying he was not a drug user when indeed, he was. He has consented to a pre-trial diversion program which could lead to no prison time for an offense that carries a maximum sentence of 12 years.[28]

The *New York Post* obtained information from the laptop and began reporting on it through their Twitter account. However, Twitter swiftly suspended the *New York Post's* account. It was later revealed, through files released by Elon Musk, that the FBI had collaborated with Twitter to suppress information related to the laptop. An article by Tristian Justice in The Federalist titled "CONFIRMED: FBI Colluded with Big Tech to Prevent Voters from Learning about Hunter Biden's Laptop" sheds light on this collaboration.[29]

The FBI leaned on Twitter to suppress the laptop story and exerted similar pressure on Facebook executives.[30] Musk's released files demonstrated that the FBI paid Twitter over $3.4 million to comply with FBI instructions, [31] using taxpayer money. The FBI is expected to remain apolitical and unbiased, but its actions show clear favoritism toward Democratic presidential candidates in the past two elections.

Such corruption within the government, regardless of the party involved, does not serve the people's best interests.

The current border policy implemented by the Biden Administration regarding the southern border poses a threat to the safety of American citizens. The adoption of an open border policy creates opportunities for criminals and terrorists to enter the country while also facilitating substantial profits for drug cartels. Among the concerning elements of this unrestricted flow across the border is the influx of the dangerous drug Fentanyl. Disturbing statistics from Families Against Fentanyl reveal that between 2020 and 2021, a heartbreaking number of individuals aged 18 to 45 tragically lost their lives due to Fentanyl overdoses—37,208 in 2020 and 41,587 in 2021.[32] It is deeply disheartening to witness the loss of our young adults being treated as acceptable collateral damage by those who prioritize granting amnesty to all illegal entrants, potentially to secure future votes.[33]

In certain states and cities governed by Democratic officials, there have been declarations of "sanctuary states" or "sanctuary cities" for undocumented immigrants. In these cases, when an individual in the country illegally is apprehended for a minor offense or misdemeanor, the local authorities neglect to notify Immigration and Customs Services (ICE) about the potential for deportation. Instead, they may release the individual back into society with minimal or no bail. This deliberate disregard for laws established by duly elected representatives contradicts the officials' sworn oath of office. Such actions deviate from the principles of a functioning republic and resemble practices found in authoritarian forms of government. Consequently, these officeholders should be subject to the impeachment or recall process, as their actions jeopardize the safety of the citizens they have pledged to protect, all in pursuit of potential political gains in the future.

Verses of Scripture

The Bible takes crime seriously. It calls for punishment when wrong is done and desires fair justice in the courts. The following verses verify this:

Psalm 11.7 For the Lord is righteous; he loves justice; the upright will see his face.

Proverbs 17.23 The wicked accept bribes in secret to pervert the course of justice.

Proverbs 18.5 It is not good to be partial to the wicked and so deprive the innocent of justice.

Proverbs 24.22-25… To show partiality in judging is not good; Whoever says to the guilty, "you are innocent,"–people will curse him, and nations denounce him. But it will go well with those who convict the guilty, and rich blessing will come upon them.

Crime is not just a social issue for politicians to debate. It is addressed in the Bible, and God has set his standards regarding it. We are wise to heed them. Given the policies advanced by many Liberals on crime, it is unsafe for Americans to have them in power. Policies that favor violent criminals because they may create a political advantage, are atrocious and are adverse to the biblical standard of crime.

Part Three

The Road to Renewal

Chapter 12

How Government Works

To form a new government, requires infinite care, and
unbounded attention; for if the foundation is badly laid
the superstructure must be bad.[1]
– George Washington

Many people vote in election after election, but they have yet to learn how Government works. A survey by the Annenberg Public Policy Center of the University of Pennsylvania in 2014 provides astonishing data on what people know about their Government in America. The results are below:

- While little more than a third of respondents (36 percent) could name all three branches of the U.S. government, just as many (35 percent) could not name a single one.

- Just over a quarter of Americans (27 percent) know it takes a two-thirds vote of the House and Senate to override a presidential veto.

- One in five Americans (21 percent) incorrectly thinks that a 5-4 Supreme Court decision is sent back to Congress for reconsideration.

- Asked which party has the most members in the House of Representatives, 38 percent said they knew the Republicans are the majority. However, 17 percent responded Democrats, and 44 percent reported that they did not know (up from 27 percent who said they did not know in 2011).

- Asked which party controls the Senate, 38 percent correctly said the Democrats, 20 percent said the Republicans, and 42 percent said they did not know (also up from 27 percent who said they did not know in 2011).[2]

Framing a Government

The survey was taken in 2014, but in all likelihood, a similar survey today would render worse results. There are some basic facts every voter should know regarding how Government works today. Ignorant and uninformed voters harm democracy. We will review some of these basic facts in this chapter, but first, we will look at how the Founding Fathers desired the Government to work. Then we can assess how far we have strayed and to what end.

On July 4, 1776, 56 brave and daring men signed the *Declaration of Independence*. Our nation considers this its birthday or date of founding. However, this date could be debated because declaring independence and winning independence are two different things. Following this declaration, our Founding Fathers and The Continental Army faced the most powerful military in the world at the time. They had faith in God and a vision for a free nation. The United States started operating under the Constitution on March 9, 1789, even though New Hampshire's ratification vote on June 22, 1788, made it the law of the land. We don't give either of these dates precedence, preferring to light the skies with fireworks every Fourth of July.

The war was costly, but God's hand intervened on more than one occasion to help the thirteen colonies win the conflict. Just as the war was no easy accomplishment, neither was the drafting and ratification of the Constitution on which our form of Government is anchored. When the war ended, the question was, "How would the colonies be aligned?" Would there be 13 individual nations (states), regional nations, or just one nation of 13 states? The latter won out, but it was far from an easy achievement. The debate was sometimes tedious, and some key states' ratification vote was very close. In the end, a representative republic form of Government was adopted based on a Constitution which began with the revolutionary words "We the People."

The debate during the convention, the content of the Constitution itself, and the *Federalist Papers* by James Madison, Alexander Hamilton, and John Jay all give valuable insight into how the Founding Fathers wanted the Government to work. Understanding the crux of the debate at this 1787 constitutional convention is essential. The 13 colonies had just won independence from a monarchy that wielded tyrannical rule and violated their God-given rights. The last thing the majority delegates wanted was to create a form of Government created by their hands that could gain similar power and once again put those rights in jeopardy.

There were no declared political parties at this debate, but there were opposing sentiments. The group known as the "Federalists" wanted the national or Federal Government to have distinct powers which the states could not challenge. The "Anti-Federalists" wanted to ensure these powers given to the Federal Government did not severely encroach on individual state rights and the liberties of citizens. Since 1782, the colonies have been operating under the Articles of Confederation, which had many flaws, and the delegates were convening to correct them. It took a little while for

203

them to realize a remodeling job would not suffice. The old would have to be discarded, and they would create a new guidance document for governing.

Forming a government through a new constitution was challenging. It had to be firm, efficient, powerful, and functional enough to execute its responsibilities. This new Government had to be strong enough to keep national unity while safeguarding the rights and liberties of the people. The new Constitution would set the form and the procedure for government operations. At the same time, it would impose restrictions on the Federal Government to protect the rights of the people and assure each of the states their authority to govern with the powers not placed in the Federal Government. This was all-important, and the Tenth Amendment in the *Bill of Rights* protects this concept. The Constitution was a restraining document on the Federal Government, so it would be unable to muster enough power to overshadow individual states without infringing on the rights and liberties of the people. Ten amendments, known as the Bill of Rights, were added to the Constitution *on December 15, 1791.* The Anti-Federalists were responsible for this action, which has been a blessing to American citizens throughout our nation's history.

According to the Constitution, the Federal Government was entrusted with three essential powers: national defense, foreign and intrastate trade, and maintaining domestic tranquility. To effectively fulfill these responsibilities, it was necessary for individual states to possess greater strength, particularly in establishing robust armies and navies. Strengthening the states was crucial for them to confront external threats effectively. If each state were to have its currency, trade among the states would be disorganized and chaotic. In the event of uprisings like Shay's Rebellion, the states would likely need to be prepared to handle such situations. The framers of the Constitution aimed to establish a government structure that granted the federal level authority in these three key areas while empowering the states to govern within their borders. James Madison's *Federalist Paper Number 45* emphasized this balance of power between the Federal Government and the States.

> The powers the proposed Constitution delegates to the Federal Government are few and defined. Those who are to remain in the State governments are numerous and indefinite. The former will be exercised principally on external objects, such as war, peace, negotiation, and foreign commerce. ... The powers reserved to the several States will extend to everything generally concerning the lives, liberties, and properties of the People, as well as the internal order, improvement, and prosperity of the states themselves.[3]

Simply stated, Madison reserved two basic roles for the Federal Government:

- A Federal currency to provide the nation with a safer, more flexible, and more stable monetary and financial system.

- A strong national defense promotes tranquility for the citizens.

The *Federalist Papers* were the campaign tool of the Federalists who wanted the Constitution ratified by the state legislatures. These essays were written to convince voters to support ratification. Madison's words laid out the appealing concept of few powers to the Federal Government and many to the states. This was the original intent of the Founding Fathers. There would be less discord in our country if this were true today.

The Constitution laid out the desire of the Founders to have checks and balances on the various branches of Government. The House of Representatives was to be elected by the people in a prescribed district, and each state was guaranteed at least one representative. Senators were to be elected by the legislatures of each state, but this was later changed to by the people in the Seventeenth Amendment in 1913. Given the survey results mentioned earlier, it might have been better if the Founders' original plan had been followed. If only 36 percent can name all three branches of Government, it leads one to doubt their qualifications to vote. This may have been their reasoning, who wanted one chamber of Congress always to be chosen by an informed segment of voters.

Checks and Balances

The legislative process involves the creation of laws by Congress, with both chambers voting on a bill, requiring a majority for it to pass. In case of disagreements between the two chambers, the bill is referred to a committee for resolution. Once it successfully passes both houses, it is presented to the President, who has ten days to sign it into law. If the President takes no action, the bill automatically becomes the law of the land. However, the President can exercise the power of veto to prevent a bill from becoming law. In turn, Congress can override a presidential veto with a two-thirds majority vote in both chambers, thereby making the law operational. These processes demonstrate the checks and balances established by the Founding Fathers.

While the President is the nation's chief executive officer, their power is not absolute. The Founders never intended for the President to possess monarchical authority. The President serves as the military's Commander-in-Chief, but only Congress has the authority to declare war. The President is privileged to appoint cabinet members, federal court judges, and Supreme Court justices, but Senate approval is required for these appointments. The appointment of Supreme Court Justices is particularly significant since the Supreme Court serves as the highest Court in the country, and its decisions carry finality and nationwide impact. The Judiciary Branch was originally designed to be the weakest among the three branches. However, over time, due to the Legislative Branch's failure to effectively "check" its reach, the Supreme Court has gradually assumed more power and has become the most influential branch today.

Supreme Court Justices are appointed for life, a measure intended by the framers to insulate federal judges from politicization. However, this arrangement lacks a mechanism to check Supreme Court decisions once made. Unlike Congress's veto power over the President, there is no override vote for Supreme Court decisions. Nevertheless, Congress can impeach a Justice, following a similar process to that of impeaching a President. History records only one instance of a Justice being impeached, but they were not removed from the bench due to the failure to meet the two-thirds majority requirement. The Supreme Court remains the sole entity capable of overturning its own decisions. Thomas Jefferson, the nation's third president and a key figure in the founding of today's Democratic Party, openly expressed his concerns about the independent position of Supreme Court justices and the challenges they posed to the nation:

> At the establishment of our Constitution, the judiciary bodies were supposed to be the most helpless and harmless government members. Experience, however, soon showed in what way

they were to become the most dangerous; that the insufficiency of the means provided for their removal gave them a freehold and irresponsibility in office; that their decisions, seeming to concern individual suitors only, pass silent and unheeded by the public at large; that these decisions, nevertheless, become law by precedent, sapping, by little and little, the foundations of the Constitution, and working its change by construction, before anyone has perceived that invisible and helpless worm has been busily employed in consuming its substance. In truth, man is not made to be trusted for life if secured against all liability to account.[4]

If Jefferson thought the worm was at work during his day, he would be stunned at what is happening today. He also felt liberty was at risk by the power judges had:

You seem . . . to consider the judges as the ultimate arbiters of all constitutional questions; a very dangerous doctrine indeed, and one which would place us under the despotism of an oligarchy. Our judges are as honest as other men, and not more so . . . and their power [is] the more dangerous, as they are in office for life and not responsible, as the other functionaries are, to the elective control. The Constitution has erected no such single tribunal, knowing that to whatever hands confided, with corruptions of time and party, its members would become despots.[5]

Despotism is adverse to liberty and freedom, but a man who drafted the *Declaration of Independence* feared the seed of tyranny was sown in the Judiciary Branch of our Government. The Liberals love this power given to the

Supreme Court. They use it as a loophole when they cannot pass the legislation they want. Abortion was made legal in 1973 in the *Roe v. Wade* case ruling, which appeased the Separation of Church and State crowd and the Liberal Left.

Today, the Left is displeased. The Supreme Court now has a conservative lean. Three of the nine justices were appointed by Donald Trump. The overturn of *Roe* in the summer of 2022 outraged Democrats, but if one goes back to the Founding Fathers' original intent, that should have happened. More similar rulings should be based on the same principles set forth by the Constitution. The Federal Government, by Supreme Court rulings, has overstepped the powers the Founders wanted the Federal Government to have. Remember those three areas of power: national military and regulating foreign and domestic trade. Has the Federal Government overstepped the boundaries put forth in the Constitution? You be the judge as you review the following items now being run by the Federal Government:

Social Security – running a national retirement program

Medicare - Obamacare – running healthcare

Welfare (Housing, Food Stamps, Medicaid) running programs for poor people

Education – placing requirements on local schools, grants for tuition programs

Student Financial Aid – running a loan program for college students.

The list could be expanded, but most Americans would easily recognize these things. It is not that these items should be ignored. Most of the above items are "Entitlement Programs." By some estimates, these programs consume 49 percent of the annual Federal budget.[6] The states could take these programs on if they so desired. However, the Federal Government was never empowered or designed to oversee any of these programs; the Founders never dreamed of this kind of overreach in power. Alexander Hamilton was a supporter of Federal Government powers, but his words sounded a warning:

> If the Federal Government should overpass the just bounds of its authority and make a tyrannical use of its powers, the people, whose creature it is, must appeal to the standard they have formed and take such measures to redress the injury done to the Constitution as the exigency may suggest and prudence justify.[7]

Hamilton talks of "injury to the Constitution." Liberal policies have damaged our nation and the Founding Fathers' original intent. But there are those seeking to rectify this. David Barton and Rick Green have developed an effective course for churches and concerned citizens called "Patriot Academy." The course trains and equips citizens to restrain Government and return to the principles outlined in the Constitution. Find out how to receive world-class leadership training by going to **www.patriotacademy.com**.

The Founders wanted the most power to stay with the states, making each a political and cultural laboratory. States excelling with effective policies would be examples for other states to copy them. Today we have predominantly Liberal states, which we call blue states, and their conservative counterparts are tagged red states. The blue states of New Jersey, New York, California, and Illinois have so oppressed their citizens with high taxes and incompetency that many people are moving from them to red states. People are voting with their feet, giving evidence that the Government in blue states is not working for the people.

Majority Matters

Rush Limbaugh used to say he was the mayor of Realville. He saw things as they really were, not as he hoped them to be. This did not mean he would stop working for change for the better, but he saw the present environment for what it is. We all will do better when we realize we live in Realville. The Government is not working as the Signers wanted it to when they framed it, but the form they gave us provides opportunities to bring about reform to get us back closer to their original intent.

One point to remember in Realville is **Majority Matters!** Every two years, we have a national or general election when members of the House of Representatives and one-third of the members of the Senate are elected. Every four years, we elect a president. The reality is that either the Democrats or Republicans will control (hold a majority) in each of these chambers. A majority in one of these legislative chambers is extremely important. Often you will hear someone say, 'I don't vote for a particular party. I vote for the best person." This is not wise today because the majority matters.

The House of Representatives is overseen by a Speaker the majority party chooses. This person has a lot of power. They assign committee seats to members and who will chair those committees. They decide what legislation comes to the floor for a vote. The Speaker and their leadership team set the agenda. The House is an important chamber because all revenue (taxes) bills must start in the House. You may recall this fact caused a problem for Obamacare. This legislation mandated every citizen to have healthcare insurance which functioned like a tax. Problematically, Obamacare did not start in the House, where only tax bills can begin; it started in the Senate. The Senate has a rule by which a bill can be filibustered by a member or members of the minority party, preventing it from seeing a vote. A 60-member majority is required to prevent the filibuster.

A bill can originate in either chamber but must be voted on by the other chamber. Most of the time, a chamber amends the bill sent to them by the other chamber, so the bill is now different. To rectify this situation, the two chambers have representatives from each that meet as a conference committee to rewrite a bill that both chambers can support. This becomes an entirely different bill on which both sides must vote. During the Obamacare debate, Democrat Ted Kennedy died, opening up a Massachusetts senate seat that Republican Scott Brown won. The Democrats lost their super majority of 60 senators meaning the filibuster was now possible. Nancy Pelosi, the Democrat Speaker of the House, had the House vote on the Senate version of Obamacare since she did not want a conference committee bill to go back to the Senate where it could now be filibustered. This meant the bill that became the Affordable Care Act (Obamacare) originated in the Senate and not the House. It took a Liberal Supreme Court ruling to save the day for Obamacare.

The party with the majority in a chamber gets to have one of its elected party members as chairperson of the committees. No bill will be placed on the docket for the committee to consider that is not approved by the committee chair. The committees have subpoena power and can demand a person to testify before them. This is very important for the Judiciary and Oversight committees that do investigations. It is very unlikely a political party will investigate one of their own. Whoever holds the majority in the House has the power of investigation.

The House also has the power of the purse. It decides what programs will be funded and the amount. The party that holds the majority in the House wields a lot of power; the majority matters. If you vote for the candidate you think is the best person and they are not part of the majority, that person will likely have difficulty being productive. This is why the authors vote for the party more receptive to the Christian faith and its positive impact on the nation's culture. Given their position on abortion, support for the LGBTQ+ agenda, and the expulsion of God from the classroom, and their platform, it is not the Democratic Party.

This is not to say all praise and adoration is given to the Republican Party. They have disappointed in the past. The Republicans have some Liberal blood in their ranks, whereas the Democrats have no conservative blood in theirs. The best we can say is the Republicans will give an ear to Christian morality and principles and note their positive influence on the culture, but listening and acting are two different things. At this point, Republicans give Christians some degree of hope where very little exists in the other party.

The Born-Alive Abortion Survivors Protection Act of 2023, which we have mentioned previously, verifies this. On January 11, 2023, the House, led by the new Republican majority, passed this bill protecting infants who survived a botched abortion. The vote was 220 to 210, and the only "NO" votes came from Democrats. This was worse than when they voted on this in 2018. Chuck Schumer, the Democrat majority leader in the Senate, said the bill was dead when it reached the Senate.[8] This means Democrats want to deny life to an infant born despite a failed abortion attempt. The Constitution's Fourteenth Amendment states that all people born in the United States are citizens. It makes no exception for those surviving an abortion. Therefore, Democrats, who take an oath to defend the Constitution, are willing to violate this oath to appease the abortion lobby and industry. We would not want to answer to God for such actions.

The Democrats would say they are protecting a woman's

right to choose or for her reproductive health. The issue is not the health of the woman who is the birth mother; it is about the health of the newborn infant who can only live if he or she is given medical care. The woman has already paid for the abortion procedure. If the child is placed for adoption at no expense to her, she achieves the goal of her abortion, not having the responsibility of raising a child. The child can now bless the lives of the adoptive parents. The bill cannot become law because the Democrat majority in the Senate will vote it down, and it will never reach President Biden's desk for signature. Would he have signed it? Our guess is "no" since past actions have him placating the Democrat donor abortion lobby instead of his Catholic faith. You see now why the majority matters. On this issue alone, we cannot see how Bible-believing Christians, who take their faith seriously, can vote for a Democrat for Congress or President.

The President you elect will appoint justices to the Supreme Court, and the Senate will confirm by a simple majority. No Liberal Democrat president will nominate to the Supreme Court a person who is pro-life, supports Christian values, and supports family values or prayer in schools. A Democrat majority in the Senate will not confirm who they believe will support conservative positions or Christian values. These two realities should influence how you vote and for whom.

Corruption Cannot be Tolerated

The Founding Fathers created checks and balances in the Constitution to restrain the power of the Federal Government because they knew that power could lead to corruption. We do not like corruption from any public servant or political party at any level. When officeholders become corrupt, they cease to be public servants and serve themselves for personal gain. The Founders had lived under a corrupt government. They wanted to avoid framing one that could quickly go down that same road.

At the time of this writing, corruption is abounding in our nation. The FBI became corrupt as it collaborated with the Democrat Party to fabricate the Russian Hoax against President Trump and prevent the truth about Hunter Biden's laptop information from being known before the 2020 election.

In January of 2023, it was discovered that President Biden had classified files in an unsecured room at the Penn Biden Center for Diplomacy and Global Engagement. Another batch was found in his garage. Presidents can declassify documents with just a sentence, but these files were from the Obama Administration when Joe Biden was vice president. Just two months previously, the FBI raided Donald Trump's home in Florida to take files they believed were top secret, which the former President says he declassified. The biased Left media started circling like sharks around the former President. Still, they circled the wagons to protect Joe Biden when he committed the same thing, and maybe worse since he was not President when he took the files and could not declassify any of them at the time—the reason we need to be concerned. Media outlets should be dedicated to seeking truth to protect the American people instead of reporting to safeguard a possible act of corruption by a president they favor. This is malpractice journalism. If corruption is allowed to be tolerated, it will be the poison that will destroy democracy. The Founders knew this and wanted a constitution to restrain the Federal Government's powers.

When the Signers framed the Constitution, they did not leave their Christian principles outside the room. As evidenced by these words from Alexander Hamilton, "For my own part, I sincerely esteem it [the Constitution] a system which without the finger of God, never could have been suggested and agreed upon by such a diversity of interests."⁹ The Founders did not conceive the degree of moral decay the nation they established would encounter in future years. If they could have looked into the future scope and seen what we are dealing with in our culture today, our Constitution would likely have content that would protect the unborn and preserve the sanctity of marriage between one man and one woman (All of the 13 colonies had sodomy laws at the time) and required Christian morality and values be taught in our public education system.

Morality Counts

John Adams, our second president, gives one of the most provocative statements regarding the Constitution:

> We have no government armed with power capable of contending with human passions unbridled by morality and religion. Avarice, ambition, revenge, or gallantry, would break the strongest cords of our Constitution as a whale goes through a net. Our Constitution was made only for moral and religious people. It is wholly inadequate to the Government of any other.¹⁰

The word "avarice" may not be familiar to many. It means a desire for wealth and material gain, a significant factor pulling many politicians to corruption. Adams' words, "Our Constitution was made only for a moral and religious people. It is wholly inadequate to the government of any other," strikes a sad note for us. Every passing year, Christians make up a smaller percentage of our nation's population. The Christian faith no longer has an influence on the culture it once had in our history.

In essence, Adams is saying if we lose our moral moorings, our nation's existence is in peril. The moral conscience the Christian faith gave our country at its founding allowed citizens to be entrusted with the rights and liberties treasured by the Founders. They believed that Christian principles would hold people's behavior in check. Now they are eroding at an ever faster speed year after year. The final destination is tyranny.

Adam's colleague and sometimes political rival, Thomas Jefferson, once wrote: "God who gave us life gave us liberty. Can the liberties of a nation be secure when we have removed a conviction that these liberties are the gift of God? Indeed I tremble for my country when I reflect that God is just, that His justice cannot sleep forever."[11]

Adams and Jefferson may have had their political differences, but they agreed there was a distinct beneficial connection between God and the liberties given to American citizens. These former presidents' words warn us that if our faith in God is lost, our liberties and the nation will follow.

Government can work better than it does, but you must be concerned enough to make it happen. People say what we write is like preaching to the choir. When 40 million Christians don't vote in a presidential election, some of the choir does not attend the concert. Some who claim a Christian identity have voted for those supporting an agenda opposed to Christian values; they are singing off-key. The choir needs a good sermon now and then to be reminded whose song they are supposed to be singing.

Chapter 13

Churches and Christians Waking Up

The preservation of the sacred fire liberty, and the destiny of the republican model of government, are justly considered deeply, perhaps as finally, staked on the experiment entrusted to the hands of the American people.[1]
– George Washington

During World War II, the soldiers learned to express their understanding of the important Biblical teaching that faith without works is dead (James 2.19) by saying, "Pray and pass the ammunition." In East Texas, the same concept is expressed with the adage, "Pray and grab a hoe."

It is time for Christians in America to "pray and grab a hoe." God has woven the principle of sowing and reaping throughout the natural world. Everything in this world that matters is affected by the law of sowing and reaping. Everything we do in life has a delayed response. For example, if you plant a seed of corn in the ground, you expect an ear of corn to grow slowly. You sow today, but you reap tomorrow. If you fail to plant today, you will not reap tomorrow.

Speaking Truth to Power

Life in the fifties was good because American society embraced the Judeo-Christian ethic for many generations before the fifties. In the sixties, our society planted a different cultural seed. Now, we are harvesting the fruit of that evil, cultural seed with an abundant harvest of evil. The future for America will be even bleaker unless we plant a different seed.

I (Rick) believe the only hope for the restoration of this nation is a return to true Christian faith. Christians across America must finally say, "*Enough is Enough.*" America will not be changed from the top down but from the bottom up. Ronald Reagan was a great American president. He stood up for traditional family values and wrote a book decrying abortion. Under his leadership, America was restored to a role of world leadership, and the communist stranglehold was broken. The "Great Satan," the mighty Soviet Union, was dismantled after seventy years of dominating one-third of the world's population, as Ronald Reagan courageously stood up to the Soviets.

As great as Ronald Reagan was as a leader, he could not restore America to her Christian heritage. That is because true change can only come from the bottom up. It begins in small towns across America. It will not happen until Christians stand up and be counted – by informing themselves of the issues confronting America and then going to the polls and expressing their convictions.

The Church and Christians have a right, even an obligation, to convey what is true. To be faithful to our Lord, we must speak the truth. This will not make us popular when the trends of society promote falsehoods. We are not to retreat from telling the truth even when we find the falsehood we are confronting is dressed in political apparel. Many young pastors and those in the ranks of church laity have been advised to stay out of politics. This was to be an area of neutrality for the Christian populace, so they were taught. As a nation, we got away with that false notion in the fifties and some years following, but it is not so today. Some political factions mean to silence and bring actual harm to the Christian faith. They wish to drive it from the public square, expel it from the schools and rid the culture of its influence. Neutrality can no longer be a position for the Christian. Jesus said, *"Whoever is not with me is against me"* (Matthew 12.30a).

When the prophet Nathan confronted David about his adulterous affair with Bathsheba, it was not likely he relished the encounter. Sin had come into the kingdom, and God put him in the position of revealing it to the offender. He was not neutral. He did not avoid the responsibility by saying, "This is related to the king, and it's a matter that I should stay clear of. God will take care of it in his way. I should not run the risk of the king's wrath on me and my family." Instead, Nathan took a stand and spoke truth to power. Sometimes God takes care of bad things by using us to take a stand to declare what is good.

In the New Testament, John the Baptist lost his head over an incident of mixing church and state when he, the preacher, called out Herod, the King, for adultery. Herod had his head cut off at the urging of his evil wife. These two examples from the Scripture remind us that good comes from the preacher getting involved in politics; sometimes, it takes a considerable toll. Still, it can be no mistake that mixing church and state, as commonly understood, is a lie and does not provide an excuse for the Church not to be involved in politics.

Every Bible-believing Christian should vote for their values in every election. When the principles of our Christian faith are challenged, and the well-being of our children is at risk, we must push back, even if the danger is from political powers.

What a Church Can Do

The American political system is a game of numbers. Whoever has the most votes wins. For more than three decades, we Christians have been failing to exercise our influence because we have failed to even show up to vote. A relatively small but radical coalition of pro-abortion, pro-homosexual, anti-religion secular humanists has been able to elect their candidates and shape the culture of America because of our neglect. The vast majority of Americans are conservative in their lifestyle and their politics. They still believe in God and want a country based on biblical values. Most Americans are ready to stand with anyone who will say, "Enough is Enough." The Liberal theories that started in the sixties have not worked and will not work in the future.

There are several things that you can do right where you live that will make a difference:

- Register everyone you can to vote.
- Enlist godly men and women who are skillful leaders to run for office.
- Get involved in the political process at every level.
- Take advantage of early voting.
- Organize a committee of laypeople in the church whose sole charge is to keep moral concerns before the congregation. (See www.saltandlightcouncil.org)
- You have influence. Everyone has influence, and most people have more than they realize. USE IT!
- Make financial contributions to campaigns where the candidate is fighting for biblical values.
- Pray for your elected officials.

Let's take a closer look at each one of these efforts to gather more helpful insight.

Register Everyone You Can to Vote

It is not necessary to tell Christians how to vote. Most will vote for their biblical convictions if informed on the issues and will be a part of a restored America. Many Christians need to realize how easy it is to register voters. In Texas, to become a voter registrar, all that is required is to go to your county courthouse, fill out an application, and receive a certificate of appointment to serve as a volunteer deputy registrar. Check to see if your state works this way. You will get a voter registration form, and with it will come the authority to register voters. It is even more accessible in states like Ohio. Anyone can distribute a voter registration form without county authorization. Forms can be taken to the church and filled out ten days before the election or announced deadline. Before every major election, tables can be stationed around the church, and those attending should be encouraged to register if they are not registered voters.

Rather than simply handing out registration forms, have a place where they can quickly be filled out and given to the county authorized person or designated person who will take the forms to the county election center. There are several ways to get people to register, and the method you employ is secondary to getting the results. If our people are not registered, they cannot vote. We will never get our country back until the majority of those who vote on election day share our values.

The pastor is the key. Voter registration drives in churches are perfectly legal and practiced by thousands of churches every election cycle. This may prove daunting, as many pastors have been misinformed about this and do not want to be responsible for leading their church into legal entanglements. With all that pastors have on their plates to do, when it comes to anything controversial, their first response is often to avoid it altogether. Part of that mindset comes from self-preservation. I (Rick) entered the ministry in 1969, and I can tell you that pastoring in today's world of social upheaval is a contact sport. Most pastors aren't looking for more battles to fight.

If you are not a pastor, schedule an appointment to see your pastor or associate pastor to discuss a voter registration drive in your church. There is no better place to find a collection of people with shared values who care about something bigger than themselves than at church. Remember, when you seek an appointment with your pastor, he is swamped and will most likely have reservations about a voter registration drive if your church has no history of such an effort. If the pastor is on board, your job is 75 percent complete, as he is the key influencer in your congregation. Typically, if he is not for something, it will not get done; if it does, it will not be as effective as it would have been with his support. Recruiting your pastor is very important. Take the time required to make your best effort.

When you schedule your meeting with your pastor, encourage him to access the website of Recover America at **www.recoveramerica.com**. You can find detailed information provided by Alliance Defending Freedom, founded by Alan Sears and comprised of over one thousand staff and volunteer attorneys committed to defending our rights as Christians.

Another good source of information is provided by attorney Kelly Shackelford, founder and President of Liberty Legal Institute. He is one of the top legal minds in the country and, more importantly, on our side. Kelly has been called to fight on the front lines of the culture war, and he has published a one-page document called "Churches and Election: What is the Law?" that has been presented to pastors around the country. You may access this document and other resources at Liberty Legal Institute's website at:

www.libertylegal.org
or our website at
www.recoveramerica.com

Thankfully, there are many examples of Pastors who will engage and laypeople who decided that if their pastor would not engage, they would. More and more pastors are taking a stand and coming to the forefront of the battle for saving America. Some of them have been referred to in earlier chapters, but here is a partial list of men and women standing in the gap, as watchmen on the wall, on behalf of righteousness, regardless of the cost. This list is incomplete but should encourage you that men and women across the country are standing up.

1. **Dr. Edwin Young** pastors the 80,000-member Second Baptist Church in Houston, Texas, where he has served since 1978. The church had 500 in attendance when he came. He served two terms as the President of the Southern Baptist Convention and has written dozens of books. He has not shied away from the key moral issues of our day and will call out politicians for improper conduct when the issues demand Biblical leadership. He is a true champion of the faith.

2. **Dr. Jack Graham** is the Senior Pastor of Prestonwood Baptist Church, one of the nation's largest churches. When Dr. Graham came to Prestonwood in 1989, the congregation responded enthusiastically to his straightforward message and powerful preaching style. Now thriving with more than 56,000 members, he never fails to address critical moral issues Biblically and routinely encourages other pastors to do the same. He also has served as the President of the Southern Baptist Convention. He is a true champion of the faith.

225

AMERICA IN THE BALANCE

3. **Steve Riggle** is the Founding and Senior Pastor of Grace Church Woodlands, in The Woodlands, just north of Houston. Grace Church Woodlands is the second mega-church Pastor Steve and his wife, Becky, have established in the Houston Metroplex in the past 30 years.

    Along with pastoring, Steve also serves as the President of Grace International, a fellowship of over 4,900 churches with more than 498,000 members, various compassion ministries, and educational institutions both nationally and internationally with ministries in 122 nations of the world.

    Pastor Steve has a warrior's heart, and has never failed to rally to the cross when a hero was needed to fight the good fight. In 2014, when Houston Mayor Annise Parker, an outspoken lesbian, demanded to see pastor's sermons that she suspected were rallying church attenders to oppose her efforts to pass a pro Transgender ordinance for the city of Houston, he spoke out publicly against the intrusion into church affairs. He opened the doors to the Grace Church 10,000 seat worship center for a rally for the seven named pastors in her lawsuit, which drew pastors from across the nation and over 7,000 Christians rallied to their defense.

    In the end, the Mayor backed down and the Ordinance allowing biological men to enter girls private spaces was never enacted. I have never witnessed a more courageous pastor nor greater visionary than Steve Riggle. He understands that pastors must engage the culture and he trains his people to stand up when needed. He is a true champion for Christ.

4. **Rev. Steve Smothermon** is the pastor of the growing Legacy Church of over 20,000 members, with campuses across New Mexico, with the main campus in Albuquerque. He courageously defied Governor

226

Michelle Lujan Grisham's orders to shut down his church throughout the Covid pandemic lockdowns, reminding the Governor repeatedly that he would obey God rather than any governmental order to close his church. He incurred her threats of being arrested and refused to pay the growing fines being imposed on Legacy Church for his refusal. The Governor finally conceded she didn't have the authority to stop Rev. Smothermon from exercising his First Amendment right to freely exercise his deeply held religious beliefs. He is a true champion of the faith.

5. **Rev. Jack Hibbs**, Senior and founding pastor of Calvary Chapel Chino Hills, based in Southern California, the Founder & President of Real Life ministry, and a nationally syndicated TV and radio host. Members of his church occupy many offices in their local and state governments. He often calls his congregation to take political action when warranted and to vote for their values on Election Day. He is a true champion of Christ.

6. **Rev. Paul Blair**, Senior Pastor of Fairview Baptist Church, Edmond, Oklahoma, and founder of the Liberty Pastors Network, comprised of more than a thousand pastors across America of every denomination, who have been through his three-day worldview seminars and who have signed a pledge to preach the word without compromise. These men are among the unsung heroes of the faith in America. Paul Blair a true champion for Christ.

7. **Rev. Dan Fisher**, Co-Pastor of Fairview Baptist Church, founder of the *Black Robbed Regiment,* and Vice President of the Liberty Pastors Network, working alongside

Pastor Paul Blair. He has written The Black Robbed Regiment, a detailed account of Pastors who stood and fought for freedom during the War for Independence. He travels across America, performing a first-person portrayal of Lutheran Pastor George Peter Muhlenberg, who resigned from his church and later became a Major General, serving on the Staff of General George Washington. Rev. Muhlenberg became a political figure in the newly independent United States. He served in the United States House of Representatives and later became a United States Senator from Pennsylvania. Dan Fisher is a true champion for Christ.

8. **Rev. Tony Perkins** serves as both Pastor and President of the Family Research Council and is their fourth and longest-serving President, joining the organization in August 2003. Described as a legislative pioneer by the national media, Tony has established himself as an innovative pro-life and pro-family policy and political leader since being elected in 1996. He served two terms as a State Representative in the Louisiana State Legislature and termed limited himself after two terms. He has stood for faith, family, and freedom without wavering. He is a true champion of Christian values.

9. **John Miller**, Senior Pastor of the Church on the Rock in Texarkana, Texas. John and I met as invited speakers for a Tea Party Rally in Tyer, Texas, in 2008. We immediately bonded and forged a great friendship. Pastor Miller is a frontline warrior in the culture war for the soul of America. During the 2020 COVID lockdown, his congregation not only remained open but grew and took the bold step of buying the closed building formerly housing a Gander's Mountain store, remodeling it, and moving while most churches drew back in fear. God honored his bold leadership and brought a buyer for the

old facilities, and they are growing and leading the city as a lighthouse of truth. Pastor Miller is a true Mighty Man of God.

10. **David Welch** is not a pastor in the traditional sense. He was a mechanic in Washington who chose to get involved in trying to save the culture. He worked for Pat Robertson's Christian Coalition, garnering such attention in his home state that he was offered a position in Washington, DC, to mobilize pastors across America.

That's how we became acquainted. When the campaign winded down, he moved his family to Houston to assist me while I was still pastoring and finally formed the Houston Area Pastor's Council, which has great influence in Texas's largest city. From there, he branched across Texas forming Area Pastor's Councils in numerous cities and finally formed the U.S. Pastors Council. In Houston, he has proven that pastors can make a difference, and he has won my great admiration for his faithfulness. He is truly a Mighty Man for Christ.

The American pulpit has a rich history. During the Revolutionary War, the British referred to the colonial preachers as "the Black-Robed Regiment." They got this tag because they gave their sermons in black robes and fanned the flames of liberty with their inspiring messages for God-given rights and freedom. The abolition movement that ended slavery was born largely in pulpits in northern states. Pastors were bold in our history, and their voices were not shy, but shy seems to be the approach many take today. One evangelical church in the Midwest had a "God and Country" concert scheduled for Veterans Day in 2021 until the pastor called those in charge and canceled it because he did not want to offend the Liberals in his congregation, which he believed to be 50 percent. When did Veterans Day become only a conservative day of remembrance? Veterans are made up of people from all political parties and fought for people of all political parties to stay free. It is time for pastors to stand up like the prophet Nathan and boldly proclaim the truth. It can be done in proper ways which do not violate any laws. Before the 2020 election, Pastor Gary Hamrick of Cornerstone Chapel in Leesburg, Virginia, presented the platform positions on key issues of the two major political parties via PowerPoint. He did not state how one should vote, but it was clearly revealed which party had a more biblical worldview on the issues.

A pastor can preach the truth and should preach the truth even if it sends people away. Paul gives Timothy sound advice:

> [3] For the time will come when people will not put up with sound doctrine. Instead, to suit their desires, they will gather around them a great many teachers to say what their itching ears want to hear. [4] They will turn their ears away from the truth and turn aside to myths. [5] But you keep your head in all situations, endure hardship, do the work of an evangelist, and discharge all the duties of your ministry. (2 Timothy 4.3-5 NIV)

If we are placating people in our churches for the sake of their financial contributions, then we are not doing well for them or the kingdom of God. Pastors must preach sermons favoring pro-life and against the sin of homosexuality.

When you see your pastor, tell him you are willing to oversee voter registration if he will give it his blessing by acknowledging the importance of Christians voting for their values on election day. The more support he gives you from the pulpit or in various columns in church publications, the more readily people will avail themselves of this service.

Enlist Godly Men and Women Who Are Skillful Leaders to Run for Office

Christians need to run for the school board, the city council, the county government, the state government, and the national office. Daniel Webster was correct when he said, "Whatever makes men good Christians makes them good citizens."[2]

John Jay was correct when he said, "Providence has given to our people the choice of their rulers, and it is the duty as well as the privilege of and interest of our Christian nation to select and prefer Christians as their rulers."[3]

If no one qualified is running for office whom we feel deserves our support, we have no one to blame but ourselves. Leaders are made, not born. People decide to run for public office for various reasons, but when you get down to basics, it is about serving. That's why we call them "public servants." People enter public office either to serve themselves or to serve others. While many noblemen and women serving in public office are not Christians, the best place to find a candidate you can trust with the public treasury is someone who has embraced the truth of Christianity. When an expert asked Jesus to name the greatest commandment, He replied, "Love the Lord your God with your heart and with all your soul and with all your mind…And the second is like it: Love your neighbor as yourself" (Matthew 22.37-39).

Someone who truly understands that concept will also realize he will answer not only to the voters but to God for how he conducts the sacred office that the voters have entrusted to him. If a man does not fear God, he will find a way to enrich himself.

When you discover that there is no one in a race, you feel you can support, consider running yourself, or start looking for someone and recruit them to run. One reason we so often lament that we have few leaders we can trust to vote for is that those who know Christ and know him intimately seldom consider they may be called to run for office. When someone who knows the Lord decides to run, they often choose the wrong race. The Bible teaches that the righteousness of God is revealed from faith to faith (Romans 1.17, KJV). There is a scriptural principle taught by that verse that means God prepares us for great things by maturing us as we obediently serve Him in lesser assignments. Training for greatness begins by doing the mundane things well, and while you may not be prepared or qualified for being President, God may want you to run for the school board or city council so He can refine you and equip you for greater office. Or He may want to use you to shape your school board to reflect what God intended it to be before Christians got too busy to invest their time in their children's education.

In 2010, when Tea Parties were active, many people wanted to run for Congress to push back on the Obama agenda. I (Steve) was working for a candidate who was indeed qualified for the office. He was a Viet Nam vet, served as the Director of Agriculture in Ohio for 16 years, and had been a candidate for Congress before. There were ten candidates in the primary, and whoever got the plurality (most votes) would be the Republican candidate in the general election. There was a candidate who was endorsed by Republican leadership and was regarded as the "establishment candidate." My guy lost to this establishment candidate by 153 votes in the primary. The other eight candidates said to me they would have preferred my candidate to the one who did win so the establishment candidate would not be victorious. Some of these eight never had a chance and pulled in less than one or two percent of the vote. Had they dropped out and endorsed my candidate, the establishment club would have lost. By running in the race, these 'no chance wannabees" help to elect the least desirable candidate who, to them, was the least conservative of the bunch. Christians must be wise when they consider running for office.

We must begin recruiting godly men and women to run for office at every level. Someone is going to make decisions politically that affect our lives. Why not a Spirit-led Christian who loves Jesus? Why not you? Pray and grab a hoe.

You must pay your dues before you print your yard signs. The American system has two major parties, the Republican Party and the Democratic Party. You must look at all the parties and decide for yourself which one, if any, best represents your values. You can begin the process by visiting their websites and reading their party platforms to determine which platform best represents your values.

A common mistake among Christians, causing many to withdraw and never get involved in politics, centers on a complete misunderstanding of the nature of politics. It would help if you had a basic understanding of political science. Universities offer courses where students can get a major in this field.

Political science means "many sciences," which describes what it does...it is the science of arriving at conclusions after examining many different ideas. Politics has often been described as "the art of the possible." It is the way we settle disagreements without bullets or force. But it also involves compromise, and that word disturbs many Christians. Amazingly, Christians who seem annoyed by compromise in politics have no problem within other areas of their lives.

People often say the lesser of two evils is still evil, and based on that equation, they justify not voting for either of the two candidates or supporting one of the two parties. We must be careful with such thinking. After all, we live in a fallen world where virtually every decision is the lesser of two evils. Everything is tainted to some degree by corruption. Politics is not the church, but it can be redeemed to the degree that sanctified men and women get involved. We have been to political gatherings where the majority of people present loved Jesus, and we have sensed His presence in a significant way, and we have been in churches where we could not sense his presence at all, not even in the pulpit.

Get Involved in the Political Process at Every Level

In 2015, Lesbian Houston mayor Annise Parker wanted to subpoena pastors' sermons and place fines on those she thought were guilty of hate speech if they preached that homosexuality was a sin. It made no difference. The Bible was on the side of the pastors. There was such an outcry from citizens that she had to withdraw her plan, as over 7,000 citizens and over 300 pastors rallied to oppose her.[4] Even though this persecution of pastors was not enacted, the intent of the Liberal Left was clearly revealed.

Few Christians know how a party platform is constructed, and consequently, they need to understand how much influence they can exert by participating in the process. Christians must acquaint themselves with the political party structure in America. Then they must "pray and grab a hoe." It is alarming that only 32 percent of people can correctly name the three branches of government. Christian people should not be among these.

In every polling precinct, immediately following an election primary, a precinct convention is held on the same evening. To participate in a precinct convention, you must vote in the primary. Very few voters participate in their precinct. Christians must acquaint themselves with this process and get involved. A few voters with strong Christian convictions can pass resolutions that reflect their biblical values and make a powerful impact.

You can be a campaign volunteer. You can put up signs, field phone calls, work a fair booth, stuff envelopes, etc. People who are candidates today often started as campaign volunteers.

Christians Must Take Advantage of Early Voting

In most states, we now have what is referred to as "early" voting. That means for a season before every actual election day, you can vote at your convenience, typically between 8:00 a.m. and 5:00 p.m. During presidential elections, there is often a Sunday when the polls are open for early voting. What a perfect opportunity this affords for Christians.

If you choose to be the one who heads up the voter registration and mobilization efforts in your church or organization, check with your voter registrar and find out when early voting takes place. If there is a Sunday when the polls are open, make sure your church family knows that. The pastor should announce these days. You can make it a social event. Encourage everyone to go out to eat that day or have the church host a lunch in connection with the effort, then bus or carpool to the voting place. The lines are typically short, and the results are fantastic. Yes, the votes are really counted. Wouldn't it be great if every Christian in America voted their convictions this next election? Early voting is one way to help make it happen. It can't happen unless every Christian in your church participates.

Organize a Committee to Keep Moral Concerns before the Congregation

Several good names for the committee have surfaced over the past few years, for example, "The Moral Action Committee" or "The Christian Action Committee." One church calls the committee the "Moral Action Ministry Team." These people keep the pastor and staff abreast of

AMERICA IN THE BALANCE

local, national, and moral concerns. In addition, this committee is an excellent resource to help register voters and distribute information about moral concerns. This committee is especially important today with the battle regarding abortion at the state level and the gains made by the transgender movement in our schools. If your church does not have a Moral Action Ministry Team, why not approach your pastor about organizing one? Why not volunteer to assist in the project?

You have Influence. USE IT!

Now, more than ever before, God needs you, and America needs you if we are to remain a free and great nation. We have missionaries stationed worldwide who are praying and looking to you and me to ensure that this free and blessed nation remains the lifeline it has been for supporting the work of the gospel worldwide. Thomas Jefferson appropriated money from the U.S. treasury to underwrite missionaries to preach to the Indians, believing evangelization would be cheaper than war.[5]

By the time a presidential election arrives, everyone knows more about the presidential candidate than they care to know. Still, when you walk into the booth, you will see dozens of candidates for lesser offices, of which you likely need to gain more knowledge.

This presents quite a dilemma. We believe that the only thing worse than not voting is voting wrong. Every time you vote, you essentially vote twice: you are voting for someone and against someone else. If candidate "A" is a good guy and candidate "B" is a bad guy, when you vote for candidate "B," you force candidate "A" to get two votes to gain one. Candidate "A" needs one vote to cancel your vote for candidate "B" and another to advance one vote. That's why we must vote right when we go to the polls.

There is no foolproof way to accomplish this feat, but tools are available to help us. I (Rick) believe the best tool available is www.ivoterguide.com, provided by the American Family Association. You can enter your zip code, obtain a list of every candidate running, and see their rating from very conservative to very Liberal. Print out their list and take it with you to vote. The best way is to obtain good voter guides from trustworthy people. Nationally, Eagle Forum and Christian Coalition have consistently offered good voter guides. They will give you good information on the national candidates, but most of your votes will be cast for state and local races. Each state is different, but Family Policy Councils, affiliated with Focus on the Family, now operate in over thirty states, and they do a good job offering voters information in the states where they operate. Another excellent resource is the Family Research Council, based in Washington, DC. Once again, you can go to the website:

www.recoveramerica.com

There, you can find links to these organizations and various voter and candidate information that is updated regularly. Finding helpful information on candidates is imperative if you want your vote to make a difference. When I (Rick) was pastoring, we had a team of members that we called our CIA (Christians in Action). I charged them with the responsibility of comprising nonpartisan information on local candidates that we then made available to our people and the people of our community. While this may sound time-consuming and labor-intensive, considering the damage one unscrupulous politician can cause, the time and investment are well worth the dividends. Christian citizenship is a duty; some are called to this ministry just as some are called to preach. If God wills that we take back our country, He also wills that someone does the necessary work. Could it be He is calling you? I'm looking for someone to pass this baton to. Will you take it and run?

A church can host candidate forums. Invite candidates by registered mail running for city council, school board, and other local offices. Set aside time for them to answer questions submitted by Christians and screened by an appointed committee to avoid pointless or inappropriate questions.

The registered mail invitations aim to prevent anyone from claiming the church is partisan or showing favoritism to those who might be Christians or aligned with their views. Registered mail records the mail and the response, even if the candidate does not appear. When a candidate fails to come, he effectively says he doesn't need the vote from the host group, or he knows his views would not curry their favor. Candidates often express their appreciation for such events. They expend a lot of time and energy trying to find people to listen to their views, and typically, they get less response from churches than any other institution. This is a great way to express appreciation and offer prayer support for the candidates and their families during the stressful time of running for public office. The use of voter guides and forums are items that can propel your influence. You can give voter guides to relatives and friends who do not attend your church, and you can invite the same to the candidate forums.

No one has greater influence in America than the preachers of America. Millions of people go to church weekly to hear what they have to say. They sincerely want to know what we think about everything, including politics. For thirty-plus years, groups like the ACLU and Americans United for the Separation of Church and State have threatened pastors with IRS complaints and even fines if they speak out on anything political. The time has come for us to courageously say we have had enough.

These groups know that the First Amendment guarantees pastors the right to speak, just as any other citizen. Your church is tax-exempt, not because it possesses a 501(c)(3) letter from the Internal Revenue Service, but because the Congress of the United States declared that the Federal Government could not tax the churches when the first tax code was written in 1913. We have been lied to and intimidated for years. Enough! America now needs the Church's voice and the pastor's leadership more than ever.

By God's grace and mercy, we now have our lawyers too. There are men like Mat Staver of Liberty Counsel, Jay Sekulow of the American Center for Law and Justice, Kirsten Waggoner of Alliance Defending Freedom (ADF), Philip Jauregui of the Judicial Action Group, and a host of others who will fight in a court of law for your right to fair speech.

We have God on our side and should not be intimidated by what man can do to us. William F. Merrill wrote these words to the song Rise are Up, O Men of God in 1911.

> Rise up, O men of God!
> Have done with lesser things.
> Give heart and mind and soul and strength
> To serve the King of Kings.
> Rise up, O men of God!
> The kingdom tarries long.
> Bring in the day of brotherhood
> And end the night of wrong!

Another way pastors can effectively change America is to get their people involved. Few things are more sobering for pastors than checking their local county voter records against their church membership files. They will typically discover that most didn't vote in the last election. We can save America, and the current downward trends can be reversed. But we must get more significant numbers of Bible-believing Americans to the polls to vote harmoniously with a Christian worldview. About 85 percent of regular churchgoers are registered to vote, and of those, only about half actually show up to vote on election day. That means only a tiny percentage of our team participates while the rest sit at home. We must get more Christians to the polls on Election Day.

Make Financial Contributions to Campaigns

I (Steve) was teaching a Sunday school class on the topic of God in American history, and I asked how many people have contributed to candidates in the recent election. No hands went up. This has to change. It is now very easy to donate via the candidate's website. It does not have to be a large amount. Just $20 or $25 from several people can make a difference. If we got one million Christians, who have never donated before to a campaign, to give in the next election, that would be 20 to 25 million dollars more for Christian candidates to use to defeat their opponent. Many of our Christian-friendly conservative candidates are outspent by sinister groups on the Left. We gladly give money to missionaries. We must regard candidates taking their Christian principles to Washington, the state capital, the county courthouse, city hall, and the school boards as our missionaries to promote and protect our Christian heritage. You should donate to close races even if they are out of state because that is where they are needed most and can make a difference. Some organizations have a PAC (Political Action Committee). One is the Family Research Council which is faith-based. You can give to them during election season, and they will benefit the cause of conservative and Christian candidates.

Contact Your Elected Officials

You should create a computer file on how to contact government officials. Various websites of government entities and officeholders provide contact information. Learn who your public servants are, from school board members to your U. S. representative and your two U. S. senators. When making contact, do not be rude or condescending. Keep your Christian character intact. You can be firm yet polite as you make your viewpoint known. Let the official know that you share your views with others in your church and that you only make financial contributions to candidates you have complete confidence in when you select who to support with a donation.

Passing the Baton…Getting People Involved

The storm clouds have gathered over America, but have you ever seen how beautiful the sun is when it breaks through such clouds? We pray that God will be pleased to grant us one more sweeping revival that will push back the paganism that is choking our land and allow us to be a part of the generation that sees the gospel preached to every living creature just before Jesus returns. Wouldn't that be great? It could happen if you and I exercise our right to participate in the process of America's renewal and use every ounce of our influence to get others to do so.

Heaven is full of great patriots who stood up in their generation and rescued this nation from the brink, and they are watching us to see if we, too, will stand. Will you stand?

The eyes of the world are fixed on the American church, eagerly anticipating its actions. We must act now, as enough is enough! Four runners pass a baton in a track relay while covering a specific distance. The smoother the exchange, the greater the likelihood of success and a victory lap. Having the fastest runners is irrelevant if someone stumbles or

241

drops the baton, as individual times are inconsequential in a relay.

Remembering that we must stay united as a team in the culture wars is important. While we may have truth and right on our side, we must not forget to work together towards a common goal. Candidates often spend exorbitant amounts of money to get noticed. As voters, we must choose candidates who truly deserve our support if we want to see real change in our nation.

Additionally, having a computer file dedicated to contacting government officials is a good idea. Plenty of websites provide contact information for government entities and officeholders. It's worth learning who your public servants are, from school board members to U.S. representatives and senators. When enough people band together and send emails regarding important issues, these officials will sit up and take notice. So don't hesitate to speak up and make your voice heard!

I (Rick) had a unique experience several years ago when I was invited to pray at the Texas Republican Party State Convention. The following day, I was invited to participate in a prayer meeting in the convention hall. To my surprise, there were hundreds of people kneeling, praying, weeping, and singing before the Lord. It was a moving experience that I will never forget. I can only imagine that the prayer meetings of our early Founders must have been similar to that morning prayer meeting.

As pastors, we are responsible for encouraging every eligible voter in our community to register and vote. If we don't take the lead in this crucial task, who will? What if millions of Christians across America decided to take over both parties? Imagine choosing between two Christian candidates instead of settling for the least offensive and most trustworthy option. It's not impossible, but it will take prayer and action from enough of us to make it happen.

Chapter 14

Epilogue:
Reflections From the Authors

Proclaim liberty throughout the land unto all
inhabitants thereof.
– Leviticus 25.10

From Rick Scarborough

I never planned to be a preacher. From my earliest recollections, I wanted to be a lawyer and enter politics because I wanted my life to make a difference. My life ran on two tracks: I was an athlete, winning a full-ride scholarship to play football in college, and I was president of our student body in high school and briefly at the university I attended.

Then everything changed for me. God turned my life around during my sophomore year in college, and I joined the Fellowship of Christian Athletes. During the same period, a pastor of a large church in our university town recruited me to be his part-time youth pastor, and that started a love affair with the ministry. Soon, I could think of nothing else. Three years later, in 1972, I entered Southwestern Baptist Theological Seminary.

The Jesus Movement had just swept across the country, and more than 2000 young men and women enrolled in SWBTS to prepare for full-time ministry. It was the most prominent theological seminary in the world at the time, and I made friends that have lasted a lifetime. We were united in our belief that we could change the world.

In 1992, in my second year of ministry at First Baptist Church of Pearland, Texas, a suburb of Houston, I heard of a high school assembly being held in our community. I took a pocket recorder and recorded the speaker's remarks. She was so out of bounds in her speech to our children that I spoke up from the assembly floor and confronted her. That resulted in quite a bruhaha, as you can imagine, but suddenly my love of ministry and love of politics merged. I began urging our people to get involved in local government, and they did. Our members soon held the majority of seats in the school board and the city council. Soon, three of our members were in the state legislature, and one, Randy Weber, now serves in the US Congress. For a season, we made profound differences in our local government. In 2002, I resigned from my pastorate and began traveling the country and encouraging pastors to engage in the culture. Many did, but most did not.

Looking back fifty years later, everything about America is worse, not better. One could conclude that we failed, but success in ministry is not measured in nickels and noses, as some have been misled to believe. It is measured in faithfulness, and by God's grace, I have been faithful and am more committed to seeing America revived than I have ever been, hence this book, *America in the Balance*. I didn't need convincing when Steve contacted me about co-authoring this book. I had already set aside two months to write my next book, and as he shared his concept with me, I was immediately convinced that we were to write it. You hold in your hand a road map back to God.

He alone can save our country. We have stepped over numerous red lines, but He has not yet brought final judgment to our nation in His grace and mercy. It is coming if we do not soon repent, but I pray that this book will open eyes and cause hearts to return to the God who gave the world this wonderful nation, the United States of America.

From Steve Feazel

My research for all my writings related to American history, culture, politics, and government has led me to conclude Christianity played an essential role in the founding of the United States of America. It did so to the extent that there would have been no United States of America if the Founders did not regard Christianity as indispensable. My PowerPoint presentation, "One Nation under God," displays an opening slide with the words, "If America was born, then Christianity was its mother."

Our Nation's founding is referred to as "The American Experiment." No nation ever came into being with the concept of government "of the people, by the people, and for the people." It was a nation conceived in liberty because the people had certain "unalienable rights" given to them by their Creator, the God of the Bible. If these rights came from God the Creator, then all people of the world had such rights. To their disadvantage, their governments or rulers did not let them benefit from those rights. Our Founding Fathers desired to create a nation where the people would embrace and enjoy these rights, and the government they would design would not infringe upon those rights.

Unalienable rights are rights people have been given which cannot be surrendered or rightfully taken away because they are the will of God. In America, the law was to be king, and the laws were to be made with the involvement of the people through a representative republican form of government. Those laws were not to be in opposition to the Word of God. Everyone would be equal under the law. All of these concepts were revolutionary for governing a nation. Before we had a revolution with muskets and canons, we had one with ink and parchment. Fifty-six men in a room in Philadelphia in 1776 took quill in hand and signed a document pledging their "Lives, Fortunes, and sacred

Honor" to establish a new nation centered on rights coming from God.

I cringe when someone says, "Politics and religion don't mix." Our Founding Fathers built our nation on the reality **that politics and religion do mix**! If our rights come from God, then integrating our Christian faith and political operations is welcomed, beneficial, and normal. The Founders saw government as actually subordinate to God with the role of being God's agent to ensure the rights God gave to the people were not infringed upon. The Christian faith is an enemy of Communism. Marx hated it, and all communist dictators held it in check or eliminated it. This is why it was so unsettling when the Communist Party in America decided not to run a candidate for President in 2020 but instead endorsed Joe Biden of the Democrat Party. Humanism believes there is no God. It holds this belief in common with Communism. These two isms find comfortable accommodations in the Democrat Party.

In the general election, I vote for the candidates of the party whose platform is the closest to the Founding Fathers' original intent. There is no way I can vote for a candidate in a party that is pro-abortion, pro-same-sex marriage, pro-transgender, pro-criminal over the victim, and pro-drag queens in schools.

Back to the Future was a popular film in 1985. We, in America, have to go back to the past so we can have a future. America will not solve its problems or end its cultural turmoil without reinserting the role of the Christian faith back into our civic life as the Founders so intended it. Once again, we can have religion being influential in politics for the benefit of the people and the protection of liberty. It's time to choose Normal over Crazy, Good over Evil.

About the Authors

Dr. Rick Scarborough is the President and Founder of Recover America, a nonprofit organization dedicated to educating and mobilizing Christians to take their faith into the civil arena, providing Biblical solutions for today's most pressing issues. He served as an itinerant evangelist for fourteen years, conducting more than 500 crusades across America and around the world. In 1990 he became the pastor of a church on the southeast side of Houston, where he led members of his congregation to run for the local school board and the city council, bringing the salt and light of the gospel into the public arena. Three of his members went on the serve in the Texas Legislature and one, Congressman Randy Weber, now serves in the U.S. House of Representatives. Dr. Scarborough's work has been featured in numerous publications and documentaries on CNN and HBO.

He has written several books, including the best-selling *Enough is Enough, Liberalism Kills Kids* and *Mighty Men Stay on Track*. He has appeared on numerous radio and TV programs. He and his wife, Tommye, make their home in Houston, TX. They have two grown children and one in Heaven. They have four grandchildren and one great grandchild.

Steve Feazel is an ordained minister in an evangelical denomination where he served as pastor. He has also taught business courses at the college level as an adjunct professor. He produced three award-winning faith-based documentaries on social issues, including the pro-life side of abortion. Besides holding a master's degree from seminary, he has an MBA from Arizona State University. His first published book, entitled, *Abduction: How Liberalism Steals Our Children's Hearts and Minds*, was coauthored with

Dr. Carol Swain. He teamed up with Gov. Mike Huckabee to write the bestselling book, *The Three C's That Made America Great: Christianity, Capitalism, and the Constitution.* His book, Voting Christian Values, won best book in the Christian Education category at the Christian Indie Awards in 2023, sponsored by the Christian Independent Publishers Association. Steve spends his time as a writer, video producer, and speaker. He and his wife, Edythe, have two grown sons and five grandchildren. They reside in central Ohio. Steve's website is www.visionword.com, and his blog is www.feazelfrontline.com.

Endnotes

Introduction

1. John Adams, Speech given on the 61st Anniversary of the Declaration of Independence July 4, 1837 in the town of Newburyport.

2. Ramesh Ponnuru, "Why can't Democrats say 'Islamic terrorism'?" December 2, 2015, https://www.centralmaine.com/2015/12/02/why-cant-democrats-say-islamic-terrorism/

3. Diana Chandler, "Pew: Muslims on pace to outnumber Jews in U.S." *Baptist Press*, January 12, 2018, https://www.baptistpress.com/resource-library/news/pew-muslims-on-pace-to-outnumber-jews-in-u-s/

4. Collins English Dictionary, 2021.

5. Franklin Graham, "Time to Take a Stand," *Decision Magazine*, November 2022, p. 2.

6. Francis Schaeffer and C. Everett Koop, *Whatever Happened to the Human Race?* Fleming H. Revell Company, 1979, p.26.

Chapter 1

1. Gouverneur Morris, letter to George Gordon, June 28, 1792

2. *Declaration of Independence,* July 4, 1776

3. The Journal of Christopher Columbus (During His First Voyage), and Documents Relating to the Voyages of John Cabot and Gaspar Corte Real, Clements R. Markham, ed. And trans. (London: 1893, 37-68.

4. Vivek Ramsey, *Nation of Victims*, Center Street, Nashville, p.175.

5. Rev. John Robison, Farewell Address to the Pilgrims Upon Their Departure from Holland, 1620. The Account by Edward Winslow in his "Hypocrisie Unmasked," 1646. https://oll.libertyfund.org/title/robinson-words-of-john-robinson-robinsons-farewell-address-to-the-pilgrims?html=true.

6. Ryan Foley, "New Mexico megachurches fined $10K for violating coronavirus restrictions,"

Christian Post, December 31, 2020, https://www.christianpost. com/news/new-mexico-megachurches-fined-10k-for-violating-covid-limits.html

7. The Mayflower Compact, "Beyond the Pilgrim Story," The Pilgrim Museum, https://pilgrimhall.org/mayflower_compact_text. htm

8. "Pennsylvania Charter to William Penn - March 4, 1681," *Pennsylvania Historical & Museum Commission,* http://www. phmc.state.pa.us/portal/communities/documents/1681-1776/ pennsylvania-charter.html

9. "Constitution of the Commonwealth of Pennsylvania – 1776," Duquesne University of Law, 2023, https://www.paconstitution. org/texts-of-the-constitution/1776-2/

10. *Constitution of Delaware 1776,* https://constitution.org/1-Constitution/cons/early_state /delaware1776.html

11. Constitution of North Carolina: December 18, 1776 Yale Law School https://avalon.law.yale.edu/18th_century/nc07.asp

12. Constitution of Vermont - July 8, 1777, https://avalon.law.yale. edu/18th_century/vt01.asp

13. Constitution of Massachusetts 1780, *Consource,* https://www. consource.org/document/ constitution-of-massachusetts-1780-10-25/

14. George Washington, *Address to the Delaware Nation, Founders Online,* May 12, 1779, https://founders.archives.gov/ documents/Washington/03-20-02-0388

15. David Barton, *The Bulletproof George Washington,* Wall Builder Press, Aledo, TX, 2002, p ???

16. Matthew Spalding, *The Founders' Almanac, (George Washington's Farewell Address, September 19, 1796),* The Heritage Foundation, Washington, DC, 2002, p 311.

17. William Federer, *America's God and Country,* Amerisearch, Inc., pp. 199-200.

18. Ibid.

19. Noah Webster, *History of the United States,* 1835.

20. SAMUEL ADAMS, LETTER TO JOHN SCOLLAY, APRIL 30, 1776.

21. Samuel Adams, *The Right of the Colonists as Christians,* 1772.

22. John Adams, *Diary of John Adams,* July 26, 1796.

23. John Adams, speech the Militia of Massachusetts on October 11, 1798.

24. John Adams, Letter to Thomas Jefferson, June 28, 1813.

25. John Adams, Letter to Thomas Jefferson, December 25, 1813.

26. Patrick Henry, Speech to Virginia Assembly, convened at Richmond, March 23, 1775, *History*, https://www.history.com/topics/american-revolution/patrick-henry.

27. A. G. Arnold, *The Life of Patrick Henry of Virginia* (Auburn and Buffalo: Miller, Orton and Mulligan, 1854), p. 250.

28. Patrick Henry, Letter to daughter, Martha, August 20, 1796.

29. "Patrick Henry Quotes 2," Death Bed June 1799, *Revolutionary War and Beyond*, https://www.revolutionary-war-and-beyond.com/patrick-henry-quotations.html

30. John Witherspoon, "American clergyman," https://www.britannica.com/biography/John-Witherspoon

31. Eric Metaxas, *If You can Keep: The Forgotten Promised of American Liberty*, Penguin, New York, New York, pp.8-9.

32. Alexis de Tocqueville, *Democracy in America,* introduction to book 1, trans. Henry Reeve, as quoted by the Gutenberg Project, accessed February 10, 2106, http://www.gutenberg.org/files/815/815-h.htm.1835-40,

33. Ibid.

Chapter 2

1. George Washington, Farewell Address, 1796.

2. *Engel v. Vitale,* June 25, 1962.

3. Letter of October 7, 1801, from Danbury, CT Baptist Association to Thomas Jefferson, from the Thomas Jefferson Papers Manuscript Division, Library of Congress, Washington, D. C.

4. Jefferson, *Writings,* Vol. XVI, pp. 281-282, to the Danbury Baptist Association on January 1, 1802.

5. Ibid.

6. Thomas Jefferson, *Writings,* Vol. XIX, pp. 449-450, at a Meeting of the Visitors of the University ... on Monday the 4th of October, 1824.

7. Ibid.

8. Jefferson, *Memoir,* Vol. IV, pp. 358-359, to Dr. Thomas Cooper on November 2, 1822.

9. Jefferson, *Writings,* Vol. XVI, p.291, to Captain John Thomas on November 18, 1807.

10. *Constitutions,* (1813), p. 364, "An Ordinance of the Territory of the United States Northwest of the River Ohio," Article III.

11. Joseph Story, *Commentaries on the Constitution of the United States,* (Boston: Hilliard, Gray, and Company, 1833), Vol. III, p. 278, §1871.

12. David Barton, *Original Intent,* (Aledo, Texas: Wall Builder Press, 2000), p. 424.

13. Jefferson, *Memoir,* Vol. III, p. 441, to Benjamin Rush on September 23, 1800.

14. Kate Mason Rowland, *The Life of George Mason,* (New York: G. P. Putnam's Sons, 1892), Vol. I, p. 244.

15. Thomas Jefferson, *The Works of Thomas Jefferson,* vol. 11, ed. Paul Leicester Ford, New York: G. P. Putnam's Sons, 1905, a quote by The Founders' Constitution. "Amendment I (Religion)," document 60, accessed January 23, 2016, http://press-pubs. uchicago.edu/founders/ documents/ amend I_religions60. html.

16. *A constitution or Frame of Government Agreed Upon by the Delegates of the People of the State of Massachusetts-Bay* (Boston: Benjamin Edes & Sons, 1780), pp. 7-8, Article III, "Declaration of Rights."

17. Mike Huckabee and Steve Feazel. *The Three Cs that Made America Great: Christianity, capitalism and the Constitution,* Trilogy Christian Publishing, Tustin, CA, 2020, p. 83-84.

18. *Wallace v. Jaffree,* 472 U. S. at 103 (1985), Rehnquist, J. (dissenting).

19. Thomas Jefferson, *The Writings of Thomas Jefferson,* vol. 15, Washington, DC: Thomas Jefferson Memorial Association of the United States, 1903, 277.

Chapter 3

1. Chris Enloe, *The Blaze*, "Tulsi Gabbard officially leaves Dem Party…" Oct 11, 2022.

2. Dictionary, https://search.yahoo.com/search;_ylt=AwrNOk9fjJBjU4QHV.JXNyoA;ylc=X1MDMjc2NjY3OQRfc gMyBGZyA3lmcC10BGZyMgNzYi10b3AEZ3ByaWQDZ3RYbX RtbzdTRGFORXNJc2J2b0NpQQRuX3JzbHQDMARuX3N1Z2c DMTAEb3JpZ2luA3NlYXJjaC55YWhvby5jb20EcG9zAzAEcHFz dHIDBHBxc3RybAMwBHFzdHJsAzIxBHF1ZXJ5A2RlZmluaXR pb24lMjBvZiUyMHJhZGljYWwwEdF9zdG1wAzE2NzA0MTk5O TA-?p=definition+of+radical&fr2=sb-top&fr=yfp-t&fp=1

3. Democratic Party Platforms, 1960 Democratic Party Platform Online by Gerhard Peters and John T. Woolley, The American Presidency Project https://www.presidency.ucsb.edu/node/273234

4. Andrew Abbott, "U.S. Military Increasingly Crippled Under Biden," Association of Mature American Citizens, July 19, 2022, https://amac.us/u-s-military-increasingly-crippled-under-biden/

5. Democratic Party Platforms, 1960 Democratic Party Platform Online by Gerhard Peters and John T. Woolley

6. Ibid.

7. Sylvan Lane, "Democrat bill would force Fed to defund fossil fuels," *The Hill*, September 15, 2021, https://thehill.com/policy/finance/572444-democratic-bill-would-force-fed-to-defund-fossil-fuels/

8. Democratic Party Platforms, 1960 Democratic Party Platform Online by Gerhard Peters and John T. Woolley

9. Baxter Dmitry, "Rasmussen Poll: Majority Of Democrats Want Communism In America," July 30, 2018, https://newspunch.com/rasmussen-democrats-communism-america/

10. Andrew O'Rielly, "Revolutionary Communist Party USA leader endorses Biden, warns followers against 'protest vote,'" *Fox News*, August 3, 2020, http://www.foxnews.com/politics/revolutionary-communist-party-head-vote-biden.

11. Sam Dorman, "House Dems quash bill mandating medical care for infants who survive abortions," *Fox News*, Feb 29, 2020, https://www.foxnews.com/politics/house-dems-bill-born-alive-abortion.

12. Nathaniel Blake, "NYT Columnist Admits Schools Are Grooming Children Into LGBT Identities, "The Federalist, April 13, 2022. https://thefederalist.com/2022/04/13/nyt-columnist-admits-schools-are-grooming-children-into-lgbt-identities/

13. Lee Brown, "Transgender kids OK for hormones at 14, surgery at 15, health group say," *New York Post*, June 16, 2022, https://nypost.com/2022/06/16/trans-kids-ok-for-hormones-at-14-surgery-at-15-health-group/

14. John Malcom, "Are Parents Being Tagged as 'Domestic Terrorists' by the FBI? Justice Department Needs to Show Its Cards," *The Heritage Foundation*, November 18, 2021, https://www.heritage.org/crime-and-justice/commentary/are-parents-being-tagged-domestic-terrorists-the-fbi-justice

15. CN Staff, "Attempted Murderer Released Without Bail In NY, Goes On To Shoot 3 More People," *Concealed Nation*, August 8, 2020, https://concealednation.org/2020/08/attempted-murderer-released-with-no-bail-in-ny-goes-on-to-shoot-3-more-people/

16. David Horowitz, *Barack Obama's Rules for Revolution: The Alinsky Model*, David Horowitz freedom Center, Sherman Oaks, CA, 2009, p. 29-30.

17. Chris Enloe, *The Blaze*, "Tulsi Gabbard officially leaves Dem Party…" Oct 11, 2022.

Chapter 4

1. Robert H. Bork, *Slouching Towards Gomorrah: Modern Liberalism and America Decline*, Regan Books, New York, NY, 2003, p. 139.

2. Bob Harper, "Democrats kicked God off the platform," *The Baltimore Sun*, September 9, 2012, https://www.baltimoresun.com/opinion/bs-xpm-2012-09-09-bs-ed-convention-god-20120909-story.html

3. Tim LaHaye and David Noble, *Mind Siege*, Thomas Nelson, Nashville, 2003, p. 69.

4. These "Czars" numbered 28 according to PolitiFact, though Judicial Watch put the number at 45. Also see: Kelly Chernenkoff, "Obama's Czars: What are They and How Much Power do they Wield," Fox News, December 24, 2015, https://www.foxnews.com/politics/obamas-czars-what-are-they-and-how-much-power-do-they-wield

5. Karl Rove, "The President's Apology Tour," *Wall Street Journal*, April 23, 2009, https://www.wsj.com/articles/ SB124044156269345357

6. Ibid.

7. Alexis de Tocqueville, <u>*Democracy in America,*</u> introduction to book 1, trans. Henry Reeve, as quoted by the Gutenberg Project, accessed February 10, 2106, http://www.gutenberg.org/files/815/815-h. htm.1835-40, <u>1835-40.</u>

8. Andrew Reed and James Matheson, *Account of a Revival*, Routledge, 1998,

9. Steve Bomboy, "The history of legal challenges to the Pledge of Allegiance," *National Constitution Center,* June 14, 2022, <u>https:// constitutioncenter.org/amp/blog/the-latest-controversy-about- under-god-in-the-pledge-of-allegiance</u>

10. Debra Viadero, "NCES Finds States Lowered 'Proficiency' Bar," *Education Week*, October 29, 2009, <u>https://www.edweek.org/ teaching-learning/nces-finds-states-lowered-proficiency- bar/2009/10</u>

11. Anya Kamenetz, "6 in 10 teachers experience physical violence or verbal aggression during COVID," *NPR*, March 19, 2022, https:// www.npr.org/2022/03/17/1087137571/school-violence- teachers-covid

12. David Horowitz, *Dark Agenda,* Humanix Books, West Palm Beach, FL, 2018. p. 63.

13. Ibid.

14. Horowitz, p. 64.

15. Nathan Mote, "The Aitken Bible," *The Heritage Post,* <u>https:// heritagepost.org/american-history/the-aitken-bible-the-first- american-bible/</u>

16. Horowitz, p. 139.

17, Kristin Hunt, "The End of American Film Censorship," *Daily Jstor*, February 28, 2018, https://daily.jstor.org/end-american-film- censorship/

18. Ibid.

19. Danny Goldberg, *Dispatches from the Culture War*: How the Left lost Teen Spirit, Miramax Books, New York, 2003, p. 229.

20. Known to one of the authors by a personal conversation of with a reliable source who has firsthand knowledge of the incident.

21. Horowitz, p. 148.

22. Horowitz, p. 150.

23. Ibid.

24. Horowitz, p. 151.

25. John Witherspoon, *The Dominion of Providence Over the Passions of Men*, May 17, 1776.

26. Ronald Reagan,

Chapter 5

1. Robert Woodson, Stated on the *Tucker Carlson Tonight Show* on the Fox News Channel, November 23, 2022.

2. Red and Black Editorial, "The Georgia Tech-Pittsburgh Sugar Bowl Controversy," December 8, 1955, https://digilab.libs.uga.edu/scl/exhibits/show/not-only-for-ourselves_/sugar_bowl

3. Rich Lowery, "Stop Lying About the Police," *National Review*, December 24, 2014, https://www.nationalreview.com/2014/12/stop-lying-about-police-rich-lowry/

4. Martin Marks, "San Francisco Elections Commission Backtracks on Sacking Director John Arntz," *California Globe*, December 17, 2022, https://californiaglobe.com/articles/san-francisco-elections-commission-backtracks-on-sacking-director-john-arntz/

5. Julia Ward Howe, *Battle Hymn of the Republic*, November 1861.

6. History.com, "The republican Party," February 1, 2021, https://www.history.com/topics/us-politics/republican-party

7. Sam Jacobs, "Democrats & Jim Crow: A Century of Racist History the Democratic Party Prefers You'd Forget," The Libertarian Institute, June 19, 2020, https://libertarianinstitute.org/articles/democrats-jim-crow-a-century-of-racist-history-the-democratic-party-prefers-youd-forget/

8. Ibid.

9. Brad Sylvester, "Fact Check: 'More Republicans Voted for the Civil Rights Act as a Percentage Than Democrats Did,'" *The Daily Signal*, December 17, 2018, https://www.dailysignal.com/2018/12/17/fact-check-more-republicans-voted-for-the-civil-rights-act-as-a-percentage-than-democrats-did/

10. Robert Woodson, Sr., "Is the Black Community a Casualty of the War on Poverty?" *The Heritage Foundation*, March 15, 1990, https://www.heritage.org/political-process/report/the-black-community-casualty-the-war-poverty

11. "Big Cities battle Dismal Graduation Rates," CBS News," April 1, 2008, https://www.cbsnews.com/news/big-cities-battle-dismal-graduation-rates/

12. Owen Strachan, "Margaret Sanger Wanted to Eliminate 'Human Weeds,'" *Patheos*, November 4, 2011, https://www.patheos.com/blogs/thoughtlife/2011/11/margaret-sanger-wanted-to-eliminate-human-weeds/

13. Martin Luther King, "I Have a Dream Speech," August 28, 1963, Washington, DC, https://www.patheos.com/blogs/thoughtlife/2011/11/margaret-sanger-wanted-to-eliminate-human-weeds/

14. Jason DeParle and Sabrina Tavernise, "Poor are Still Getting Poor, but Downturn's Punch Varies, Census Data Show," *NYTimes.com*, Sept. 15, 2011, https://www.nytimes.com/2011/09/15/us/poor-are-still-getting-poorer-but-downturns-punch-varies-census-data-show.html

15. Per Bylund, Tweet on *Twitter,* Nov. 15, 2015.

Chapter 6

1. ALEX EPSTEIN, *THE MORAL CASE FOR FOSSIL FUELS*, PORTFOLIO PUBLISHING, EDMONTON, ALBERTA, CANADA, 2014. P. 48.

2. "1200 'Scientists' Claim That Climate Change Is Not Real. Here's The Truth," *The Quint,* September 7, 2022, https://www.thequint.com/climate-change/1200-scientists-claim-that-climate-change-is-not-real-heres-the-truth

3. "Al Gore's Climate Change Hypocrisy Is As Big As His Energy-Sucking Mansion," *Investor's Business Daily*, August 3, 2017, https://www.investors.com/politics/editorials/al-gores-climate-change-hypocrisy-is-as-big-as-his-energy-sucking-mansion/

4. Ibid.

5. Gabriel Hayes, "John Kerry mocked for speech on WEF's almost extraterrestrial plan' to save the planet: 'Liberal delusion,'" January 17, 2023, https://www.foxnews.com/media/john-kerry-mocked-speech-wefs-almost-extraterrestrial-plan-save-planet-liberal-delusions.

6. Joseph Curl, "IRONY ALERT: Biden's 'Climate Czar' John Kerry owns $12 Million Beachfront Home," *Daily Wire*, Nov. 24, 2020, https://www.dailywire.com/news/irony-alert-bidens-climate-czar-john-kerry-owns-12-million-beachfront-home

7. David Mikkelson, "Are These John Kerry's Houses?" *Snopes*, April 1, 2004, https://www.snopes.com/fact-check/home-on-the-million-dollar-range/

8. **Chriss Street, "No One Cares How Many Predictions Earth Day Founders Got Wrong," *Breitbart*, April 22, 2014, https://www. breitbart.com/national-security/2014/04/22/no-one-cares-if-earth-day-founders-got-it-wrong/**

9. **Maxim Lott, "Eight Botched Environment Forecasts," Fox News," https://www.foxnews.com/science/eight-botched-environmental-forecasts**

10. **Marc Morano, "UN Global Warming Author Defends Erroneous Claims, January 5, 2011, *Newsmax*. https://www. newsmax.com/MarcMorano/Michael-Oppenheimer-U-NIPCC/2011/01/05/id/381916/**

11. **Bob Reiss, "Examining Hansen's prediction about the West Side Highway," *Skeptical Science*, February 15, 2011, https:// skepticalscience.com/Hansen-West-Side-Highway.htm**

12. **David Goeller, (Associated Press), "Scientists Cite Pollution for Overheating Earth," *The Sumter Daily Item*, June 12, 1986, p.5D.**

13. **Besty Reed, "Arctic expert predicts final collapse of sea ice within four years," *The Guardian*, September 17, 2012, https:// www.theguardian.com/environment/2012/sep/17/arctic-collapse-sea-ice**

14. Sha Hua, "China, India Complicate Biden's Climate Ambitions," April 22, 2021, https://www.wsj.com/articles/china-india-complicate-bidens-climate-ambitions-11619116604

15. *Investor's Business Daily*, August 3, 2017.

16. *Investor's Business Daily,* August 3, 2017.

17. OFFICE OF THE PRESS SECRETARY OF THE WHITE HOUSE, "FACT SHEET: THE RECOVERY ACT MADE THE LARGEST SINGLE INVESTMENT IN CLEAN ENERGY IN HISTORY, DRIVING THE DEPLOYMENT OF CLEAN ENERGY, PROMOTING ENERGY EFFICIENCY, AND SUPPORTING MANUFACTURING," *THE WHITE HOUSE,* FEBRUARY 25, 2016, HTTPS://OBAMAWHITEHOUSE.ARCHIVES.GOV/THE-PRESS-OFFICE/2016/02/25/FACT-SHEET-RECOVERY-ACT-MADE-LARGEST-SINGLE-INVESTMENT-CLEAN-ENERGY

18. Emma Newburg; *Schumer-Manchin reconciliation bill has $369 billion to fight climate change* — Published by CNBC, Thursday, July 28, 2022 Updated Monday, August 22, 2022.

19. Stephen Moore, "Follow the (Climate Change) Money," *Heritage Foundation,* Dec. 18, 2018, https://www.heritage.org/environment/commentary/follow-the-climate-change-money

20. Ibid.

21. Ibid.

22. "What is U.S. electricity generation by energy source?" *U.S. Energy Information Administration,* Nov. 2022, https://www.eia.gov/tools/faqs/faq.php?id=427&t=3

23. Kirk Chrisholm, "144 Products Made from Petroleum And 4 That May Shock You," *Innovative Wealth,* 2023, https://innovativewealth.com/inflation-monitor/what-products-made-from-petroleum-outside-of-gasoline/

24. **John Eidison, "The hidden agenda 'climate change,'" *American Thinker,* Oct 2, 2018,** https://www.americanthinker.com/blog/2018/10/the_hidden_agenda_behind_climate_change.html**.**

25. Ibid.

26. Ibid.

27. Ibid.

28. Ibid.

29. "Climate Report to UN: Trump right, UN wrong – Skeptics Deliver Consensus Busting 'State of the Climate Report' to UN Summit," *Climate Depot,* **Nov.15, 2016,** https://www.climatedepot.com/2016/11/15/skeptics-deliver-2016-state-of-the-climate-report-to-un-summit-everything-you-been-told-about-global-warming-is-wrong/

30. "BURN IN HELL: NYT Warmist Paul Krugman to those whose 'deny' global warming: 'May you be punished in the afterlife for doing so' — Calls 'denial' an 'almost inconceivable sin,'" *Climate Depot,* March 15, 2013, **https://www.climatedepot.com/2013/03/15/ burn-in-hell-nyt-warmist-paul-krugman-to-those-whose- deny-global-warming-may-you-be-punished-in-the-afterlife- for-doing-so-calls-denial-an-almost-inconceivable-sin/**

31. Ibid.

32. **Nell Frizzell, "Is Having a Baby in 2021 Pure Environmental Vandalism?"** *British Vogue,* **April 25, 2021, https://www.vogue. co.uk/mini-vogue/article/having-a-child-sustainable**

33. "Gore: 'Fertility management' is needed to reduce the number of Africans to help 'control the proliferation of unusual weather,'" *Climate Depot,* January 27, 2014, https://www. climatedepot.com/2014/01/27/gore-fertility-management-is- needed-in-africa-to-help-control-the-proliferation-of- unusual-weather/

34. **Hanna Panreck, "Russian-British comedian mocks wokeness in Oxford Union speech: 'Train young minds to forget,'"** *Fox News,* **January 15, 2023, https://www.foxnews.com/media/ russian-british-comedian-mocks-wokeness-oxford-union- speech-trained-young-minds-forget.amp**

Chapter 7

1. Ronald Reagan, "Abortion and the Conscience of the Nation" *The Human Life Journal,* (1983)

2. Jennifer L. Holland, "Abolish Abortion: The History of the Pro-Life Movement in America," Organization of American Historians, November, 2016, https://www.oah.org/tah/issues /2016/ november/abolishing-abortion-the-history-of-the-pro-life- movement-in-america/

3. History.com Editors, "Roe v. Wade," *History.com,* June 24, 2022, https://www.history.com/ topics/womens-rights/roe-v-wade.

4. **https://www.youtube.com/watch?v=ouJuKOuiX0U**

5 Harry Blackmun, *Roe v Wade,* Supreme Court, January 22, 1973, p.156.

6. Report, Subcommittee on Separation of Powers to Senate Judiciary Committee S-158, 97th Congress, 1st Session 1981.

7. Bernard N. Nathanson, "Deeper into Abortion," New England Journal of Medicine 291 (1974): 1189Ð90.

8. Bernard Nathanson, *Aborting America* (Garden City, NY: Doubleday, 1979).

9. Shettles and Rorvik, *Rites of Life*, Zondervan, Grand Rapids, MI, January 1, 1983, p. 103.

10. Kenneth Poortvliet, "Feticide: Definition, Laws & Cases," https://study.com/academy/lesson/feticide-definition-laws-cases.html 11. Theresa Waldrop, Stella Chan and Holly Yan, "Scott Peterson sentenced to life in prison after being spared a death sentence," CNN, December 8, 2021, https://www.cnn.com/2021/12/08/us/scott-peterson-resentencing/index.html

12. "Vanderbilt-pioneered fetal surgery procedure yields positive results," Research News, Vanderbilt university, Feb. 9, 2011, https://news.vanderbilt.edu/2011/02/09/vanderbilt-pioneered-fetal-surgery-procedure-yields-positive-results/

13. Cleveland Clinic, "Fetal Development: Stages of Growth," https://my.clevelandclinic.org/health/articles/7247-fetal-development-stages-of-growth

14. "Media Hides Fact: Planned Parenthood Does 40% of Abortions," *Life News,* http://www.lifenews.com/2012/09/05/media-hides-fact-planned-parenthood-does-40-of-abortions/ Matthew Clark Sep 5, 2012

15. HTTP://WWW.OPENSECRETS.ORG/ORGS/SUMMARY.PHP?ID=D000000591, OPEN SECRETS.ORG, CENTER FOR RESPONSIVE POLITICS

16. "Planned Parenthood Racism," *Students for Life*, 2021, https://studentsforlife.org/learn/planned-parenthood-racism/

17. Ibid.

18. Michael J. New, "Planned Parenthood's Annual Report: Abortion Increases, Health Service Declines," *National Review,* September 11, 2022, https://www.nationalreview.com/corner/planned-parenthoods-annual-report-abortion-increases-health-service-declines/

19. Jonathan Cahn, *The Return of the Gods,* Frontline, Lake Mary, FL, 2022, pp. 106-107.

20. Virginia Allen, "New Study Shows Women Deeply Regret Their Abortions, Experience Tremendous Guilt and Shame," *Life News,* Oct. 10, 2022, https://www.lifenews.com /2022/10/10/new-study-shows-women-deeply-regret-their-abortions-experience-tremendous-guilt-and-shame/

21. Anders Hagstrom, "Canada offered assisted suicide to a Paralympian veteran who wanted a wheelchair lift installed: report," *Fox News,* December 4, 2022, https://www.foxnews.com/politics/canada-offered-assisted-suicide-paralympian-veteran-wanted-wheelchair-lift-installed-report.

Chapter 8

1, Francis Schaffer, *The Great Evangelical Disaster,* Crossway Books, Westchester, IL, 1984, p. 139.

2. Catalina Gonella, "Survey: 20 of Millennials Identify as LBGTQ," *NBC,* March 31, 2017, https://www.nbcnews.com/feature/nbc-out/survey-20-percent-millennials-identify-lgbtq-n740791

3. Ibid.

4. Michael Swift, *"Gay Revolutionary."* Reprinted from The Congressional Record of the United States Congress. First printed in Gay Community News, February 15-21, 1987

5. Time Magazine, January 21, 1966

6. San Francisco Gay Men's Choir, *We'll Convert Your Children,* July 1, 2021. https://www.youtube.com/watch?v=cgmvWm4cBSM

https://video.search.yahoo.com/yhs/search?fr=yhs-iba-syn&ei=UTF-8&hsimp=yhs-syn&hspart=iba&param1=a4ynsxR6Qey%2F0eSxI5Q2QWGaMGHGeDm6lxv4fe0djnAnpZaJymph22gktDOxVL7J&param2=9dUI1n2R0BLDxNuWfiP4aWyjOZc2NBa%2Bx2opBYQCDMSB7nBAfwbAzkkglZNKi5o21u72Jm8TatlnU7NDGbP7F8Lft0aXvravgWuUt1wLTDRGoZDy1s38eFH2mqhQf7J35YCbQdFh0U0Q40PE25%2BEeG%2Bt%2By660cfFWnTypqgOdcDU8rmhfheCq5BmzLuS0tlndBvtceJN%2Fj7IfcdPbfc0BVUx56544U4eY3%2FNMaa0femhbNeERWzGAB1onuaBVb8KBcMTzihvtKlzHcesn2zLF5wBAbeBVEPdyMcNiKCtQFSsep09yPgL0TmnVb5%2F4pG0dbvXtwu6ygaJAlNp0jMGjQ%3D%3D&param3=NwVEMR%2FzKcG52XsVBYEh2zk2Yklq85vdfspZPoqz2M1qypHRDDTed5vIiOf0QJloIYNIhURx5ygk43IbuWBmnfLApzQNuNyJQuCIFEosygzUObTBvpAdBKtFCFkedGtzXg8BZPONEY8XN9MMyOktF%2BE4VeouGczuAQBfnb1Yu5TS1nz%2F3QlePiRMGKUuKNZsDhvIJDHXcbEZBu%2BKZ%2FuzN2XH%2BqyG3zhHQmFnpo%2F80wq2wk4rZQLrJD3enHCK7hy3TDyxk9VlKDV8fBsUhey5hLLzPfSikdGrbcyWXK1SpugNfztjhLtRuTX6ZX1t4olvhv3EoCcT14JeIOrdqCtHLLeUIDXcQq8v4YnyWjzp%2Bdk0gNNPSZoSMpbvlTi0Vb9ryPfRD9ia3IcFjwPu5qA3depJrilJNOUxa26J2e3f1o%2FRPgeJagClsVD3CjHYsZZtS%2F5vRu%2FuWVng1fHOcq%2FW2Q%3D%3D&param4=osbqGOAihfqej3VgdRohXsM83DSHqSE%2Bd3qqKDLsPlE%3D&p=san+francisco+gay+mens+chorus&type=asbw_8923_CHW_US_tid20115#id=2&vid=e1dc3addb6c2ace959733f877ebd2b10&action=click

7. NURITH AIZENMAN, "HOW TO DEMAND A MEDICAL BREAKTHROUGH: LESSONS FROM THE AIDS FIGHT," *NPR*, Feb. 19, 2019, HTTPS://WWW.NPR.ORG/SECTIONS/HEALTH-SHOTS/2019/02/09/689924838/HOW-TO-DEMAND-A-MEDICAL-BREAKTHROUGH-LESSONS-FROM-THE-AIDS-FIGHT

8. "Stop the Church," Wikipedia, September 24, 2022, https://en.wikipedia.org/wiki/Stop_the_Church#:~:text=Stop%20the%20Church%20was%20a%20demonstration%20organized%20by,53%20of%20whom%20were%20arrexsted%20inside%20the%20church.

9. NURITH AIZENMAN, "THE OTHER SIDE OF ANGER: HOW TO DEMAND A MEDICAL BREAKTHROUGH: LESSONS FROM THE AIDS FIGHT," *NPR*, FEB. 19, 2019, HTTPS://WWW.NPR.ORG/SECTIONS/HEALTH-SHOTS/2019/02/09/689924838/HOW-TO-DEMAND-A-MEDICAL-BREAKTHROUGH-LESSONS-FROM-THE-AIDS-FIGHT

10. Michael Spector, "How ACT UP Changed America," *New Yorker Magazine*, June 6, 2021, https://www.newyorker.com/magazine/2021/06/14/how-act-up-changed-america

11. Tim LaHaye, *The Battle for the Mind*, Fleming H. Revell, Grand Rapids, MI, 1980, pp. 87-88.

12. LaHaye, p.??

Chapter 9

1. David Roach, "He, She, Huh? Pronoun Campaign 'cultural Marxism,'" *Baptist Press*. September 13, 2016, https://www.baptistpress.com/resource-library/news/he-she-huh-pronoun-campaign-cultural-marxism/

2. Staff, *OUT Magazine*; 8/17/22, https://www.out.com/drag/2022/8/17/10-most-followed-social-media-queens-world#media-gallery-media-1

3. Outtravler staff, "10 Most Followed Drag Queens in the World," *OUT Magazine*, 8/17/22, https://www.khou.com/article/news/local/houston-public-library-admits-registered-child-sex-offender-participated-in-drag-queen-storytime/285-becf3a0d-56c5-4f3c-96df-add07bbd002a

4. The Associated Press, "Test scores drop to lowest levels in decades during pandemic, according to nationwide exam," *NBC News*, Oct. 24, 2022, https://www.nbcnews.com/news/us-news/test-scores-dropped-lowest-levels-decades-pandemic-according-nationwid-rcna53659

5. Anna Miller, "Even in Idaho," *The American Mind*, Feb. 1, 2022, https://americanmind.org/memo/even-in-idaho/#:~:text=School%20administrators%20in%20 Coeur%20d%E2%80%99Alene%20manipulated%20an%2011-year-old,to%20tell%20her%20parents%20about%20her%20new%20 identity.

6. Molly Sprayregen, "Mother sues school claiming teachers made her kid change gender identity," *LBGTQ Nation*, January 24, 2022, https://www.lgbtqnation.com/2022/01/mother-sues-school-claiming-teachers-made-kid-change-gender-identity/

7. Samantha Kamman, "Missouri AG investigates transgender clinic accused of hundreds of children," *The Christian Post*, February 14, 2023, Missouri AG investigates transgender clinic accused of harming hundreds of children.

8. Ibid.

9. Ibid

10. Michael w. Chapman, "Johns Hopkins Psychiatrist: Transgender is 'Mental Disorder;' Sex Change 'Biologically Impossible,'" *CNS News*, November 26, 2020, https://www.cnsnews.com/article/national/michael-w-chapman/johns-hopkins-psychiatrist-transgender-mental-disorder-sex

11. Staff, "Don't Be Bullied in the Pronoun War," *Daily Citizen*, May4, 2022, https://dailycitizen.focusonthefamily.com/dont-be-bullied-in-the-pronoun-war/

12. Kendall Tietz, "Judge Finds Skirt-wearing Teen Boy Guilty of Sexually Assaulting female Classmate in Loudoun Country School Bathroom," *The Daily Caller*, Oct. 26, 2021, https://dailycaller.com/2021/10/26/skirt-teen-loudon-county-public-schools-sexual-assault-guilty/and Hannah Natanson, "How and why Loudoun County became the face of the nation's culture wars," *Washington Post,* July 5, 2921, https://www.washingtonpost.com/local/education/loudoun-schools-transgender-student-rights/2021/08/10/3b7c894e-f9f7-11eb-943a-c5cf30d50e6a_story.html

13. Emily Zinos, "LGBT crusaders have gone too far. People are starting to tune out." *Life Site*, August 1. 2019, https://www.lifesitenews.com/opinion/lgbt-crusaders-have-gone-too-far-people-are-starting-to-tune-out/

14. "Why Permission from a Child or Underage Teen Doesn't Count," *Stop It Now*, 2022, https://www.stopitnow.org/ohc-content/why-permission-from-a-child-or-underage-teen-doesnt-count.

Chapter 10

1. The Northwest Ordinance, July 23, 1787, **Officially titled "An Ordinance for the Government of the Territory of the United States North-West of the River Ohio," the Northwest Ordinance was adopted on July 13, 1787, by the Confederation Congress, the one-house legislature operating under the Articles of Confederation. https://www.archives.gov/milestone-documents/northwest-ordinance**

2. Noah Webster, A collection of Papers, Literary, and Moral Subjects, (ed. 1843), preface Noah Webster Dictionary, 1828 https://libquotes.com/noah-webster/quote/lbw9n5e

3. Noah Webster, Noah, "Notable Quotes," *Webster's 1828 Dictionary - Online Edition*. Retrieved April 10, 2019. https://en.wikipedia. org/wiki/Noah_Webster

4. "John Dewey Chronology" 1934.04.08, 1936.03.12, 1940.09, and 1950.09.11. "What Humanism Means to Me," first published in *Thinker 2* (June 1930): 9–12, as part of a series. Dewey: p. lw.5.266 [*The Collected Works of John Dewey, 1882–1953*, The Electronic Edition]

5. John Dewey, *The Unseen Hand*, A. Ralph Epperson, Publius Press, 1985, p. 298

6. David T. Koyzis, "The Sixties and the Evolution of Liberalism," *First Things*, May 17, 2010. https://www.firstthings.com/blogs/ firstthoughts/2010/05/the-sixties-and-the-evolution-of-liberalism

7. Dale Mineshima-Lowe, "American Civil Liberties Union," The First Amendment Encyclopedia, 2009 and June 2021, https:// mtsu.edu/first-amendment/article/1166/american-civil-liberties-union

8. J. A. Reisman and E. W. Eichel, *Kinsey, Sex and Fraud: The Indoctrination of a People*, NCJ 3181, United States Department of Justice, 1990, https://www.ojp.gov/ncjrs/virtual-library/ abstracts/kinsey-sex-and-fraud-indoctrination-people

9. "John Dewey," *Great Pedagogical Thinkers*, https://www. pedagogy4change.org/john-dewey/

10. Ibid.

11. Breck Dumas, "Virginia mom confronts school board over graphic sexual materials in school." *Fox News*, Sept. 24, 2021, https:// www.foxnews.com/us/fairfax-mom-confronts-school-board-over-graphic-sexual-materials-in-school

12. Dan Whitcomb, "Declaration of Independence Banned at Calif School," Reuters, www.reuters.com, Nov. 24, 2004.

13. Ibid.

14. Ibid.

15. "Yes to 'The Vagina Monologues' but No to 'West Side Story,' *Fox News.com,* Partial transcript for *The O'Reilly Factor*, January 14, 2003, accessed February 10, 2016, http://www.foxnew.com/story/2004/01/15/yes-to-vagina-monologues-but-no to-west-side-story.html.

16. Marc A. Thiessen, "The danger of critical race theory," Woonsocket Call, Nov. 13, 2021, https://www.pressreader.com/

17. Ibid.

18. Learn more about *IndoctriNation* at www.indoctrinationmovie.com

19. Tammy Bruce, *The Death of Right and Wrong*, Prima Publishing, Roseville, CA, 2003, pp. 162-164.

20. David Limbaugh, *Persecution,* (Washington, DC: Regnery Publishing Co, 2003), pp. 132-133.

21. D. Kassy Dillion, *"Oklahoma governor praises passage of 'empowering' school choice bill in state's House"* Fox News," *Feb. 23, 2023,*https://news.yahoo.com/exclusive-oklahoma-governor-praises-passage-103047863.html?fr=sycsrp_catchall

Chapter 11

1. Thomas Jefferson, First Inaugural Address, March 4, 1801.

2. James Madison, Federalist Paper Number 51, February 8, 1788.

3. Francis Schaeffer, *A Christian Manifesto,* Crossway Books, Westchester, Illinois, 1981, p. 99.

4 Schaeffer, p. 100

5. Thomas Paine, *Common Sense,* January 10, 1776.

6. Samuel Adams, Addressing the state legislature of Massachusetts as Lieutenant Governor in 1794.

7. John Quincy Adams, *The Jubilee of the Constitution* 1839, pp. 13-14.

8. Alexander Hamilton, *The Farmer Refuted* Feb. 23, 1775, *Hamilton Papers.*

9. James Wilson, *Of the General Principles of Law and Obligation,* *1791.*

10. George Mason: As argued in Robin v. Hardaway, Virginia General Court, 1772.

11. Noah Webster, *History of the United States,* 1832.

12. Franklin Graham, "Crime and No Punishment," *Decision Magazine,* March 1, 2022, https://decisionmagazine.com/franklin-graham-crime-and-no-punishment/

13. Alfred S. Regnery, "Why Are Liberals Anxious to Free Violent Criminals From Prison?" *Breitbart,* May 16, 2016, https://www.breitbart.com/politics/2016/05/16/regnery-why-are-liberals-anxious-to-free-violent-criminals-from-prison/

14. "Racial and Ethnic Disparities in the Criminal Justice System," *National Conference on State Legislatures,* May 24, 2022, https://www.ncsl.org/civil-and-criminal-justice/racial-and-ethnic-disparities-in-the-criminal-justice-system

15. Ibid.

16. Most Ridiculous Lawsuits Ever," July 7, 2009, https://Terrence Dickson, of Bristol, ... besteverawards.wordpress.com/2009/07/27/most-ridiculous-lawsuits-ever-ever/#:~:text=Man%20gets%20stuck%20in%20garage%20after%20burglary%2C%20sues,could%20not%20get%20the%20garage%20door%20to%20open.

17. Zaid Jilani, "The Deadly Consequences of 'Defund the Police,'" *National Review,* Feb. 1, 2021, https://nationalreview.com/2021/02/the-deadly-consequences-of-defund-the-police/

18. Ryan Young and Devon M. Sayers, "Why police forces are struggling to recruit and keep officers," CNN, February 3, 2022, https://www.cnn.com/2022/02/02/us/police-departments-struggle-recruit-retain-officers/index.html

19. Associated Press, "76,000 California inmates now eligible for early releases," *Fox News,* May 1, 2021, https://www.foxnews.com/us/california-plans-early-release-for-76000-prison-inmates-

including-violent-felons

20. AFP Editor, "Bail Reform Isn't Working," American Free Press, July 6, 2020, https://americanfreepress.net/bail-reform-isnt-working/

21. Post Editorial Board, "Sorry, new state stats don't support no-bail – they show what a disaster it's been," *New York Post*, September 22, 2022, https://nypost.com/2022/09/22/new-state-stats-dont-support-no-bail-they-show-what-a-disaster-its-been/

22. Hannah Nightingale, "BREAKING: Waukesha massacre suspect high in pretrial risk assessment but was released anyway," *PM,* December 2, 2021, https://thepostmillennial.com/breaking-waukesha-massacre-suspect-pretrial-risk-assessment

23. Jerry Dunleavy, "Durham report: Five key takeaways from the bombshell findings into Trump-Russia investigation," May 16, 2023, *Washington Examiner*, https://www.washingtonexaminer.com/news/justice/durham-report-takeaways-trump-russia-investigation-fbi-doj

24. Marshall Cohen, "FBI offered Christopher Steele $1 million to prove dossier claims, senior FBI analyst testifies," *CNN*, October 14, 2022, https://www.cnn.com/2022/10/11/politics/steele-dossier-fbi-durham-danchenko/index.html

25. Dunleavy, Durham Report

26. Miranda Devine, *Laptop from Hell*, Post Hill Press, Nashville, TN, 2021.

27. "ICYMI: Comer & Oversight Committee Members Present Evidence of Influence Peddling by Biden Family," *Committee on Oversight and Accountability*, May 10, 2023, https://oversight.house.gov/release/icymi-comer-oversight-committee-members-present-evidence-of-influence-peddling-by-biden-family%ef%bf%bc/

28. Press Release, "Tax and Firearm Charges Filed Against Robert Hunter Biden," June 20, 2023, United States Attorney's Office, District of Delaware, https://www.justice.gov/usao-de/pr/tax-and-firearm-charges-filed-against-robert-hunter-biden

29. Tristian Justice, "CONFIRMED: FBI Colluded With Big Tech To Prevent Voters From Learning About Hunter Biden's Laptop," *Federalist,* August 26, 2022, https://thefederalist.com/2022/08/26/confirmed-fbi-colluded-with-big-tech-to-prevent-voters-from-learning-about-hunter-bidens-laptop/

30. Ibid.

31. Elizabeth Nolan Brown, "The FBI Paid Twitter $3.4 Million for Processing Requests," *Reason,* Dec. 19, 2022, https://reason.com/2022/12/19/the-fbi-paid-twitter-3-4-million-for-processing-requests/

32. Audrey Conklin, "Fentanyl overdoses become No. 1 cause of death among US adults, ages 18-45: 'A national emergency,'" *"Fox News,* December 16, 2021, https://www.foxnews.com/us/fentanyl-overdoses-leading-cause-death-adults

33. Jordon Boyd, "While Biden Beckons Illegal Immigrants, Democrats Are Working To Let Them Vote In US Elections" *The Federalist,* March 16, 2021, https://thefederalist.com/2021/03/16/while-biden-beckons-illegal-immigrants-democrats-are-working-to-let-them-vote-in-us-elections/

Chapter 12

1. George Washington, Letter to John Augustine Washington, May 31, 1776

2. Michael Rozansky, "Americans know surprisingly little about their government," Annenberg Public Policy Center of the University of Pennsylvania, September 17, 2014, https://cdn.annenbergpublicpolicycenter.org/wp-content/uploads/2018/03/Civics-survey-press-release-09-17-2014-for-PR-Newswire.pdf

3. James Madison, *Federalist Paper Number 43.*

4. Thomas Jefferson, Letter to A. Coray, October 31, 1823.

5. Thomas Jefferson, Letter to William Jarvis, Sept. 28, 1820

6. Merrill Matthews, "We've Crossed The Tipping Point; Most Americans Now Receive Government Benefits," *Forbes,* July2,

2014, https://www.forbes.com/sites/merrillmatthews /2014/07/02/weve-crossed-the-tipping-point-most-americans-now-receive-government-benefits/?sh=4cea50853e6c

7. Alexander Hamilton, *The Federalist Paper No. 33.*

8. Lawrence Richard, "Born-Alive Act Pelosi, Schumer melt down after new bill requires care for babies born during failed abortion," *Fox News*, January 12, 2023, https://www.foxnews.com/politics/born-alive-act-pelosi-schumer-melt-down-new-bill-care-babies-born-abortion

9. **Alexander Hamilton, Statement after the Constitutional Convention (1787),** https://thefederalistpapers.org/founders/hamilton/alexander-hamilton-statement-after-the-constitutional-convention-1787.

10. John Adams, Address to the Military, October 11, 1798.

11. Thomas Jefferson, (1905). Andrew A. Lipscomb and Albert Ellery Bergh (ed.). *The Writings of Thomas Jefferson.* Vol. 1. p. 211. "A Summary View of the Rights of British America: Set Forth in Some Resolutions Intended for the Inspection of the Present Delegates of the People of Virginia, Now in Convention / by a Native, and Member of the House of Burgesses". World Digital Library. 1774. Retrieved 2013-08-03.

CHAPTER 13

1. George Washington, *First Inaugural Address*, April 30, 1789.

2. Daniel Webster, Speech at Plymouth, Massachusetts, December 22, 1820.

3. John Jay, Letter to John Murray (12 October 1816) as published in *The Life of John Jay (1833) by William Jay*, Vol. 2, p. 376

4. Todd Starnes, "Houston Mayor drops bid to subpoena pastors' sermons," *Fox News*, May 7, 2015, https://www.foxnews.com/opinon/houston-mayor-drops-bid-to-subpoena-pstors-sermons

5. David Barton, *Original Intent, The Courts, the Constitution, and Religion*, Wall Builders, Aledo, TX, 2000.